Organizational Change for Corporate Sustainability

The sustainability of business, both economically and ecologically, is one of this century's central debates. While corporations can have positive effects on society and the environment, they can also impact negatively. This book raises important questions like, 'how do corporations become truly sustainable?'

Organizational Change for Corporate Sustainability brings together global issues of ecological sustainability, human resource management, corporate citizenship and community renewal to create a unified approach to global sustainability. Outlining the long-term corporate benefits of sustainability, it examines the changes required in organizations to achieve true sustainability. Using specific examples of incremental and transformational changes, it is relevant to anyone studying or working in the areas of management, human resource management, environmental studies, sustainability or organizational studies.

Dexter Dunphy is Distinguished Professor at the University of Technology, Sydney, where he directs research on corporate sustainability in the Graduate School of Business. An experienced researcher and consultant in the fields of organizational change and corporate sustainability, he is published internationally.

Andrew Griffiths is Senior Lecturer and Research Fellow in the Technology and Innovation Management Centre at the University of Queensland where he researches and publishes in sustainability, innovation and organizational change.

Suzanne Benn is Research Associate in the School of Management at the University of Technology, Sydney, where she researches corporate sustainability.

Understanding Organizational Change

Series editor:
Dr Bernard Burnes

The management of change is now acknowledged as being one of the most important issues facing management today. By focusing on particular perspectives and approaches to change, particular change situations, and particular types of organization, this series provides a comprehensive overview and an in-depth understanding of the field of organizational change.

Titles in this series include:

Organizational Change for Corporate Sustainability
A guide for leaders and change agents of the future
Dexter Dunphy, Andrew Griffiths and Suzanne Benn

Organizational Change
A processual approach
Patrick Dawson

Organizational Change for Corporate Sustainability

A guide for leaders and change agents of the future

Dexter Dunphy, Andrew Griffiths and Suzanne Benn

Routledge
Taylor & Francis Group

LONDON AND NEW YORK

First published 2003
by Routledge
11 New Fetter Lane, London EC4P 4EE

Simultaneously published in the USA and Canada
by Routledge
29 West 35th Street, New York, NY 10001

Routledge is an imprint of the Taylor & Francis Group

Typeset in Times by Keystroke, Jacaranda Lodge, Wolverhampton
Printed and bound in Great Britain by The Cromwell Press, Trowbridge, Wiltshire

British Library Cataloguing in Publication Data
A catalogue record for this book is available from the British Library

Library of Congress Cataloging in Publication Data
A catalog record for this book has been requested

ISBN 0–415–28740–5 (hbk)
ISBN 0–415–28741–3 (pbk)

Contents

List of illustrations

Figures

Tables

Notes on the authors

Dexter Dunphy is Distinguished Professor, University of Technology, Sydney, a position he took up in January 2000 after seventeen years as Professor at the Australian Graduate School of Management. Dexter holds the degrees of BA(hons), MEd(hons) and DipEd from Sydney University and PhD in Sociology from Harvard University. His main research and consulting interests are in corporate sustainability, the management of organizational change and human resource management. His research is published in over seventy articles and eighteen books, including: *The Sustainable Corporation: Organizational Renewal in Australia* (co-authored with Andrew Griffiths, Allen and Unwin, Sydney, 1998); *Sustainability: The Corporate Challenge of the Twenty-first Century* (co-edited with others, Allen and Unwin, Sydney, 2000); and *Beyond the Boundaries: Leading and Re-creating the Successful Enterprise* (with Doug Stace), McGraw-Hill, Sydney, 2001.

Andrew Griffiths is a Senior Lecturer in Technology and Innovation Management at the University of Queensland. His areas of research include: the management of corporate change and innovation; strategic issues relating to the pursuit of corporate sustainability; and e-commerce and innovation. Andrew's doctorate from the University of New South Wales, Sydney, examined the relationship between organizational strategies and industry responses to competitive threats. He has co-authored two books: *The Sustainable Corporation: Organizational Renewal in Australia* (co-authored with Dexter Dunphy, Allen and Unwin, Sydney, 1998) and *Sustainability: The Corporate Challenge of the Twenty-first Century* (co-edited with others, Allen and Unwin, Sydney, 2000).

Suzanne Benn is Research Associate in the Corporate Sustainability Project at University of Technology (UTS), Sydney. She co-ordinates the undergraduate teaching programme, Sustainable Enterprise, and lectures in the MBA programme at UTS in Organizational Change and Analysis. Suzanne holds a bachelor's degree in chemistry from the University of Sydney and post-graduate qualifications in education. She also holds a masters degree in Science and Society and a doctorate in Science and Technology Studies from the University of New South Wales, Sydney.

Series editor's preface

It is an accepted tenet of modern life that change is constant, of greater magnitude and far less predictable than ever before. For this reason, managing change is acknowledged as being one of the most important and difficult issues facing organizations today. This is why both practitioners and academics, in ever growing numbers are seeking to understand organizational change. This is why the range of competing theories and advice has never been greater and never more puzzling.

Over the past hundred years or so, there have been many theories and prescriptions put forward for understanding and managing change. Arguably, the first person to attempt to offer a systematic approach to changing organizations was the originator of Scientific Management, Frederick Taylor. From the 1930s onwards, the Human Relations school attacked Taylor's one-dimensional view of human nature and his over-emphasis on individuals. In a parallel and connected development, in the 1940s, Kurt Lewin created perhaps the most influential approach to managing change. His planned approach to change, encapsulated in his three-step model, became the inspiration for a generation of researchers and practitioners, mainly – though not exclusively – in the USA. Throughout the 1950s, Lewin's work was expanded beyond his focus on small groups and conflict resolution to create the Organization Development (OD) movement. From the 1960s to the early 1980s, OD established itself as the dominant Western approach to organizational change.

However, by the early 1980s, more and more Western organizations found themselves having to change rapidly and dramatically, and sometimes brutally, in the face of the might of corporate Japan. In such circumstances, many judged the consensus-based and incrementally focused OD approach as having little to offer. Instead, a plethora of approaches began to emerge which, whilst not easy to classify, could best be described as anti-OD. These newer approaches to change were less wary than OD in embracing issues of power and politics in organizations; they did not necessarily see organizational change as clean, linear and finite. Instead, they viewed change as messy, contentious, context-dependent and open-ended. In addition, unlike OD which drew its inspiration and insights mainly from psychology, the newer approaches drew on an eclectic mix of sociology, anthropology, economics, psychotherapy and the natural sciences, not to mention the ubiquitous postmodernism. This has produced a range of approaches to change with suffixes and appellations such as emergent, processual, political, institutional, cultural, contingency, complexity, chaos and many more.

It is impossible to conceive of an approach which is suitable for all types of change, all types of situations and all types of organizations. Some may be too narrow in applicability whilst others may be too general. Some may be complementary to each other whilst others are clearly incompatible. The range of approaches to change, and the confusion over their strengths, weaknesses and suitability, is such that the field of organizational change resembles more an overgrown weed patch than a well-tended garden.

The aim of this series is to provide both a comprehensive overview of the main perspectives on organizational change, and an in-depth guide to key issues and controversies. The series will investigate the main approaches to change, and the various contexts in which change is applied. The underlying rationale for the series is that we cannot understand organizational change sufficiently nor implement it effectively unless we can map the range of approaches, and evaluate what they seek to achieve, how and where they can be applied, and, crucially, the evidence which underpins them.

Series editor
Bernard Burnes
Manchester School of Management,
UMIST

Acknowledgements

This book is the culmination of two years of collaborative work between the three authors. However, it builds on more years of their collective experiences in consulting, research and teaching about organizational change, human resource management, social responsibility and ecological sustainability. Each of the authors was involved in undertaking case studies, interviewing managers and change agents, supervising and co-ordinating research students, presenting conference papers and publishing journal articles. All these activities provided a rich set of resources that we have drawn on in the book. In particular, however, we acknowledge the special contribution played by Suzanne Benn and Phyllis Agius in tracking down, synthesizing and organizing much of the research material which appears in various chapters.

In writing this book, the three authors each took primary responsibility for particular chapters: Dexter for Chapter 1: Setting the agenda, Chapter 3: The sustaining corporation, Chapter 8: The transformational path and Chapter 9: Leading towards sustainability; Andrew for Chapter 5: Achieving sustainable efficiencies, Chapter 6: Sustainability: the strategic advantage, and Chapter 7: The incremental path; Suzanne for Chapter 3: The drivers of change, and Chapter 4: Compliance and beyond.

While we took individual responsibility for writing these chapters, the end product of each chapter was the result of the work of all three authors and of a handful of selected reviewers. We express our particular gratitude to all those in the organizations we studied. We thank them for the interview time and research material they so generously provided and hope that we have given a fair and balanced view of their contribution to sustainability. We also thank other researchers whose published work we have accessed and summarized where relevant.

The following people gave us valuable feedback on drafts of particular chapters: Phyllis Agius, Lino Caccavo, Graham Cavanagh-Downs,

Professor Gavan McDonell, Professor Serge Mukhi, Dr Renato Orsatto, Professor Ian Palmer, Stuart Smith, Professor Doug Stace, Philip Sutton and Dr Dedee Woodside. We also wish to acknowledge the contribution of Jodie Benveniste and Philip Sutton to the original Sustainability Phase Model that we have modified for use in this book. We are also indebted to Philip Sutton for providing us with the term 'sustaining corporation' to describe our 'ideal' sustainable corporation. We sincerely thank Frank Hubbard of Worthwhile Projects Pty Ltd for permission to quote from his Sustainability SMART© system. We are grateful to Joseph Agius for his creativity and excellent service in providing the phase designs and graphics for other illustrations.

Several institutions have supported this project. Dexter and Suzanne thank Professor Tony Blake, Vice Chancellor of the University of Technology (UTS), Sydney, who supported the establishment of the Sustainable Corporation Project, as well as Peter Booth, Dean, Faculty of Business, UTS, and Professor Thomas Clark, Head, School of Management, UTS, who provided valuable ongoing support. Andrew thanks Professor Richard Badham, Director of the Centre for Change Management at the University of Wollongong, and Professor Lyn Grigg, Director of the Technology and Innovation Management Centre at the University of Queensland, for providing time, space and resources to pursue this project.

Phyllis Agius read, typed and formatted the full text with patience and accepted our many revisions with good humour. We thank her for going beyond the call of duty in helping us meet our tight deadlines and for the many improvements and intellectual contributions she made to our individual chapters. Without her enthusiasm and commitment the task of completing this book would have been more onerous.

We are also deeply indebted to our families. Dexter would like to thank his partner Francine for her interest and enthusiasm for the project and his children Mark, Kristen and Roger for their good humour in accepting that 'Dad's writing another book'.

Andrew would like to thank Jenine for her patience and understanding of the consuming focus involved in writing the manuscript and for the late-night debates on creating better societies. He would like to dedicate these efforts to Jenine and his children, Meg and Liam, in the prospect of creating sustainable futures.

Suzanne would like to thank her partner, the environmental lawyer Andrew Martin, for his ongoing advice and support and for his own passionate commitment to our Australian environment. As always, she thanks her three adventuring sons, Steven, Andrew and Thomas, as the source of so much inspiration and joy.

This book outlines critical challenges facing corporations in the new millennium. We hope that the ideas we present here provoke readers to take up the challenge of creating sustainable corporations that support human welfare and a viable future for all life on the planet.

Part I
Towards third wave corporations

1 Setting the agenda for corporate sustainability

- Why corporate sustainability?
- The evolution of the corporation
- Phase models of sustainability
- Change agent roles and the phase model
- Appendix: Phases in the development of corporate sustainability

Why corporate sustainability?

We are faced with an extraordinary situation. Never before in the history of the world has the viability of much of the life on this planet been under threat from humanity; never before have so many of the world's people experienced such material wealth and so many others lived in abject poverty; never before have so many had such interesting and fulfilling work and so many others such degrading work or no work at all. If we are to live healthy, fulfilling lives on this planet in the future, we must find new life-affirming values and forge new patterns of living and working together.

The critical situation in which we find ourselves has been brought about by multiple causes but one important contributing factor is the rise of the corporation. Corporations are the fundamental cells of modern economic life and their phenomenal success in transforming the earth's resources into wealth has shaped the physical and social world in which we live. The powerful dynamism of modern organizations has transformed nature and society. The central question to be answered in this century is whether the current model of the corporation needs to be modified to contribute to the continuing health of the planet, the survival of humans and other species, the development of a just and humane society, and the creation of work that brings dignity and self-fulfilment to those undertaking it. And if so, how?

In this book we argue that some traditional organizational values and forms are not sustainable and, unless significantly reshaped, will continue to undermine the sustainability of society and the planet. Corporations have contributed to the problems outlined above and they must therefore be part of the answer. Fortunately their transformation is already underway, driven in part by the changing demands of modern society and also by the leadership of far-sighted and responsible people within and outside corporations who see the need for change. However, for the transformation to be successful, many more change agents are needed. Some of the most important changes in history have been created by people of vision and imagination who were not content simply to react to events about them but to envisage the possibility of a different world and to initiate action to bring the new reality into being. They were often regarded as deluded or heretical at the time but later celebrated for their foresight and courage.[1]

This book is written to assist change agents to drive the necessary changes faster and farther while there is time. We discuss key issues in the debate around the nature of sustainability but not at great length. For those interested in taking this further we provide references to some of the key books and articles which are the focus of this theoretical debate. Our view is that this debate will now be most fruitfully engaged through the process of reconstructing organizations so they support a sustainable world. The current crisis is too urgent to wait for consensus; we need to start out on the path towards sustainability by generating new models of organizational action that support social relationships and the natural world. The time to debate abstract theories is past; what we need now is to embed our theories in action and to engage in dialogue around working models.

In our view, many corporations need to change significantly the way they do business. However, we are not arguing that corporations are the enemy. We are arguing that new circumstances require new responses. The crises faced by humanity can only be resolved by the use of concerted corporate action. Corporations are instruments of social purpose, formed within society to accomplish useful social objectives. If they do this, they have a right to a continued existence, a licence to use resources, and a responsibility to produce socially beneficial products and services. However, if they debase human life, act with contempt for the community of which they are part, plunder and pollute the planet, and produce 'bads' as well as 'goods', they forfeit their right to exist. They become unsustainable because they are unsustaining. The single-minded pursuit of short-term profitability for shareholders or owners does not justify a 'couldn't care less' approach to people and the planet.

Responsible resource stewardship is a universal requirement for all of us, individually and collectively.

This book examines the transition to the organization of the future that functions as an instrument for the fulfilment of human needs and the renewal of the biosphere. We define key steps along the way and indicate how to make an incremental transition from step to step or, in some cases, a transformative leap to the fully sustainable and sustaining corporation. This is therefore a guidebook for corporate change agents – executives, managers and members of the workforce, external consultants, community activists – who are dissatisfied with the status quo in organizational life and who dream of a new organizational world where individuals are cherished, the community is supported and the natural environment nourished as a matter of course as the organization goes about its core business. Nothing less than this is worthy of our humanity, our intelligence and our ingenuity.

The distinctive contribution of this book is that it concentrates on how to implement the changes that make organizations more sustainable themselves and also more sustaining of the environment and society. In doing this, we draw on leading-edge change theory from management and the social sciences. So this book is a practical and informed tool for creating sustainable corporations that are part of the solution to keeping a world that is fit to live in. It is an invitation to you to be part of the future solution – a responsible agent of creative change.

For those who are prepared to act with purpose and direction in reshaping the organizational world, this is perhaps the most exciting period in human history. Each generation faces its challenges. But this and the next two or three generations will be decisive in determining whether more humans than have ever lived on this planet can create the collaborative institutional forms needed for our survival and the survival of those other precious life forms who share this planet with us. And beyond survival, to create innovative institutional forms to provide us all, and those who come after us, with a quality of economic, social and cultural life that nurtures and develops our human capabilities.

That is the challenge we deal with in this book. In meeting this challenge, we must redesign many of our organizations. So we begin here with a short discussion of the evolution of the institution which is the focus of our book: the corporation. Because corporations share so many common features and are so pervasive, we can easily assume that the corporation is an immutable social form. But it is not – it has already undergone substantial redefinitions over time. How did the corporation arise? Why was it created? How has it evolved and how can we redesign it for human and ecological sustainability?

The evolution of the corporation

The corporation as we know it today is a relatively modern invention but its historical roots can be traced back to the Roman Empire.[2] The Romans realized that social institutions were vulnerable to turnover among members and the founders' deaths. So, to ensure continuity, they adopted the fiction of an institution having an identity, like a supra individual, independent of its members.[3]

The notion was later carried across into Church canon law with an added distinction made between ecclesiastical and lay corporations. Ecclesiastical corporations promoted religious matters; lay corporations were formed for municipal governance, manufacturing and commerce. This was the origin of the commercial corporation as we know it today. Under British law, this idea was developed further. The law enshrined the right of the monarch to grant a charter to organizations that allowed them to operate. The sovereign's consent was absolutely necessary to the formation of any corporation and he or she had the right to revoke the charter at any time.

Many of the British settlements in North America were founded by corporations under charter from the British crown and were defended by British troops. For instance, Cecilius Calvert was given a charter by Charles I to found the colony of Baltimore. In return for a grant of 4 million hectares of land, he agreed to pay the king 'two Indian arrows a year plus one fifth of any gold or silver discovered'.[4]

After the foundation of British colonies in North America, this kind of control by the British crown became a source of irritation to many American citizens. The 'Boston Tea Party', which sparked the American Revolution, was a citizen protest against the right of the British Parliament to favour the East India Company, incorporated under charter from the British Crown, by allowing it to ship tea to America without paying import duties.[5] Arguments about the rights of corporations are not a novel phenomenon.

When the United States finally won its independence, its citizens were determined to bring corporations under the control of their elected legislatures. As a result, the constitutions of most American states today retain the authority to grant charters to corporations; the laws define the scope of corporate activities and retain the right to revoke charters once they are granted.[6] In the early 1800s, charters for corporations such as banks, insurance companies and turnpike operators were in fact revoked for a variety of reasons.

However, in the late nineteenth century, corporations fought these laws and succeeded in gaining greater autonomy. A major turning point was a US Supreme Court decision in *Santa Clara County* v. *Southern Pacific Railroad* that a private corporation was a 'natural person' under the US Constitution. This simply clarified and legitimized the idea of the corporation being 'one person in law' which originated with the Romans and was perpetuated by the Church and English law. However, the decision allowed large, wealthy corporations equal rights with individual citizens, local communities and other groups who might not be able to match the funds needed for legal confrontation over issues of community concern.[7] In reality, large corporations were increasingly able to write their own rules for action. Recent corporate scandals such as the Enron collapse in the USA have made this very clear and create increased pressure for corporations to be made more accountable. The difficulties associated with holding organizations accountable for compliance to legal requirements and legitimate community expectations will be discussed in Chapters 3 and 4.

The rise of the multinational corporation and the internationalization of financial markets has taken the power of the modern corporation to the point where it can represent a formidable challenge to the authority of the nation state, let alone small groups of citizens. Global corporations operate across political boundaries and so escape overall surveillance by particular nation states. The wealth of the largest global companies exceeds that of most nations and this has given them unprecedented power. The existence of large-scale power discrepancies does not in itself guarantee that the power will be used irresponsibly but it does create the potential for the misuse of power. Throughout corporate history many corporate chieftains have used their power rapaciously and irresponsibly. For example, a coalition of oil companies and large construction firms in the USA planned and efficiently brought about the demise of the US railroad system to favour the construction of a vast network of interstate highways. But of course, there are also plenty of instances of corporate leaders exercising social and environmental responsibility. In fact, there is a growing divide between those corporate leaders who have embraced the responsibilities of corporate citizenship and those who, through ignorance or design, continue to exploit natural and human resources.

Are corporations evil?

It is a naive and simplistic view that portrays corporations as evil by their very nature. Almost everything we depend on in our modern world is the product of corporations – from the food we eat, the clothes we wear to the phones and computers we use to communicate with each other. We cannot do without corporations. What is important, however, is that we exercise sufficient collective control over the way in which they operate to ensure they support rather than destroy the ecological and social fabric we depend on.

Throughout the history of corporations, there has been a continuing debate over how the corporation should be defined, including its legal constitution, its social responsibilities, its role in environmental protection, and the constituency to which it is accountable. The core of this debate can be summarized as the argument about whether the role of the corporation is simply to create financial wealth for its owners or to contribute to the well-being of a wider range of stakeholders, including the community, the environment and future generations.

This debate has gone on for as long as 'modern' corporations have existed and its history is too long and complex to trace here. The debate has included, for example, fierce critiques of the legitimacy of the slave trade; sabotage of the 'dark satanic mills' that blighted the lives of workers and devastated England's 'green and pleasant land'; large-scale demonstrations against nuclear power plants; experiments in 'industrial democracy'; the rise of 'green' political parties; organizational innovations such as 'the triple bottom line'; demonstrations against globalization. Since corporations came into being, each generation has engaged with and continued this debate which has shaped corporations as we know them today.

Most recently a critical issue in the debate has been the relative virtues of the prevailing neoliberal economics ('economic rationalism') versus 'stakeholder capitalism'. Neoliberal economics, led by the economist Milton Friedman, argues that the role of the corporation is simply to maximize short-term returns to shareholders. The widespread acceptance of this point of view, especially by economic advisers to governments, has been influential in shifting considerable power from the public to the private sector, the ongoing privatization of government services, the deregulation of major industries and markets and the creation of international competitive 'free trade' markets. Critics of this viewpoint argue that these changes have had destructive consequences for other important stakeholders – employees, customers, suppliers, governments, local communities, future generations, other species of planetary life, and the environment. A recent shot across the bows of the neoliberal economists has been fired by Allen Kennedy in his book *The End of Shareholder Value* which argues vehemently against what he sees as the legitimation of 'pure greed'.[8] At least some of the destructive consequences of corporate activity result from the relentless drive for short-term profitability at the expense of longer-term sustainability – an issue we shall return to later in this book. Kennedy suggests reforms to create genuinely sustainable wealth for all the corporation's stakeholder groups, not only its shareholders.

The nature of the modern corporation, and the philosophy of economic neoliberalism that supports it, has been strongly influenced by the success of the US economy and the history of leading US corporations. The culture of modern capitalism has evolved from the experiences of a multitude of corporations developing on a continent with enormous unexploited and virtually free natural resources. For example, at the time of European settlement, the number of bison on the North American continent was estimated at between 30 and 60 million. They were the most economically valuable wild animals that ever inhabited the American continent. When a halt was called to their slaughter in the late 1800s only 600 survived. The passenger pigeon, once the most numerous bird in North America and on the planet, did not survive the onslaught of the hunters' guns – they were completely exterminated.[9] Despite depredations of this magnitude, the size of the continent ensured that, for the formative two centuries of US capitalism, the torrent of ecological destruction and the increasing waste and pollution emitted in converting resources into wealth could be absorbed by nature. The wealth that was generated enabled the USA to become the most powerful nation on earth with a business culture dominating the late twentieth and early twenty-first century.

As a result, most corporations today operate under accounting rules and cultural assumptions that reward them for disregarding many of the social and environmental consequences of their activities. They 'externalize' many costs of ongoing operations to the community, the environment and future generations. Neoclassical economics, based on the experience of environmental plenty, still assumes that many inputs from the natural and social environments, like air and parenting, are free goods because there are no financial charges made for them. In addition, the goods and services produced by the firm are given value but the 'bads' and 'disservices' created at the same time are often neither identified nor costed and charged back to the corporation. The discourse of business and economics largely defines out ecological and community issues. Hence in the most significant business decisions, these issues are ignored because they are invisible – the decision makers have no cultural categories for them – or, if perceived, the issues are regarded as irrelevant or of marginal importance. In fact, they are of increasing importance for survival of life on this planet and for social justice and they must become central to strategic decision making. We need a new economics that redefines economic capital to include nature and people.[10]

So we face a situation where corporate decision makers, many of whom are well intentioned, community-minded citizens, make decisions which cumulatively are having a catastrophic impact on the planet and on the global community. And they are supported in this pattern of decision making by consumers (us) who reward them by purchasing goods and services they produce. We are all captives of a culture of capitalism that, over 200 years, produced enormous wealth and an increased standard of living for large numbers of people. But the costs of continuing on this path, using the same methods, are now threatening to destroy our ability to use the wealth in the creation of healthy, satisfying lives and also threatening the viability of such a life for future generations. We have become, in the words of Tim Flannery, 'future eaters'.[11] Most of us have a stake in our current culture and are threatened by any substantial critique of it. We sense that we must, at least for the sake of our children and future generations, start to do some things differently. But the size and the complexity of the issues are daunting and we are caught in a spider web of cultural categories that constrain our effective action. Change must begin with us – but where can we begin?

> Like it or not the responsibility for ensuring a sustainable world falls largely on the shoulders of the world's enterprises, the economic engines of the future.
>
> *Source*: Stuart Hart, Kenan Flagler Business School[12]

Making a start

Wherever we are in society and the world of work, we can engage in the debate about the social role of the corporation. All of us can contribute to a redefinition of corporations to ensure they become major contributors to sustainability rather than social and environmental predators undermining a world fit to live in. There is a huge opportunity here to ensure that all corporations are instruments of a broader social purpose than the generation of short-term wealth for shareholders. Of course shareholders deserve a return on their investment. As we shall show, in most cases this return is enhanced rather than reduced by sustainable practices. We think it is vital that corporations make profits – but not at the cost of destroying the future viability of society and the planet.

The sustainability debate is currently being engaged in three ways: first, at the intellectual level as the immensity of current unsustainable practices is documented and we all become aware of the considerable challenges of changing these practices; second, at the level of corporate action, as hundreds of thousands of members of boards of management, executives, managers, supervisors, members of the workforce, external consultants, non-government organizations and community groups take a multitude of actions on a daily basis that impact on issues of social and environmental sustainability; third, at the level of consumption, as we collectively create the powerful patterns of financial rewards that shape the economy. If we continue to purchase products that strew our world with waste and poison our environment, we cannot blame the captains of industry for the resulting destruction. If we are to make corporations instruments of renewal, the debate must be engaged at these three levels: through forging a powerful new ideology that creates a compelling vision of a future world fit to live in, and implementing the practical actions in the workplace and in our consumption patterns that will bring the vision into being.

A new approach to economics has developed in recent years to deal with the fact that traditional economics has largely taken the ecological and social environment for granted. This approach recognizes that economics must take 'natural capital' (ecosystems) and 'social capital' (relationships between people) into account. Neoclassical economics treats the economy as a closed system, with negative results, such as pollution, treated as 'externalities' which can be ignored in economic terms. Similarly some of the world's most critical resources are treated as 'free' inputs and accorded no value unless they acquire economic worth in the process of production. Ecological economics, by contrast, makes such externalities an integral part of the economic system. Ecological economics is a new field of study which integrates principles from ecology and economics. As a result of the increasing importance of these new approaches, economists are recognizing the implications of ecological functioning and resilience for human welfare. For instance, biological resources such as trees and fish and ecological services such as erosion control and climate stabilization depend on maintaining certain levels of ecosystem functioning.[13]

The depletion of natural and social resources and the accumulation of toxic wastes or rising crime rates can be consequences of economic decisions that seem 'rational' in traditional economic terms. But in the new economic models their social and economic effects are included rather than excluded. It is fair to say that in these new models some 'rational' decisions begin to look insane. For instance, the decision to build bigger, more technologically efficient fishing fleets to maximize harvests of fish from the world's oceans looks rational – but only on the assumption that the supply of fish is inexhaustible.

This book makes a contribution at all three levels: to the intellectual agenda for change; to the strategies for corporate action; and to changing consumption patterns. We outline the need for sustainability, identifying the gap between where we are now and where we need to be, and then we provide a detailed discussion of the kinds of strategic actions that are needed to carry us forward.

In accomplishing this, we outline developmental phases that lead to the fully sustainable organization, that is, an organization that is itself sustainable because its stakeholders including its employees will continue to support it. But it is also a sustaining organization because it is sustaining the wider society and the ecological environment. Since 1992, when the leaders of the world's governments gathered in Rio to endorse the principles of sustainable development, they have struggled with the challenge of integrating the social, environmental and economic principles that sustainability requires. Corporations which develop according to our integrated model will make a major contribution to ensuring that the world progresses along this path.

Phase models of sustainability

Various authors have described the historical processes by which corporations have moved towards supporting ecological sustainability.[14] Studies of historical stages underlying moves towards corporate social responsibility (or as we refer to it here, human sustainability) are more rare. An exception is a model proposed by Austin. Austin proposed that corporations develop relationships with other non-profit organizations according to a 'collaboration continuum'. In this continuum, the relationship can develop from the philanthropic phase through a transactional relationship, such as sponsorship, to an integrated phase. In this stage profit and non-profit share a common aim.[15] Our interest in phase theories such as this is not primarily to develop historical understanding, although that is useful, but more importantly to understand the paths corporations must travel to reach a full commitment to a comprehensive model of sustainability that covers both human and ecological issues. If we are to move corporations towards full sustainability, we must be able to identify the stage where they are now so we can determine how to move forward.

Much can be learned by examining the history of moves towards sustainability in particular industries. For example, Hoffman has made a detailed analysis of the movement towards ecological sustainability in the chemical industry in the USA.[16] He distinguishes four stages, from 1962, when environmental issues were rarely discussed, to 1993 when the chemical industry and its key stakeholders increasingly adopted a proactive stance, viewing the environment as offering a set of strategic opportunities. In between, the chemical corporations reacted defensively and were met by tough governmental regulations; the initiative then moved from government to environmental activists. Finally the leading US chemical companies absorbed what they had seen as 'heretical' ideas, acted more responsibly, and found that the result was actually beneficial in business terms.

There is a great deal of overlap in models such as this, despite differences in the names given to the various phases and different numbers of phases. Clearly any generalized phase model is a high-level abstraction from the bewildering diversity of corporate life. Nevertheless, ideal type models of this kind have a long history in the sciences – without such a model it is difficult to compare and contrast individuals, organizations, communities.[17]

In writing this book, we reviewed current models in the ecological and management literature and also drew on our own organizational experience and research. We also reviewed the parallel but unrelated literature on the developmental phases of the movement towards human sustainability in corporations.[18] The result is a comprehensive model of the developmental phases through which corporations progress towards both human and ecological sustainability. This model is central to the approach to change outlined in this book; we summarize it here and explain it in more detail in subsequent chapters.

The sustainability phase model

The phase model is designed as a tool for making meaningful comparisons between organizations to assess their current commitment to and practice of behaviours relevant to two kinds of sustainability: human and ecological. The phases outline a set of distinct steps organizations take in progressing to sustainability. There is a progression from active antagonism,[19] through indifference, to a strong commitment to actively furthering sustainability values, not only within the organization but within industry and society as a whole.

We can use the phases to characterize an organization's characteristic way of treating the human and natural resources it employs. We can also use them to trace the historical trajectory that the organization has taken in getting to where it is and to chart possible paths forward.

The phases we distinguish are:

1 Rejection
2 Non-responsiveness
3 Compliance
4 Efficiency
5 Strategic proactivity
6 The sustaining corporation.

We do not assume that a firm necessarily progresses through the phases step-by-step on an 'improving' trajectory. To the contrary, an organization may leapfrog phases or regress by abandoning previously established sustainability practices. Significant shifts are often triggered by changes such as the appointment of a new CEO, stakeholder pressure, new legislation, economic fluctuations, or the loss of committed enthusiasts.

What are the distinguishing characteristics of each of these phases?

1 **Rejection** involves an attitude on the part of the corporation's dominant elite that all resources – employees, community infrastructure and the ecological environment – are there to be exploited by the firm for immediate economic gain. On the human side, employees are regarded simply as industrial 'cannon fodder': there is no commitment to developing them, and health and safety measures are ignored or paid 'lip service'. There is a strong belief that the firm simply exists to maximize profit and any other claims by the community are dismissed as illegitimate. The firm disregards the destructive environmental impacts of its activities and actively opposes any attempts by governments and 'green' activists to place constraints on its activities.

2 **Non-responsiveness** usually results from lack of awareness or ignorance rather than from active opposition to a corporate ethic broader than financial gain. Many of the corporations in this category embody the culture of the past century, concentrating on 'business as usual', operating in conventional ways that do not incorporate sustainability issues into corporate decision making. The firm's human resource strategies, if they exist, are focused mainly on creating and maintaining a compliant workforce. Community issues are ignored where possible and the environmental consequences of the firm's activities are taken for granted and, if negative, disregarded.

3 **Compliance** focuses on reducing the risk of sanctions for failing to meet minimum standards as an employer or producer. In organizations at this stage, the dominant elite emphasizes being a 'decent employer and corporate citizen' by ensuring a safe, healthy workplace and avoiding environmental abuses that could lead to litigation or strong community action directed towards the firm. However, they are primarily reactive to growing legal requirements and community expectations for more sustainable practices. A recent shift has seen the development of co-regulatory practices. Instead of the traditional 'command and control' approach of governmental regulation, industry, NGOs and governments are collaborating to develop new systems of voluntary compliance. This shift represents a transition from compliance towards later phases.

4 **Efficiency** reflects a growing awareness on the part of the dominant elite in the corporation that there are real advantages to be gained by proactively instituting sustainable practices. In particular, human resource and environmental policies and practices are used to reduce

costs and increase efficiency. There is, for example, a growing awareness in many firms that what is defined as 'waste' derived from the production process may be a valuable resource to another firm. (For example, the spent hops from a brewery may be valuable as cattle feed and therefore sold rather than dumped.) Similarly, investment in training may involve expense but result in compensating added value through increased quality of products and services. While moves towards sustainability may involve additional expense, they can also have significant payoffs in terms of generating income directly or indirectly. This is the beginning of the process of incorporating sustainability as an integral part of the business.

5 **Strategic proactivity** moves the firm further along the sustainability path by making sustainability an important part of the firm's business strategy. The firm's strategic elite views sustainability as providing a potential competitive advantage. Consequently they try to position the organization as a leader in sustainable business practices: with advanced human resource strategies that help make the organization an 'employer of choice', with 'corporate citizenship' initiatives that build stakeholder support and with innovative, quality products that are environmentally safe and healthy. The commitment to sustainability, however, is strongly embedded in the quest for maximizing longer-term corporate profitability, that is, it is motivated by intelligent corporate self-interest.

6 **The sustaining corporation**, the final phase, is one where the strategic elite has strongly internalized the ideology of working for a sustainable world. If it is a 'for profit' company, the organization still pursues the traditional business objective of providing an excellent return to investors, but voluntarily goes beyond this by actively promoting ecological sustainability values and practices in the industry and society generally. Its fundamental commitment is to facilitate the emergence of a society that supports the ecological viability of the planet and its species and contributes to just, equitable social practices and human fulfilment.

These are only broad summaries of these categories. For the sake of simplicity of presentation our summaries assume consistency in an organization's sustainability stance across the human and ecological areas. This is an oversimplification. In reality an organization can have quite different philosophies in each area. The organization as a whole, for instance, may have relatively enlightened human resource and social responsibility strategies that place it in Phase 5 for human sustainability

(HS5), yet be simultaneously pursuing an unsustainable ecological strategy and so be in Phase 2 in ecological sustainability (ES2). For example a mining company may invest strongly in the training and development of its employees and subcontractors and also in local community development (HS5), but it may operate environmentally polluting mining operations (ES2).

A fuller version of the model, which allows for differences of this kind, is given in the Appendix at the end of this chapter. We suggest that, on finishing this chapter, you skim read this, and identify where the organization you are involved in would be appropriately placed on these two important dimensions. As we mentioned above, we shall be dealing with each of these phases in much more detail later in the book and you can check out the specific implications of our argument for your particular organizational situation.

Change agent roles and the phase model

The phase model represents the path forward to corporate sustainability. Progress on that path can only take place through the action of various change agents. In Chapter 9 we review the kinds of change agents who can impel the corporation forward on this trajectory and briefly outline their particular roles in the process. In that final chapter, we discuss these roles in more detail. Different change agent roles are critical in different phases. Nevertheless at this point you may wish to identify which kind of change agent you are so that, as you read on, you can take particular note of how you can contribute to the progressive redefinition of those organizations you can influence. This will help clarify how you can contribute to creating a more sustainable world.

The range of potential change agents includes those who work in corporations and those outside who wish to influence them. Internal change agents are board members, CEOs, executives, managers, supervisors, professionals in staff roles and other members of the workforce. External change agents include politicians and bureaucrats, investors, consultants, suppliers and subcontractors, financial analysts, social and ecological activists and other key stakeholders such as community groups, regulators and consumers. Throughout this book we shall argue that all have legitimate roles to play and that concerted action among different kinds of change agents will be needed to create the significant changes we are advocating.

The way these change agents exert influence varies – we shall take these up in more detail in Chapter 9, but some examples are useful here. Executives may exert influence through the exercise of authority: for example, through interpersonal influence in informal networks or through ensuring that their organization markets only sustainable products. Consumers may help dramatize a key environmental issue or organize a boycott of company goods if they do not meet acceptable environmental standards. Concerted action between internal and external change agents can be particularly powerful in bringing about significant change and we shall be illustrating how this can be orchestrated. Leadership in corporate change is not only exercised by senior executives; in our final chapter we show how the most powerful force for shaping the sustainable corporation of the future will be the collaborative initiatives of a variety of change agents. This book is a contribution to an emerging social movement based on implementing sustainability principles.

We hope that you now have an understanding of the exciting task we have set ourselves in this book and have begun to see where you can contribute to the significant social shift on which our collective future depends. The rest of the book will help you deepen your understanding of your potential role and maximize your influence in this change process. To guide your path through the book, we give below a brief overview of the contents of each chapter. You may wish to read the chapters in a linear fashion or identify where you think your organization lies on the path to sustainability and leap ahead to read that first. This chapter outline will help assist you to decide which way to go.

However, we do suggest that you start by reading Chapters 2 and 3. Chapter 2 develops a broad overview of the political, economic and social environment in which we as change agents will be operating. We all need a realistic description and assessment of the forces that will restrain our attempts to influence corporate strategic action as well as those drivers of change that we can draw on to support what we are doing. Then Chapter 3 outlines the sustaining corporation working actively for a fully sustainable world. If we are to lead change, we must have a view of what the ideal organization will be like. Chapter 3 presents our view of the ideal organization of the future.

The story is told of a young emperor in ancient China who was exploring the labyrinthine interior of his palace. In his wanderings he came upon a room in which the palace butcher was carving carcasses. He watched the butcher at work for some time and was surprised to find that he didn't stop to sharpen his carving knife. The emperor inquired: 'My good man, I am surprised to see that you do not sharpen your knife. Surely with such work it must frequently become blunt?' The butcher replied: 'Your Highness is correct in perceiving that for this work the sharpest of knives is necessary. However, I seldom need to resharpen my knife as I cut where there is least resistance.' As change agents, we too need to learn how to work with the grain rather than against it, to act with skill and sure timing to ensure that our limited energy has maximum impact in bringing about movement towards the fully sustainable corporation.

Chapter 2 is designed to provide a basis for understanding the context of political and social forces in which our action is a small but potentially powerful part. If we understand the major forces that are transforming the world, we can align our energy with those forces already moving society in the direction we support. In this way even small actions may be amplified to create transformational change rather than neutralized and dissipated by countervailing forces. Chapter 2 presents the context for change and Chapter 3 the ultimate goal for change.

Chapters 4–6 then discuss the major steps organizations typically take as they move beyond the phases of rejection and non-responsiveness. Organizations in these first two phases are what we refer to as 'first wave corporations'. Their attitudes of antagonism or indifference to the compelling need to create a more sustainable world reflect the lingering persistence of a collapsing corporate model. In this 'first wave' model, the corporation simply exists to exploit human and natural resources for profit, regardless of the impact of this on the current world or the world of the future. Organizations of this kind have not yet faced, in any sense, the issue of this century, an issue bluntly expressed by Lines:

> The regenerative and assimilative capacities of the biosphere cannot support even the current levels of consumption, much less the manifold increase required to generalize to higher standards of living worldwide. Still less can the planet afford an ever-growing human population striving to consume more per-capita.[20]

Chapter 4 deals with Phase 3 of our sustainability development model – compliance. In this phase, organizations seek to minimize the risk of ignoring the increasing demand, from governments, communities and activist organizations, for environmental protection and social justice. The chapter outlines the issues to be addressed at this stage in complying with relevant environmental and social legislation and in meeting the demands of key stakeholders. The chapter also points to the benefits for the corporation in going to 'compliance plus', that is, voluntarily exceeding legislative requirements and stakeholder expectations by playing a more proactive role in launching further sustainability initiatives.

This sets the scene for Chapter 5 which deals with Phase 4 of our model, efficiency. In this stage, organizations start to reap the positive rewards of concerted action on environmental and social issues. Chapter 5 discusses the nature of efficiency, enlarging the concept well beyond cost-cutting exercises. In particular it shows how the sustainability perspective creates a new mindset that can reveal three successive and cumulative cycles of efficiency-orientated measures. Each of these cycles brings important business benefits as well as contributing to the well-being of the community and the natural environment. At this point organizations often discover how wasteful are many of the traditional production or service processes they have used. Redesign of products, production flows and service systems generates significant returns. For example, recycling carpets (Interface) or remanufacturing office machine components (Xerox; Fuji-Xerox) can save millions of dollars as well as benefiting the community and environment by eliminating toxic waste from landfill.

Chapter 6 moves on to Phase 5: strategic proactivity. At this phase, sustainability becomes important in the organization's strategic repositioning. New competitive advantages can be gained, for example, by moving into rapidly expanding markets for alternative energy (BP) or becoming involved in projects designed to help regenerate communities. An example of the latter was Lend Lease Corporation's successful Bluewater retail shopping complex near the UK end of the Channel Tunnel. This massive infrastructure project took place in a community with high unemployment. Lend Lease built a training centre on site to train local unemployed people for jobs in building and, later, as the completed complex came on line, in retail skills. Its effective example of contributing to community renewal has led to further substantial construction projects for Lend Lease in Europe – most recently its development arm, Bovis, was selected as the preferred tenderer to build a £200 million hospital at Romford on the outskirts of London.[21]

Strategic proactivity is an exercise in enlightened self-interest on the part of the corporation. However Phase 6, the sustaining corporation, represents a move beyond enlightened self-interest to a reinterpretation of the nature of the corporation itself – its redefinition as an integral, self-renewing element of the whole society in its ecological context, which also actively seeks to sustain and renew the context in which it operates. Rather than placing our discussion of the sustainable corporation after Chapter 6, we have positioned it, as our ultimate goal, immediately after Chapter 2.

Chapters 5 and 6 deal with what we regard as 'second wave corporations'. Second wave corporations represent the dominant business ideology in today's world, particularly the world of large corporations. Second wave corporations at least accept the rhetoric of adopting a view of enlightened self-interest, that is, promising policies that bring wider benefits than short-term financial returns to shareholders. Second wave corporations often fall short of these ideals for various reasons which we shall discuss later. What we are seeking in this book is to assist the transition of first wave corporations into second wave corporations; to find ways to turn the rhetoric of second wave corporations into the reality of realistic action and, where possible, to support the move of more second wave organizations into third wave organizations that are truly sustainable and sustaining.

The final part of the book takes up the issue of the implementation of change. Corporate change is a theme that permeates the entire book but in Part IV we concentrate on defining pathways towards sustainability, that is, on making corporate change that moves organizations towards sustainability.

Many organizations will prefer to make changes slowly, systematically building on the achievements of one phase as they move into the next. So in Chapter 7 we discuss how to progress incremental change. For example, BP spent most of the 1990s transforming the global company from a rigid, slow-moving hierarchical organization to a networked, fast-moving, agile company. This was a long-term, substantial and sustained investment in their workforce worldwide. This significant investment in renewing the corporate culture and building corporate capabilities proved its worth, for example, in meeting the crisis of the terrorist attack on the USA of 11 September 2001. Within hours of the attack their global executive team knew exactly how each country they operate in was reacting to the unfolding crisis. Within days they had formulated and launched a comprehensive response. According to Greg Bourne, Regional President, BP Asia/Pacific Holdings Ltd, this would have been impossible in the old BP. This change programme did transform the organization 'but in an incremental fashion over a nine year period'.[22]

Other organizations will want to make widespread, rapid and quite radical alterations to the business they are in, the way they do business, their structure, their corporate culture (or all of these). The choice of a transformative path is often driven by a desire to seize new strategic opportunities or it may come from the organization facing a major threat to its viability. Chapter 8 outlines how this can be done and provides examples such as the Australian airline Qantas which has had several periods of transformative change as it privatized its operations.

Finally, Chapter 9 takes up the issue of how corporate change can be led. We discuss how a variety of change agents, occupying different kinds of roles and acting individually or collectively, can create the momentum needed to create more sustainable organizations. All of us can exercise leadership where we are. If you already are or wish to be a leader in creating this new social reality, the sustainable and sustaining organization, we dedicate this book to you. You will find it useful in the challenging task that lies ahead.

Appendix: Phases in the development of corporate sustainability

 Phase 1: Rejection

Human sustainability (HS1)

Employees and subcontractors are regarded as a resource to be exploited. Health and safety features are ignored or paid 'lip service'. Disadvantages stemming from ethnicity, gender, social class, intellectual ability and language proficiency are systematically exploited to advantage the organization and further disadvantage employees and subcontractors. Force, threats of force and abuse are used to maintain compliance and workforce subjection. Training costs are kept to a minimum necessary to operate the business;

Ecological sustainability (ES1)

The environment is regarded as a 'free good' to be exploited. Owners/managers are hostile to environmental activists and to pressures from government, other corporations, or community groups aimed at achieving ecological sustainability. Pro-environmental action is seen as a threat to the organization. Physical resource extraction and production processes are used which directly destroy future productive capacity and/or damage the ecosystem. Polluting by-products are discharged into the biosphere causing damage and expenditure on personal and professional development is avoided. The organization does not take responsibility for the health, welfare and future career prospects of its employees nor for the community of which it is a part. Community concerns are rejected outright.

threatening living processes. The organization does not take responsibility for the environmental impact of its ongoing operations nor does it modify its operations to lessen future ecological degradation.

 ## Phase 2: Non-responsiveness

Human sustainability (HS2)

Financial and technological factors dominate business strategies to the exclusion of most aspects of human resource management. 'Industrial relations' (IR) or 'employee relations' (ER) strategies dominate the human agenda with 'labour' viewed as a cost to be minimized. Apart from cost minimization, IR/ER strategies are directed at developing a compliant workforce responsive to managerial control. The training agenda, if there is one, centres on technical and supervisory training. Broader human resource strategies and policies are ignored, as are issues of wider social responsibility and community concern.

Ecological sustainability (ES2)

The ecological environment is not considered to be a relevant factor in strategic or operational decisions. Financial and technological factors dominate business strategies to the exclusion of environmental concerns. Traditional approaches to efficiency dominate the production process and the environment is taken for granted. Environmental resources which are free or subsidized (air, water and so on) are wasted and little regard is given to environmental degradation resulting from the organization's activities. Environmental risks, costs, opportunities and imperatives are seen as irrelevant or not perceived at all.

 ## Phase 3: Compliance

Human sustainability (HS3)

Financial and technological factors still dominate business strategies but senior management views the firm as a 'decent employer'. The emphasis

Ecological sustainability (ES3)

Financial and technological factors still dominate business strategies but senior management seeks to comply with environmental laws and to minimize the is on compliance with legal requirements in industrial relations, safety, workplace standards and so on. Human resource functions such as training, IR, organization development, total quality management (TQM) are instituted but there is little integration between them. Basically the organization pursues a policy of benevolent paternalism with the expectation of employee loyalty in response. Community concerns are addressed only when the company faces risk of prosecution or where negative publicity may have a damaging impact on the company's financial bottom line. Compliance is undertaken mainly as a risk-reduction exercise.

firm's potential liabilities from actions that might have an adverse impact on the environment. The most obvious environmental abuses are eliminated, particularly those which could lead to litigation or strong community action directed against the firm. Other environmental issues, which are unlikely to attract litigation or strong community action, are ignored.

 ## Phase 4: Efficiency

Human sustainability (HS4)

There is a systematic attempt to integrate human resource functions into a coherent HR system to reduce costs and increase efficiency. People are viewed as a significant source of expenditure to be used as productively as possible. Technical and supervisory training is augmented with human relations (interpersonal skills) training. The organization may institute programmes of teamwork around significant business functions and generally pursues a value adding rather than an exclusively cost reduction strategy. There is careful calculation of cost–benefit ratios for human resource expenditure to ensure that efficiencies

Ecological sustainability (ES4)

Poor environmental practice is seen as an important source of avoidable cost. Ecological issues that generate costs are systematically reviewed in an attempt to reduce costs and increase efficiencies by eliminating waste and by reviewing the procurement, production and distribution process. There may be active involvement in some systematic approach such as Total Quality Environmental Management (ISO 14001). Environmental issues are ignored if they are not seen as generating avoidable costs or increasing efficiencies.

are achieved. Community projects are undertaken where funds are available and where a cost benefit to the company can be demonstrated.

 ## Phase 5: Strategic proactivity

Human sustainability (HS5)

The workforce skills mix and diversity are seen as integral and vitally important aspects of corporate and business strategies. Intellectual and social capital are used to develop strategic advantage through innovation in products/services. Programmes are instituted to recruit the best talent to the organization and to develop high levels of competence in individuals and groups. In addition, skills are systematized to form the basis of corporate competencies so that the organization is less vulnerable to the loss of key individuals. Emphasis is placed on product and service innovation and speed of response to emerging market demands. Flexible workplace practices are strong features of workplace culture and contribute to the workforce leading more balanced lives. Communities affected by the organization's operations are taken into account and initiatives to address adverse impacts on communities are integrated into corporate strategy. Furthermore, the corporation views itself as a member of community and as a result contributes to community betterment by offering sponsorship or employee time to participate in projects aimed at promoting community cohesion and well being.

Ecological sustainability (ES5)

Proactive environmental strategies supporting ecological sustainability are seen as a source of strategic business opportunities to provide competitive advantage. Product redesign is used to reduce material throughput and to use materials that can be recycled. New products and processes are developed that substitute for or displace existing environmentally damaging products and processes or satisfy emerging community needs around sustainable issues (reforestation; treatment of toxic waste). The organization seeks competitive leadership through spearheading environmentally friendly products and processes.

Phase 6: The sustaining corporation

Human sustainability (HS6)

The organization accepts responsibility for contributing to the process of renewing and upgrading human knowledge and skill formation in the community and society generally and is a strong promoter of equal opportunity, workplace diversity and work–life balance as workplace principles. It adopts a strong and clearly defined corporate ethical position based on multiple stakeholder perspectives and seeks to exert influence on the key participants in the industry and in society in general to pursue human welfare, equitable and just social practices and the fulfilment of human potential of all. People are seen as valuable in their own right.

Ecological sustainability (ES6)

The organization becomes an active promoter of ecological sustainability values and seeks to influence key participants in the industry and society in general. Environmental best practice is espoused and enacted because it is the responsible thing to do. The organization tries to assist society to be ecologically sustainable and uses its entire range of products and services to this end. The organization is prepared to use its influence to promote positive sustainability policies on the part of governments, the restructuring of markets and the development of community values to facilitate the emergence of a sustainable society. Nature is valued for its own sake.

Notes

1 D. Dunphy and A. Griffiths, *The Sustainable Corporation: Organizational Renewal in Australia*, Sydney: Allen and Unwin, 1998.

2 A nineteenth-century legal law text, *Stephen's Commentaries*, notes that Plutarch gave the credit for this to Numa who, 'finding on his accession the city torn to pieces by two rival factions of Sabines and Romans, thought it a prudent and politic measure to subdivide these two into many smaller ones, by instituting separate societies of every manual trade and profession' (H.J. Stephen, *New Commentaries on the Laws of England*, 2nd edn, London: Henry Butterworth, 1848, pp. 118–19).

3 They referred to these entities as *universitates* or *collegia*, meaning 'gathered together'. In the Middle Ages, universities and colleges were among the first organizations to be granted charters to operate independently of Church control.

4 *Time-Life History of the World*, 'Powers of the crown', Amsterdam: Time-Life Books, 1990, p. 151.

5 This special treatment meant that the East India Company could undercut its competition in the American colonies. The American colonists objected to paying British taxes without the right of political representation and they resented a British-based corporation being given a competitive advantage in American trade. So some Bostonians, dressed as Indians, emptied an East India Company cargo of tea into the harbour, creating a confrontation with the Crown that led to the revolutionary war. *Time-Life History of the World,* 'Winds of revolution', Amsterdam: Time-Life Books, 1990, pp. 103–5.

6 'Ending corporate governance', < http://www.ratical.org/corporations> (accessed 17 December 2000).

7 <http://www.ratical.org/corporations/TcoBeij.html> (accessed 17 December 2000).

8 A. Kennedy, *The End of Shareholder Value: Corporations at the Crossroads*, London: Orion Business, 2000.

9 T. Flannery, 'The lonesome prairie', *Good Weekend, Saturday Herald,* Sydney, 3 March 2001, 35–41; T. Flannery, *The Eternal Frontier: An Ecological History of North America and its Peoples*, Melbourne: Text Publishing Company, 2001.

10 P. Hawkins, A. Lovins and H. Lovins, *Natural Capitalism: Creating the Next Industrial Revolution*, London: Earthscan, 1999.

11 T.F. Flannery, *The Future Eaters: An Ecological History of the Australasian Lands and People*, Port Melbourne: Reed Books, 1994.

12 S. Hart, 'Beyond greening: strategies for a sustainable world', *Harvard Business Review*, Jan–Feb 1997, 67–76. This quote p. 76.

13 D. Pearce and E. Barbier, *Blueprint for a Sustainable Economy*, London: Earthscan, 2000.

14 C.B. Hunt and E.R. Auster, 'Proactive environmental management: avoiding the toxic trap', *Sloan Management Review*, 1990, 31, 7–18; A.J. Hoffman, *From Heresy to Dogma: An Institutional History of Corporate Environmentalism*, San Francisco: New Lexington Press, 1997; A.J. Hoffman, 'Institutional evolution and change: environmentalism and the US chemical industry', *Academy of Management Journal*, 1999, 22(4), 351–7; A. Schaefer and B. Harvey, 'Stage models of corporate greening', *Business Strategy and the Environment*, 1998, 7, 109–23; N. Roome, 'Developing environmental management strategies', *Business Strategy and the Environment*, 1992, 4, 154–65; R. Freeman, J. Pierce and R. Dodd, 'Four shades of green', in R. Freeman, J. Pierce and R. Dodd (eds), *Environmentalism and the New Logic of Business*, Oxford: Oxford University Press, 2000, pp. 37–62; V. Fung, *The Management of Ecological Information: Understanding How Organizations Approach and Structure Sustainability Issues*, Honours Dissertation, School of Management, Queensland University of Technology, 2000.

15 J. Austin, *Strategic Collaboration Between Non-profits and Businesses*, Working Paper, Harvard University, 1999.

16 Hoffman, 'Institutional evolution and change', 351–7.

17 For a recent discussion and analysis of the stage model approach, see
A. Kolk and A. Mauser, 'The evolution of environmental management: from
stage models to performance evaluation', *Business, Strategy and the
Environment*, 2002, 11, 14–31.

18 Dunphy and Griffiths, *The Sustainable Corporation*.

19 We do not imply here, of course, that all organizations start the journey from
a position of active antagonism to sustainability. Some organizations are
actually founded on strong ethical commitments (Phase 6) – they are
however the exception, rather than the rule.

20 W.J. Lines, *Open Air Essays*, Sydney: New Holland Publishers, 2002,
pp. 126–7.

21 C. Cummins, *Sydney Morning Herald*, 1 March 2002, Business Section,
p. 23; 'Case example 12 – Lend Lease Bluewater', in B. Hirsch and
P. Sheldrake, *Inclusive Leadership*, Melbourne: Information Australia, 2000,
pp. 141–2.

22 Personal communication in an interview with Dexter Dunphy undertaken as
part of the PriceWaterhouseCooper's CEO *Snapshot on Culture*, Sydney,
January 2002.

2 The drivers of change

- Issues of global survival
- Emerging forces driving sustainability
- External drivers of change
- Internal drivers of change
- Conclusion

Issues of global survival

On 11 November 2001, Kofi Annan told the General Assembly of the UN:

> One is tempted to say that we must now focus all our energies on the struggle against terrorism, and on directly related issues. Yet if we did so we should give the terrorists a kind of victory. Let us remember that none of the issues that faced us on September 10 has become less urgent. The number of people living on less than one dollar a day has not decreased. The number of people dying of Aids, malaria, tuberculosis, and other preventable diseases has not decreased. The factors that cause the desert to advance, biodiversity to be lost and the earth's atmosphere to warm, have not decreased.[1]

Sustainability is now widely held to be the desirable path forward for organizations. The notion has an increasing purchase on legitimacy. Yet there is still little agreement on what sustainability means or how we can achieve it. Consequently, governments and corporations are struggling with issues of survival and renewal – for themselves, for the human community and for the ecosphere.

We see five key issues pressuring corporations to become more responsible global citizens. The first issue is poverty. There are still 1.2 billion poor people in the world.[2] Second, much of the material wealth is owned by the major corporations of the developed world.

Third, the negative effects of globalization and industrialization are largely impacting on the developing world and are linked with the loss of traditional localized cultures and community life.[3] There has been a pattern of special pleading and avoidance on the part of some self-interested nations and corporations which has both limited the ability of international agreements to address these inequities and increased the social pressure on corporations to be more responsible citizens.

Fourth, the failure of the international community of nations and individual corporations to address these concerns is now a subject of intense interest to an increasingly aware and communicative global audience. Society is less willing to take lack of scientific evidence as a reason for inaction in the cause of environmental and social well-being. Much more is demanded from the corporation by a wider range of stakeholders, including many who have come together under the wide umbrella of sustainability. Finally, national governments are experimenting with a number of ways to use market and legislative mechanisms to encourage change in terms of more corporate accountability and innovation for sustainability.

The findings of the most recent *Living Planet Report* clearly indicate that existing policies have failed to deal with the planetary impacts of industrialization and globalization. The report estimated that, while the state of the Earth's natural ecosystems has declined by about 33 per cent over the last thirty years, the ecological pressure of humanity on the Earth has increased by about 50 per cent over the same period.[4] Raised awareness and new technological developments across society have delivered some hope. For instance, air pollution in many cities has decreased and the share of people in developing countries with access to clean drinking water has increased. But even the sceptics agree we should be able to do better than create a world with 800 million starving people,[5] where the number of people living in extreme poverty is still at 1.2 billion, a figure little changed since 1990.[6]

The destructive environmental and social side-effects of the combination of population growth and increased consumption have contributed to these issues of global survival. How do we address these issues? What role should corporations, governments and individuals play in creating a more desirable future? Central to the resolution of these issues is the need for all sectors of society to co-operate in changes designed to promote human and ecological sustainability. In this book, we support the position that the health of the natural environment does not have to be traded for the sake of human and economic development. If corporations integrate human and ecological sustainability into their business planning, then community, marketplace and workplace concerns can be addressed alongside those of the planet.

Emerging forces driving sustainability

The Earth Summit in 1992 endorsed the need for a positive relationship between the environment and business and introduced the concept of 'sustainable development', generally understood to mean development which meets the needs of the present generation without compromising the ability of future generations to meet theirs. Since then, integrating the social, environmental and economic dimensions of sustainability into a holistic process has proven a major challenge to business managers, community activists, politicians, bureaucrats and theoreticians. Consequently, the sustainability debate ranges over questions such as: How can we value and measure natural resources? How can we distribute ecological resources between and within generations? How can we build human capabilities in corporations and in society rather than destroying them?

We argue that these issues can only be resolved through forging creative alliances between citizens, governments and corporations. The complex issues of sustainability need to be addressed by a new political force: a mix of private and public actors, including empowered public interest groups, corporations, multinational organizations, national and international governments and industry associations. This kind of concerted action is needed to address the sustainability deficits that have emerged as a result of both 'command and control' regulation, where compliance is required to set requirements or standards legislatively, and market-based measures, such as environmental taxes and tradable permits. In this new order, corporate actors will be rewarded for their proactive engagement with issues of sustainability and their contributions to the welfare of society and the biosphere. This is not simply idealism – it is an emerging reality. An example here is the significant contribution that the environmental technology industries are making to the success of some economies, such as Sweden. However, we have a long way to go to make this new reality simply the way we normally do business.

This chapter looks at the external and internal forces causing corporations to shift to a more socially and responsible position. External pressures on the firm come from governments, community members, consumers, customers and market expectations, other corporations, industry associations, and other non-government organizations. The internal drivers are corporate leaders and change agents who see the benefit of the business case for sustainability. Marketing, human resource and operations managers are now making decisions influenced by sustainability factors.[7] Employees, shareholders and investment companies are assessing the firm's performance against sustainability criteria such as the maintenance of intellectual, knowledge and social capital, commitment and values, risk management and, increasingly, an innovative corporate culture. All are factors that will assist in the long-term survival of the firm in the new economy.[8]

Another driver of change underpins the increasing interest that corporate leaders are taking in sustainability. There is a moral purpose to the shift that goes beyond rational utility and business advantage. This new issue is responsibility: to future generations and to the world as we know it today. Leading writers talk of new models for corporations that will dictate a new way of doing business. For these writers, the firm, like any other aspect of society, is a living organizm in an interconnected ecological community, where caring for others is the long-term function of each community member.[9]

External drivers of change

Globalization and corporate consolidation

Since the 1970s, deregulation and privatization have replaced state intervention as the political imperatives of global politics. The accepted orthodoxy is that policies of neoliberalism such as deregulation and free trade will shift resources to underdeveloped countries, which will in turn increase their wealth. Furthermore, by embracing globalization, countries can share in economic progress and efficiency. Through a near-blind acceptance of these economic ideals we have reached a situation whereby the complex and global operations of financial markets and major corporations go beyond the power of national governments. Now almost three-quarters of the world's trade is controlled by the top 500 corporations, intra-firm trade accounts for approximately one-third of all world trade and fifty-one of the world's largest economies are corporations.[10] The recent consolidation of corporate power across service, manufacturing and extractive industry sectors has raised questions concerning the defencelessness of individual members of society.[11]

Some corporations are now in a position of unprecedented power. This raises the issue of how this power is exercised and for whose benefit. The trend towards world-wide corporate consolidation has led to an emotive debate about political influence, democratic input, labour standards, human rights and inequities within and between nation states. As writers such as David Korten put it, if global corporations and financial markets continue to be accountable only to the financial bottom line, society will face more environmental destruction, the marginalization of persons, communities, cultures and the creation of learned incapacity and helplessness.[12] In other words, the belief systems associated with neoliberalism are open to question and debate.

Social and environmental impacts of globalization

Globalization has opened markets, dispersed capital and grown investments and has been endorsed by most leaders of developing and developed countries. But globalization is also reinforcing and extending inequities in human living standards. Global activity, such as increased trade and financial flows, disproportionately benefits the richer countries. For example, the USA receives two-thirds of all international investment while most developing countries receive little.[13]

Environmental degradation has social costs and social deprivation has environmental costs. As the Executive Director of the United Nations Environment Program (UNEP), Klaus Toepfer, has pointed out: 'Fifty percent of the world's peoples now live in cities and often the most toxic element in the environment is poverty.'[14] The environmental costs of the global increase in industrial activity are also distributed unevenly between nations.

Recent measurements reveal global temperature and the increase in atmospheric CO_2 at all-time highs. Each new set of measurements confirms the link between global warming and carbon emissions. Climate change is now accelerating so fast that the Arctic is expected to be ice free in summer within the next fifty years. Other effects include the wholesale destruction of coral reefs and the potential for a drastic alteration of the social and economic life of many countries.[15] The weather-related damages associated with global warming have the most disastrous effects on the poorer, uninsured nations. In the floods of 1998, for instance, two-thirds of Bangladesh was submerged.[16] Even critics of the Kyoto Protocol on Climate Change agree that global warming has massive costs and that the 'developing countries will be hit much harder' by the rises in temperature.[17]

Inequities of this magnitude feed more social unrest, which in turn exacerbates social inequities and wreaks more environmental destruction. The implication for corporations becomes only too apparent. Do they defend and take part in this system that contributes to these social and environmental problems or do they shift activities to become part of the solution?

Ulrich Beck, the German sociologist, argues that since many of these social and environmental impacts are global, incalculable in scale, uninsurable and irreversible, coping with them is beyond the capacity of the traditional institutions of science, law and political systems.[18] For instance, the costs and long-term effects of the fallout of the nuclear incident at Chernobyl in 1986 and the leak of methyl isocyanate gas at the Union Carbide factory in Bhopal, India in 1984 are still in dispute, perhaps still to be reckoned with. Likewise, there is much uncertainty concerning the precise nature of the relationship between the build-up of greenhouse gases in the atmosphere and global warming.[19] The debates and uncertainties associated with the outbreak of bovine spongiform encephalopathy (BSE) in the United Kingdom and the use of genetically modified (GM) organisms to produce foodstuffs reflect a public loss of faith in the ability of our institutions to deal with these risks and uncertainties. As John Browne, President of BP, put it in his recent Reith Lecture: 'We are in a world without certainty – except for the certainty of change.'[20]

In situations of such uncertainty, disagreement between scientific experts is exploited by interest groups. In the dispute over the sinking of the oil-rig, the Brent Spar, for instance, both Shell (the owners of the vessel) and Greenpeace (opposed to the sinking) weighed into the debate, each with their own expert advisers on hand.[21] In the recent debate over the safety of GM technology, the British newspaper the *Observer* obtained a secret report showing that Monsanto deliberately worked to have pro-genetic modification supporters appointed to key international food safety committees and established a network of scientists to write articles critical of the anti-GM cause.[22] Partly as a result of such activities, Monsanto's reputation has suffered considerably.

In the UK, a national agency has been established to help the response to a variety of risks from environmental, terrorist and health issues. It represents an attempt to counter the threat of chemical and radiation weapons, the unknown causes of disease and their alarming spread.[23] A recently published US study, conducted by the National Cancer Institute and the Centers for Disease Control and Prevention, estimates that 15,000 deaths from cancer can be attributed to Cold War nuclear tests and that everyone living in the US had been exposed to fallout.[24]

'Globalization from above'

Two sets of actors have emerged on the global stage in reaction to these social and environmental effects of industrialization. From above, government representatives are negotiating international agreements, such as the response to diminishing world oil reserves, the nuclear non-proliferation treaties, GATT, the World Economic Forum, the World Trade Organization and the intergovernmental agreements on the environment.[25] However, national governments experience difficulties in co-operating in the implementation of the intergovernmental agreements concerning sustainability for various reasons, including unemployment, economic conditions and the activities of various interest groups. This puts the onus on multinational corporations to take more responsibility for their actions.

The World Commission on Environment and Development (WCED) was established by the United Nations in 1983 and was chaired by Gro Harlem Brundtland. The WCED report, *Our Common Future*, was the first attempt by an intergovernmental body to promote global dialogue on sustainability.[26] The report takes appropriate sustainable development or progress to be development which 'meets the needs of the present without compromising the ability of future generations to meet their own needs'.[27]

This view of appropriate development was promoted at the Second United Nations Conference on the Environment and Development (UNCED), held in 1992 in Rio de Janiero. It was the largest ever Heads of Government meeting, with more than 170 countries represented. The Conference endorsed the major action plan Agenda 21. The 400-page Agenda 21 has been widely taken as a blueprint for the implementation of sustainable development and the integration of economic growth with environmental responsibility. Since then the international community has developed a range of treaties and agreements, which are designed to monitor 'progress' largely according to this definition. Ten global treaties and hundreds of regional and bilateral agreements have been negotiated.[28] The precautionary principle is emerging as a key aspect of these international agreements.

The precautionary principle

The precautionary principle is defined in Principle 15 of the Rio Declaration on Environment and Development 1992 as follows:

In order to protect the environment, the precautionary approach shall be widely applied by States according to their capabilities. When there are threats of serious or irreversible damage, lack of full scientific certainty shall not be used as a reason for postponing cost-effective measures to prevent environmental degradation.

International agreements have now embraced the precautionary principle. International treaties and protocols such as under the Convention on the Prevention of Marine Pollution by Dumping of Wastes and Other Matter (London Convention) emphasize the need for caution when there is a lack of conclusive evidence of cause–effect relationships. The 1996 Protocol to the London Convention states that:

If a waste is so poorly characterized that proper assessment cannot be made of its potential impacts on human health and the environment, that waste shall not be dumped.

In another example of the application of this principle, the Paris Convention for the Prevention of Marine Pollution from Land-based Sources places the burden of proof on those who propose change, even when there is no scientific evidence to prove a causal link between emissions and effects.[29]

Application of the precautionary principle in such agreements can have major implications for corporations. In situations where scientific evidence is inconclusive, the decision making becomes political, rather than scientific. In other words, application of the precautionary principle would imply involvement of as many stakeholders as possible.[30] With environmental law a rapidly expanding field, many more corporate development projects are likely to be challenged under the precepts of this principle. It is now enshrined, if not yet fully applied, in national legislatures as well as in international agreements.

Responses to 'globalization from above'

Corporate and government irresponsibility and equity issues in the development of treaties and agreements are putting business under pressure to implement voluntary sustainability measures to supplement the international agreements. Compliance with some agreements, such as the International Labour Organization's Convention 169 Concerning Indigenous and Tribal Peoples in Independent Countries, remains inadequate.[31] Many treaties remain unratified by influential signatory nations and international policing measures are not determined. The USA consumes 24.8 per cent of the world energy, 18.5 per cent of the forest product and 28.7 per cent of materials, yet has not ratified the Basel Convention, the Convention on Biological Diversity, the Kyoto Protocol or the Convention to Combat Desertification.[32] As well, the 'imposition' of treaties on less-powerful nations has been the cause of much resentment from North to South.[33] In an attempt to discredit intergovernmental agreements, some corporations and nations have exploited the scientific uncertainty associated with complex environmental issues.[34] For instance, the Global Climate Coalition (GCC), composed largely of corporations with fossil fuel-related commercial interests, sponsored a massive advertising campaign designed to shift public opinion against the Kyoto Protocol. Other coalitions formed by corporate activists include the Global Climate Information Project (a coalition of business, farm and labour groups), the Coalition of Vehicle Choice (funded by car manufacturers) and the Information Council on the Environment (a coal industry front group).[35]

But faced with the increasingly evident effects of global warming and rising consumer 'green power'[36] some industry leaders are beginning to take action. Key supporting corporations have deserted the GCC. Companies such as BP and Shell are gearing to the challenge of developing new forms of energy and have joined the new group founded by the Pew Centre, the Business Environmental Leadership Council. Greg Bourne, Regional Vice President of BP in Australia and South Asia, has stated that growing environmental and social concerns should not be seen as impediments to business growth, but 'the beginning of a new path for all of us'.[37]

Multinational corporations, particularly those whose reputation is most at risk because of their high profile, have reacted to the difficulties associated with developing and monitoring international agreements by supporting voluntary international codes of behaviour. Many codes now exist. They include the Valdez Principles, the US Business Principles for Human Rights of Workers in China and the Business Charter for Sustainable Development. Other corporations have taken part in the creation of measurement and reporting systems. For instance, the ISO 14000 series for systems of environmental management was created by the collaboration of ninety standard-setting groups from 100 different countries. More than 7,800 sites are now registered for ISO 14001 certification.[38] Among these sites are some of the world's most powerful corporations. Another group, the Coalition for Environmentally Responsible Economies (CERES), in partnership with the United Nations Environment Programme (UNEP), has convened the Global Reporting Initiative (GRI) to develop indicators to assess corporations in terms of their economic, environmental and social performance.

A precautionary model for development

The difficulty encountered so far in ensuring social and environmental health in the face of global capitalism is also putting pressure on the UN to take on broader and more binding responsibilities. At the World Economic Forum in Davos in 1999, UN Secretary Kofi Annan challenged business to support a Global Compact he called 'Globalization with a Human Face'.[39] The compact is intended to promote human rights, just labour standards and good environmental practices and marks an attempt by the UN to lead both the private and public spheres in the direction of a more equitable and ecologically sustainable model of development.

Although the 'globalization from above' movement has to date demonstrated a limited capacity to implement sustainability,[40] there is evidence of corporations co-operating pro-actively to lend more support to sustainability. Some world and corporate leaders are showing that they are willing to push for development which is more cautious and self-reflective. As well, an equally powerful force is swelling up from below.

'Globalization from below'

Organized by transnational NGOs and spread largely on the internet, 'globalization from below' is an initiative directed against the perceived self-seeking manipulations of elite nation states and transnationals driving 'globalization from above'.[41] The aims of 'globalization from below' are diffuse and the vision for the future is not clearly specified. But the message is clear on two counts. The 'globalization from below' movement, and the criticism of Western 'imperialism' surrounding the events of September 2001, indicate the extent to which some constituent groups in society are opposed to Western developmentalism. Second, influential environmentalists, such as Paul Hawken and Dr Vandana Shiva, whose books and articles have a world-wide audience, are leading anti-globalization protesters in support of decentralized decision making on sustainability issues.[42] In this debate, many multinationals have been targeted by demands to deliver more sustainable outcomes.

A recent global campaign by environmental associations and human rights groups illustrates the influence of globalization from below. Skanska, the Swedish construction firm, pulled out of an international consortium which proposed to build the Ilisu Dam in eastern Turkey. It did so to save its environmental reputation, at risk because of the global publicity given the project. Environmentalists and human rights activists, using the internet as a communication tool, claimed that the dam would cost 25,000 Kurds their homes and would potentially cut the flow of the river Tigris into Iraq.[43]

The networked society

'Globalization from below' highlights two important points for corporations. First, globalization and the information revolution have also given the general public the means for self-critique and self-transformation. As awareness of the limitations of our traditional institutions spreads, we are moving towards what Hazel Henderson has termed 'the networked society'. Henderson argues that the most noticeable current political trend has been the advance of citizen organizations and movements. They are now a distinct third sector in the world holding the private and public sectors more accountable. More access to information has helped empower citizens, consumer choice, employees and socially responsible investors. 'The information society has created new winners – and morphed into the "age of truth"'.[44]

Second, with increased public awareness of sustainability issues, customer and market expectations are looking to more responsible products and services. The 1999 Millennium Poll sponsored by PriceWaterhouseCoopers showed that two in three citizens wanted companies to go beyond their traditional goal of maximizing shareholder value and consider broader societal goals. In a firm-specific study in 1998, the great majority of the major customers of Hewlett-Packard mentioned an ISO 14001-certified environmental management system, documentation of continuous improvement against environmental performance objectives and clear environmental attribute information for their products as criteria they use when making purchasing decisions. More than 50 per cent of the companies said they would expect energy-efficient, safe products.[45]

Alliances for sustainability

The second force driving the corporate shift to sustainability is the formation of new alliances in the name of sustainability. In this new global reality, alliances and networks are forming between social and natural scientists, business, local government, community and other social actors whose allegiances cross established boundaries. The media, information systems and ad hoc 'coalitions of opposites', such as those between NGOs and business organizations, are increasingly influential in all aspects of society. The Global Reporting Initiative, for instance, gathers input from environmental, human rights and industry association NGOs. Consumer action and mass boycotts and protests are forcing corporations to defend their actions. The open-ended nature of the sustainability ethic gives it the power to bring together, at least to the discussion table, people and groups with very different political and ideological perspectives. Some supporters advocate greening of business models which work within the current model of capitalism and democracy and support continuing technological innovation and economic growth.[46] Others argue that this approach merely encourages the continuing exploitation of ecological resources, rather than guiding us towards a more harmonious relationship with nature.[47] Other critics argue that a reliance on technical solutions for sustainable development and their diffusion to the countries of the South represents just another exploitative, special-interest-based relationship between North and South.[48] Still others take the long-term value of life on Earth to be the crucial component of the sustainability ethic; an approach incompatible with the standard approach from economics of discounting the future.[49] 'Social ecologists', on the other hand, argue that human beings will continue to exploit nature if they continue to exploit each other, as in current conditions of global capitalism.[50]

Because of the capacity of sustainability to bring together different factions of society, a wide range of environmental and human rights organizations have emerged as a powerful force for corporate change, operating at both national and international levels in co-operation with corporations. Some have become heavily involved as gatekeepers of national deregulatory reforms and in co-operative arrangements at the international level.[51]

According to Professor George Molenkamp of KPMG Environmental Consulting, leading corporations are now moving beyond an environmental focus. There is a growing awareness of internal and external social issues, and broader interpretations of the meaning of corporate stakeholders.[52] Dynamic partnerships between these newly recognized stakeholders are bringing about major shifts in corporate attitudes and practices. The Global Reporting Initiative, as mentioned, is one. In another instance, the NGO Global Forest Watch provides maps indicating the whereabouts of old growth forests and other data for the Ikea corporation to enable purchasing of forest products according to sustainable criteria. Another example is the partnership formed between the World Wide Fund for Nature (WWF) and the Unilever Corporation, at the time the world's largest supplier of frozen fish, with the aim of developing incentives to support sustainable fishing. The Marine Stewardship Council was developed as a result of this alliance.[53] The community-based Landcare movement in Australia, which aims to foster sustainable natural resource management, has formed many partnership arrangements with corporate supporters such as the major mining firm Rio Tinto, the resources company BHP, and Fuji Xerox. Sponsorship agreements can influence corporate support for sustainability. Examples include more precautionary labelling on paint tins for safe disposal and the development of an approved environment policy by the manufacturer of home-brand paints. McDonald's was refused partnership because of its lack of policy on waste reduction.[54]

As pointed out, informed consumer choice has been fanned by global information networks. Successful community-initiated legal action suits and consumer boycotts of companies concealing negative environmental effects have led citizen action groups to seek the role of corporation stakeholders. For instance, good neighbour agreements are increasingly common, with corporations and neighbourhoods working together to develop win–win solutions in problem solving. Examples of outcomes from such agreements include safety audits conducted by local residents, commitments to local hiring and research into best available alternatives.[55] The Responsible Care code followed by many chemical companies, for instance, requires each of the companies to form a community consultative committee.

Corporations are learning from relationships with other sectors. They are learning to be mission- and board-led, and their employees are learning the value of social cohesiveness and a shared sense of responsibility. They can gain in legitimacy, while keeping to their central business focus.[56] They are recognizing the growing demand from across society for more participatory decision making and accountability.[57] In the process they have learnt the value of strategic alliances and of sustainability.

The mining industry faces new challenges

A new and independent study group, Mining, Minerals and Sustainable Development (MMSD), has been established with the aim of assisting the mining industry solve the problem of how to satisfy demand for minerals while addressing the social, environmental and community impact of their industry. MMSD has established an assurance group comprising twenty-five representatives from the mining industry, the union movement, investment houses and NGOs, including environmental activists, who will evaluate the integrity of the project. So far, the group has established eight areas of priority attention. These include environmental and land management issues, national economic development, sustainable markets and consumption patterns.[58]

The dangers of 'greenwash'

The UK Turnbull Report has recently emphasized the need to build reputational capital, pointing out that 'a company's social, ethical and environmental working practices can make or break a brand name and affect share prices'.[59] The implications for share price, and thus for investment decisions by large investment funds, and for employee perceptions of corporate trustworthiness and values make reputation a powerful driver of change. Shareholders are increasingly concerned at the loss in value of their stocks in the case of failure to meet government regulations or community expectations. The Asian financial crisis, the Nike child labour issues, the Lockheed bribery scandal and the alleged involvements of Shell in the internal political situation in Nigeria have all contributed to corporate leaders shifting their attitude to sustainability away from a narrow focus on technical aspects of environmental problem solving to a more holistic approach which includes social concerns such as human rights and community impacts. In the emerging discourse of corporate citizenship, sustainability, reputation and performance are inextricably linked.

Nike under pressure

In 1996, Nike's reputation suffered a major blow when a magazine in the USA published a photo of a Pakistani boy sewing together a Nike football. The next year, Nike's progressive image was damaged further when a *New York Times* front page article revealed human rights abuses at its subcontractors' factories in Vietnam.[60] The article was based on an inspection report by Ernst & Young that described workers at the factory near Ho Chi Minh City being exposed to carcinogens in parts of the plant which exceeded local legal standards by 177 times; 77 per cent of the employees were said to suffer from respiratory problems. The report revealed that employees at the site, which is owned and operated by a Korean subcontractor, were forced to work 65 hours a week, far more than Vietnamese law allows, for US$10 a week.

More recently, Nike's reputation suffered further damage when they allegedly fired workers at the Kuk Dong factory in Mexico. Those fired had led protests against rotten food, low wages, refusal to pay maternity benefits and unwillingness to provide adequate safety equipment. In October 2000, MIT Professor Dara O'Rourke reported on the monitoring of human rights at Nike by PriceWaterhouseCoopers. O'Rourke noted that the PriceWaterhouseCoopers' monitors often failed to question workers on certain employee rights issues and that, even when they did so, Nike rejected their findings. In this instance, Nike also gave the responsibility for education on labour rights to factory management, despite the fact that factory workers accuse management of refusing them labour rights.[61]

Pressure from investors

More informed shareholders are demanding a role in corporate decision making. Not only can shareholder activism be extremely damaging to the reputation of the corporation, but shareholders are now using sustainability as a measure of financial success. Sustainability indices such as the Dow Jones Sustainability Index are outperforming other indices.[62] The financial markets are generally requiring more information on standards of accountability and the financial services industry is now under considerable pressure to provide for ethical investment.[63] Currently, the ethical investment sector in the USA represents 13 per cent of all dollars under management, with more than US$13 trillion invested.[64] The Socially Responsible Investment (SRI) industry is a major growth sector of the financial services industry, growing by a factor twelve times that of the wider managed funds sector.[65]

The UK government has recently passed legislation to regulate pension funds so that they have to take account of the environmental, social and ethical impacts of their investments. The funds are evidently prepared to take a strong stance on these issues. In a survey of the twenty-five largest UK pension funds, around 70 per cent of the funds said that they would implement SRI principles through active engagement rather than simply boycotting specific industry sectors such as tobacco and alcohol.[66] This initiative of the UK government reflects a general shift in the policy making of national governments towards supporting sustainability.

National governments: the failure of command and control

As a result of a number of environmental issues in the 1970s and early 1980s, governments became aware that existing 'command and control' policies could not deal with cases where industry was acting irresponsibly. Government agencies also began to recognize that ecological problems represented complex issues for which there may be no clear yes or no answers. Scientific risk assessment would not necessarily provide the answers. Furthermore, it became apparent that in many cases of public policy making concerning the environment and occupational health and safety, the public was effectively excluded by corporate capture of the regulatory agency.[67] The Love Canal episode acted as an awakening call to government and business that environmental irresponsibility could not continue.

Love Canal

In this episode, public authorities in the USA were held responsible by an outraged community for allowing development, including the building of expressways, housing and schools, upon and beside an abandoned storage dump containing 21,800 tons of toxic chemical waste. Not only did the episode focus intense public attention on incidents concerning toxic materials and wastes but it drew public attention to the collusion between industry and government.

After a federal emergency was called in 1978, the US government moved to pass into law the Comprehensive Environmental Response, Compensation and Liability Act (CERCLA or Superfund). Under Superfund, both government and corporation are deemed responsible for toxic site clean-up. Superfund gave the US Environmental Protection Agency (EPA) the administration of such tasks as the location, investigation and cleaning up of hazardous waste sites and the right to charge companies for site clean-up as well as taxing chemicals and petroleum industries for such operations.[68]

New approaches to change

Since the Brundtland Report and the Rio Conference, business has been drawn into a system of co-regulation, where government, business and community are all expected to play a part in sustainable development and pollution prevention. Many members of the public, and increasing numbers of industry and government leaders, recognize that government alone cannot bear the responsibility for decisions taken by industry. Corporate capture has remained an issue[69] but is increasingly challenged. In a recent example, prior to Kyoto, the Australian Bureau of Agricultural and Resource Economics (ABARE) produced a report predicting major costs to Australia in jobs and income if the proposed emission targets were met. The Australian government used this report to support their argument to raise rather than to lower Australian emission levels. The ABARE report was extensively criticized by leading academics (131 economists signed a statement that criticized the report for over-estimating the costs and underestimating the benefits). The ABARE model was subsequently exposed as being 80 per cent funded by the fossil fuel industry.[70]

In order to prevent these practices, community representatives are playing a more prominent role in the negotiations between government and industry. For instance, a Community Consultative Committee has effectively acted as a watch-dog on negotiations between the New South Wales EPA and Orica (previously ICI Australia). The negotiations have concerned the disposal of the largest stockpile in the world of hexachlorbenzene (HCB), a toxic organochlorine compound.

During the 1990s, co-regulation has also meant the development of new forms of legislation designed to integrate sustainability principles into the decision making of business. Many governments are examining incentives to prompt business recognition of the new reality that moral and ethical responsibility can co-exist with financial success. The user pays principle has emerged as a key driver of corporate change. In essence, governments are now working towards ensuring that those who create the risks pay for them.[71] Taxes such as consumer fees for the disposal of appliances (applied in Japan), legislation for producer responsibility (in Sweden and the Netherlands) and pollution taxes in many countries are examples.[72] In the USA, Superfund represents an early attempt by government to force corporations to internalize environmental costs.

Incentives-based and polluter-pays strategies include load-based licensing and tradable permits to encourage reduction of pollution. In load-based licensing, companies are charged licence fees which vary according to the amount of pollution they discharge. Other economic policy tools include tradable rights to natural resources to encourage efficient resource management, innovative design and cleaner production. Examples of such incentives include vehicle emission quotas, landfill taxes, and 'green taxes', such as carbon taxes (as in Denmark), congestion taxes (as in Singapore) and vehicle return bonuses. The British government has recently formulated policy incentives designed to encourage the local energy industry to source alternative sources of energy. Energy companies not using 'green' technologies will pay about twice the price for their fuel supplies. The initiative is geared to develop a new industry sector, such as wind turbine construction, as well as to enable Britain to meet its obligations to reduce greenhouse gas emissions under the Bonn and Kyoto agreements.[73]

New reporting requirements and concepts

The 'Porter Hypothesis' is that better designed regulation can lead to greater innovation, reduce uncertainty, raise corporate awareness and signal areas of potential resource inefficiency. Because this argument was advanced by a person widely regarded as the leading thinker in corporate strategy, it has been influential in the debate during the late 1990s concerning the framing of the environment–competitiveness relationship.[74] Although many writers have taken issue with Porter's perspective on the government–corporate relationship, the debate overall has created support for the idea that a properly designed and strictly regulated framework can prod managers to abandon ingrained ways and static models of thinking and operate for a more innovative approach to sustainability.

Accompanying the push for greater regulation is increased pressure on corporations to employ better assessment and measurement techniques in activities relevant to sustainability.[75] Accordingly, governments have become involved in the setting of sustainability targets, indicators, reporting requirements, standards and a variety of other initiatives designed to effect change in corporate behaviour. Research indicates that government initiatives have been responsible for an increased rate of publishing of health and safety and environmental reports in all countries except the USA. Bigger companies, with a higher public profile or under regulatory pressure from a number of countries, are also more likely to report. Further pressure is also placed on organizations to report by voluntary sector-specific agreements such as the Responsible Care programme of the chemicals sector.[76]

Polluter pays: new challenges for business

The adoption of the Closed Substance Cycle and Waste Management Act by the German Houses of Parliament in 1994 marked a new dimension in waste management by defining new responsibilities for business and requiring strategic planning to eliminate waste. By codifying product responsibility for parties who develop, manufacture, process, and treat or sell products, the Act represented one of the first attempts to implement a strong interpretation of 'polluter pays'. It also signalled an emerging emphasis on institutional transparency and certification – key measures associated with co-operation, co-regulation and trust. Above all, the Act was an attempt by government to shift business attitudes in the direction of the circular economy.[77]

Community right to know

In 1986 the Emergency Planning and Community Right to Know Act (EPCRA) was enacted in the USA. Through EPCRA, Congress mandated that a Toxic Release Inventory (TRI) be made public. Section 313 of EPCRA specifically requires manufacturers to report the release to the environment of more than 600 designated toxic chemicals. The reports are submitted to the US Environmental Protection Agency (EPA) and state governments. On 11 May 2000, the US EPA announced toxic emission figures for seven new sectors now included in the TRI in addition to the manufacturing sector.[78] It noted that the 1998 TRI showed a 45 per cent decrease – 1.5 billion pounds – among manufacturing industries monitored over 11 years (1988–98) and that, compared to the last TRI report, releases for those industries declined by 90 million pounds.

Ecological modernization

Porter's argument that regulation can force or 'enlighten' corporations to employ the environment as a 'competitive opportunity' has been taken up by some governments in Northern Europe and Japan.[79] These governments have initiated policies geared to encourage the emergence of a specific sector, which focuses on the development of green technology, or environmental services. This powerful approach, termed 'ecological modernization' by academic writers, sees scientific and technological advances as an answer to the dilemma of how to provide for continued economic growth without negative impact on the environment. The basic argument is that we do not have to create a new political economy to achieve sustainability. It is enough to ensure that innovative environmental goods and services become a source of profit.[80] This approach is also co-regulatory, its proponents arguing that market, government and NGOs all have a role to play in industrial transformation incorporating more ecologically friendly principles.[81] Indeed, many of the governments, such as Japan, Sweden, Norway and Germany, which have been most successful in shifting the economy away from a dependency on unsustainable production technology towards green production technology, have a tradition of close associative relations between industry, business and government.[82]

As a result of applying these strategies, the eco-industry sector in Europe now provides up to 3.5 million jobs. Currently, the core eco-industries in the EU, not including renewable energy and energy efficiency equipment and services, supply around half of the world market of €300 billion per year. With a massive expansion forecast for regions such as China, South America and South-East Asia, the world market is expected to increase to €740 billion by 2010.[83]

Globalization and the information society, informed consumers and shareholders, and new roles and policy making on the part of NGOs and national governments are major external pressures on corporations to take a more ethical stance in their business dealings in terms of respect for the rights of current and future generations. The traditional distinction between external and internal drivers is useful to highlight another set of pressures, to do with efficiency, risk management and business advantage. We can think of these pressures as the internal drivers of sustainability.

Internal drivers of change

Traditionally government and other external actors have been the major forces for corporate sustainability. More recently, internal factors are putting pressure on companies to reconsider their product design, human resource development, marketing and operations management strategies in light of business ethics and environmental and social responsibility. Each of these internal factors can be analysed in terms of business value. In a 1998 survey of 481 companies, the consulting firm Arthur D. Little found that 83 per cent of these companies saw business value in implementing sustainable initiatives.[84]

The costs of non-compliance

The most obvious internal pressure on managers in this context is cost avoidance. But the firm now needs to consider costs to its reputation in the eyes of its employees as well as external stakeholders such as shareholders, suppliers and consumers. The costs of non-compliance can be devastating for corporations, a point emphasized by a recent survey which showed that 85 per cent of US manufacturers have a corporate policy requiring compliance with the environmental standards in the country with which they do business.[85]

Being competitive means reducing costs. As we have indicated, governments are still experimenting with measures to ensure increased sustainability. As we have shown above, most governments impose penalty measures for non-compliance. Corporations which do not address social and environmental requirements face fines, workers' compensation cases, criminal convictions and payment of clean-up costs. The potential for damage liability can make non-compliance a significant business risk. Some examples:

- In the USA, the total corporate liability costs for asbestos-related diseases has been estimated at US$30 billion, far more than the product ever earned its manufacturers. In a recent court decision in South Africa, more than 300 workers in an asbestos mine were awarded damages. Claims by the multinational company that it could not be held accountable for the actions of subsidiary companies were discounted. A major concern of the workers' lawyers was that if larger settlements were won, there appeared a strong likelihood that the company would be bankrupted.[86]

- The Swiss pharmaceutical firm Roche has recently put 8,000 of its workers through training programmes to ensure they follow national and international laws, as a result of some of the world's largest pharmaceutical companies being fined more than US$700 million for operating an illegal price-fixing cartel.[87]
- In another incident, Esso was found guilty of eleven breaches of the Occupational Health and Safety Act after an explosion and fire at its Australian plant at Longford caused the death of two people and injured many others. Esso was fined US$1 million and is currently facing an additional class action seeking damages of US$650 million.[88]

The costs of inadequate protection are now taking precedence over a narrow focus on the costs of compliance. For instance, reducing the sulphur dioxide emissions that cause acid rain has been calculated to place an additional cost on Chinese industry of US$4–6 billion annually. Even the annual environmental and human health damage from a single megawatt coal-fired power station in Northern China has been calculated as more than US$39 billion.[89]

Despite the extent of such liabilities, direct costs may not be the only cost issue pushing corporations towards compliance. Indeed, for very large companies, sums of over US$50 million would need to be involved to make a difference.[90] But the costs go beyond financial liability. Many countries, such as the USA, provide for mandatory gaol sentences for managers who knowingly pollute, and authorities in the USA are increasingly vigilant in enforcing such regulations.[91]

Employee awareness

Another survey of more than 1,000 US manufacturers showed that 81 per cent have adopted formal mechanisms through which environmental considerations are addressed in everyday business and operating decisions.[92] Internal aspects of the firm can add to an explanation of these trends. With increased environmental and occupational health and safety awareness amongst employees, managers have to be seen to address requirements for employee safety as well as address environmental regulations. Wilkinson, Hill and Gollan warn that if the gap is not addressed between rhetoric and reality in this area, 'then the likely outcome will be an exodus of bright and enthusiastic people to organizations that do'.[93] According to Michael Anderson, Head Social

Responsibility Funds, AMP, tobacco companies and others with a negative public image are paying employees approximately 20 per cent more in order to get people to work for them.[94]

Leadership and risk management

A recent address by Malcolm Brinded, Shell UK Country Chairman, outlines the changed attitudes of progressive corporate leaders towards health, safety and environment risks:

> Not least is the fact they cannot be averaged. Failures in health, safety and environmental risk management may result in harm to people, and I think all of us recognise that the personal safety of anyone involved with our businesses overrides all other priorities.[95]

Brinded agrees that corporate leadership in this area is crucial to the need to change skills, attitudes and behaviours, but points to the importance of public opinion in the evaluation of the risk. He admits that Shell's poor communication led to the débâcle over the decommissioning of the Brent Spar. Their independently verified technical assessment of the risks involved was not supported by everyone. According to Brinded, Shell began to realize that 'some decisions need to be driven by values and not decided solely on the basis of sound science'.[96]

A leader's perspective: key trends in risk management

- The need for public trust
- The need for a partnership approach
- The role of personal leadership and workforce involvement
- The use of the law as a lever for safety management
- The public demand for a risk-free world[97]

Public opinion often seems only the opinion of activist NGOs, but it is now also the opinion of employees and shareholders. It has become very costly to operate companies which are not socially responsible.

Maintaining awareness of the precautionary principle and consultation with a wide range of stakeholders when assessing environmental risk can deliver business advantages. Reinhardt, for instance, describes a situation where plans for timber-harvesting and the building of a pulp mill using chlorine bleaching in the forest areas of Northern Alberta were modified according to demands made by local farmers, aboriginal residents and environmental activists. The modified plans, which included forest-management plans and reduced pollution level, cost little compared to the gains in the long-term stability of the project. Reinhardt argues that the 'environmental goods' traded were well worth it in return for 'an insurance policy against regulatory difficulties, sour community relations, business interruptions and related cost shocks'.[98] This issue highlights the importance of leadership in taking a strategic view of shifting corporations towards sustainability.

The knowledge-based organization

In the information-based economy, corporations are looking to long-term survival through the development of knowledge systems, stores of social capital and a culture of innovation. These aspects of human sustainability in turn enable the firm to take a position of more environmental responsibility. A position of corporate sustainability requires a firm both to be responsible to employees and to look to its own needs for long-term survival. In this context, managers are being influenced by a significant body of research which indicates that organizations last longer if they have clearly identified their values and goals.[99] The work of Collins and Porras is particularly notable in this regard. In their study of a number of visionary companies, these writers found that, compared to non-visionaries, these companies had an ideology which was made up of core values and purpose. It is this sense of core values which employees identified with and to which they developed commitment. Profit was important but it was not the defining feature of these visionary companies.[100] According to this research, an organization which has a clear sense of its mission for sustainability will more than survive – it can become a visionary organization and thrive in the long term.

Knowledge management is also drawing attention to the value of an organization's human resources.[101] Motivation, qualifications and commitment, when combined with a significant store of 'corporate memory', are a major asset to the corporation. Companies are increasingly dependent on employees who can work co-operatively and contribute to the social capital of the organization.[102] Social capital is fundamental to the successful working of the new organizational forms such as the network organization and communities of practice.

As prized employees hunt for the firm with a strong sense of values, there are real rewards in becoming an employer of choice. Firms need employees who can give high levels of customer service and 'who are sufficiently motivated by the company's mission and prospects to stay and aspire to higher levels of productivity. The importance of teamwork, loyalty and skills is becoming doctrine in almost every industry.'[103]

Recent work also indicates a relationship between human resource policies, the successful implementation of the Environmental Management System (EMS) and its maintenance as a strategic business and risk management tool. This research concludes that EMS programmes are more successful if factors such as training, empowerment, teamwork and rewards are addressed.[104]

Natural capitalism: the business advantage

The perspective of 'natural capitalism' has been much publicized. If firms persist with the win–win business logic of 'natural capitalism', profiting from increasing the productivity of natural resources, closing materials loops and eliminating waste, shifting to biologically inspired production models, providing their customers with efficient solutions, and reinvesting in natural capital, they can gain a commanding competitive advantage.[105]

Business advantage is also offered through the organizational restructuring required by following the principles of industrial ecology. Tracking material and energy flows over the whole producer/consumer cycle reduces the likelihood of 'suboptimal solutions' and 'unintended consequences'.[106]

At Hewlett-Packard, for example, their Environmental Strategies and Solutions programme 'confirmed that sustainability does offer companies a strategic competitive advantage'.[107] This conclusion was based on the premise that the planet is a closed system which will eventually face limits. In these circumstances, the firm would be in a new social and economic situation, and would have to deal with the challenges of a new business environment. According to Hewlett-Packard, incorporating sustainability into its core business strategies would 'enable HP to transform potential environmental liabilities such as climate change, resource exhaustion and the energy crisis into strategic business opportunities and competitive advantage'.[108]

A culture of innovation

Managers are also recognizing the links between an organizational culture of innovation and one designed to deliver sustainability. Practices designed to enhance human sustainability and social capital within the organization (such as empowerment, teamwork and continuous learning) are linked to the capacity to innovate and escape from rigid models of operation and production. Arguably, implementing more sustainable practices creates an organizational culture that facilitates both resource productivity and product differentiation.[109]

A number of companies have been successful in employing a strategy of environmental product differentiation. Reinhardt points out that such a strategy will be successful if consumers are prepared to pay more, if the benefits can be communicated readily and if the innovation is unique long enough for a profit to be made.[110] Corporations face an accelerating rate of change and an increasingly complex society. For these business conditions, innovation depends on cultural and structural characteristics of the organization. Both sets of characteristics are linked to the organization's capacity to engage with sustainability. Cultural factors such as those associated with the learning organization also underpin a culture of precaution. Structural factors such as an internal network culture, employee participation and the capability to develop community partnerships also support human sustainability. In other words, innovation, business concept redesign and sustainability can be readily linked in a dynamic relationship aimed at delivering long-term business advantage.

Importantly, such qualities enable the corporation to be more responsive to the external drivers of change. An organization geared to innovation is ready to take up government incentives for 'ecological modernization'; that is, it can readily translate social and moral issues into market issues and can exploit the potentially huge market that ecological sustainability, in particular, represents. But more than that, such an organization can more critically reflect on the possibilities of new relationships between nature, society and technology that will mark a new, more sustainable age.[111]

Conclusion

This chapter began by asking why managers are moving to address the challenges of human and ecological sustainability. In large part, the answer is that the new reality for managers is that business success and sustainability are inextricably linked. Social and environmental health are essential aspects of corporate survival. Some managers are reacting primarily to the reputational and litigious risks associated with the increasingly global reach of corporations, to the actions of internationally mobilized human rights and environmental activists and to international and national agreements and regulations concerning environmental protection and social and environmental justice. International and national governments are experimenting with a variety of policy incentives and models of governance to ensure corporate accountability.

But many other managers are also taking proactive measures in the struggle to conserve resources, minimize waste and contribute to social and ecological renewal. More companies are moving beyond compliance with government regulations to accreditation under voluntary schemes such as ISO 14001. This delivers benefits from recognition by the community, customers and other stakeholders. Importantly, corporations are increasingly influenced by new alliances being formed across the range of corporate stakeholders. Community representatives and NGOs are working with firms to develop the knowledge and social capital required for the shift to sustainable products and processes.

Shareholders and investors are also looking to more than financial success in the assessment of performance. Their selection of investments increasingly takes into account reputation and performance on the longer-term factors of social and ecological sustainability. Investors are also placing more value on the human capabilities and commitment that the organization has built. In the new economy the building of knowledge systems, social capital and other strategies designed to increase and sustain human capability are vital to corporate performance.

More and more employees have strong expectations of workplace safety and heightened environmental awareness; they are searching for more meaningful work, particularly for work that makes a social and ecological contribution as well as providing an income.

In this context, the principles of industrial ecology, of community, interconnectedness and co-operation can be seen as a model for the way forward for corporations wishing to move towards sustainability. They provide a framework for new levels of resource productivity and generate new strategic directions. More importantly, they serve as a way of understanding the corporation as a moral entity.[112]

The following chapters take us along the spectrum of corporate sustainability stances. However, it is in the next chapter that we outline our vision for the corporation of the future – the sustaining corporation.

Notes

1　H. Kempf, 'Is US power a force for good or evil?', *Le Monde* 8 January 2002; *Guardian Weekly*, 17–23 January 2002, 29.

2　B. Lomborg, *The Skeptical Environmentalist*, Cambridge: Cambridge University Press, 2001, pp. 48–9.

3　A. Giddens, *Beyond Left and Right*, Cambridge: Polity Press, 1994, p. 206.

4　World Wide Fund for Nature, *Living Planet Report*, London: WWF, 2000.

5　Lomborg, *Skeptical Environmentalist*, p. 330.

6　C. Flavin and K. Topfer, 'Foreword', in Worldwatch Institute, *Vital Signs: 2001–2002*, London: Earthscan Publications, 2001, pp. 11–13.

7　A. Wilkinson, M. Hill and P. Gollan, 'The sustainability debate', *International Journal of Operations and Production Management*, 2001, 21(12), 1492–502.

8　Ibid.; D. Dunphy and A. Griffiths, *The Sustainable Corporation*, Sydney: Allen and Unwin, 1998.

9　Ibid.; J. Ehrenfield, 'Industrial ecology: paradigm shift or normal science', *American Behavioural Scientist*, 2000, 44(2), 229–41; R. Starkey and R. Welford, 'Conclusion. Win–win revisited: a Buddhist perspective', in R. Starkey and R. Welford (eds) *Business and Sustainable Development*, London: Earthscan Publications, 2001, pp. 353–7.

10　D. Korten, *The Post-corporate World: Life after Capitalism*, San Francisco: Berrett-Koehler, 1999; D. Korten, 'The responsibility of business to the whole', in R. Starkey and R. Welford (eds) *Business and Sustainable Development*, London: Earthscan Publications, 2001, pp. 230–41.

11　M. Renner, 'Corporations driving globalisation', in L. Brown, M. Renner and B. Halwell, *Vital Signs 1999–2000*, London: Worldwatch Institute and Earthscan Publications, 1999, pp. 136–7.

12　Korten, *Post-corporate World* and 'The responsibility of business to the whole'.

13　J. Langmore, 'A callous snub to the world's poor', *Sydney Morning Herald*, 27 June 2000, 15.

14　K. Toepfer, UNEP Executive Director, address to the Third Global Forum of Parliamentarians on Habitat, 28 July 2000.

15 L. Brown, 'Overview: the acceleration of change', in L. Brown, M. Renner and B. Halwiel, *Vital Signs: 2000–2001*, London: Worldwatch Institute and Earthscan Publications, 2001.

16 Ibid.

17 Lomborg, *Skeptical Environmentalist*, p. 301.

18 U. Beck, 'Risk society and the provident state', in S. Lash, B. Scherszynski and B. Wynne (eds) *Risk, Environment and Modernity*, London: Sage Publications, 1996, pp. 27–43.

19 R. Harding (ed.), *Environmental Decision-making*, Annandale: Federation Press, 1998.

20 J. Browne, 'Business', Reith Lecture no. 3, BBC Radio 4, 26 April 2000. (Series title: 'Respect for the earth: can sustainable development be made to work in the real world?')

21 H. Tsoukas, 'David and Goliath in the risk society', *Organization*, 1999, 6(1), 499–528.

22 P. Kelso, 'Greenpeace activists cleared in GM crop case', *Guardian Weekly*, 28 September–4 October 2000, 9.

23 S. Boseley, 'Agency created to fight bioterrorism and diseases', *Guardian Weekly*, 17–23 January 2002, 11.

24 J. Borger, 'Fallout', *Sydney Morning Herald*, 4 March 2002, 10.

25 Falk, quoted in U. Beck, *World Risk Society*, Cambridge: Polity Press, 1999, p. 38.

26 World Commission on Environment and Development, *Our Common Future*, Oxford: Oxford University Press, 1987.

27 Ibid., p. 8.

28 H. French, 'Environmental treaties gain ground', in Brown *et al.*, *Vital Signs: 2000–2001*, pp. 134–5.

29 A. Deville and R. Harding, *Applying the Precautionary Principle*, Annandale: Federation Press, 1997.

30 Cameron and Wade-Gery quoted in R. Harding and E. Fisher, 'Introducing the precautionary principle', in R. Harding and E. Fisher (eds) *Perspectives on the Precautionary Principle*, Annandale: Federation Press, 1999, pp. 2–26.

31 T. Moser and D. Miller, 'Multinational corporations' impacts on the environment and communities in the developing world: a synthesis of the contemporary debate', in R. Starkey and R. Welford (eds) *Business and Sustainable Development*, London: Earthscan Publications, 2001, pp. 218–29.

32 D. Hunter, *Foreign Policy in Focus*, joint project of the Interhemispheric Resource Centre and the Institute for Policy Studies, at http://www.foreignpolicy-infocus.org/papers/environment/ (accessed 23 March 2002).

33 V. Shiva, 'The greening of the global reach', in W. Sachs (ed.) *Global Ecology*, London: Zed Books, 1993, pp. 149–56.

34 L. Brown, *The Rise and Fall of the Global Climate Coalition*, Worldwatch Institute Report, Alert 2000–6, 25 July 2000, Washington, D.C.: Worldwatch Institute.

35 S. Beder, *Global Spin*, Melbourne: Scribe Publications, 2000.
36 D. Murphy and J. Bendell, 'Getting engaged: business–NGO relations on sustainable development', in R. Starkey and R. Welford (eds) *Business and Sustainable Development*, London: Earthscan Publications, 2001, pp. 288–312.
37 G. Bourne, 'A complete health check', in *Social and Environmental Australian Location Report*, BP Australia, 2000.
38 B. Daily and S. Huang, 'Achieving sustainability through attention to human resource factors in environmental management', *International Journal of Operations and Production Management*, 2001, 21(12), 1539–52.
39 The United Nations and Business at http://www.un.org/partners/business/ (accessed 23/01/02).
40 Ehrenfeld, 'Industrial ecology'.
41 U. Beck, *World Risk Society*, Cambridge: Polity Press, 1999, p. 37; R. Falk, 'The making of global citizenship', in B. van Steenbergen (ed.) *The Conditions of Citizenship*, London: Sage Publications, London, 1994.
42 J. Palmer, 'Vandana Shiva', in J. Palmer (ed.) *Fifty Key Thinkers on the Environment*, London: Routledge, 2001, pp. 313–21.
43 P. Brown, 'Swedish firm deals blow to British-backed dam project', *Guardian Weekly*, 28 September–4 October 2000, 11.
44 H. Henderson, *Beyond Globalization: Shaping a Sustainable Global Economy*, West Hartford, Conn.: Kumarian Press, 1999.
45 L. Preston, 'Sustainability at Hewlett-Packard: from theory to practice', *California Management Review*, 2001, 43(3), 26–38.
46 E. von Weizsacker, A.B. and L. Lovins, *Factor 4: Doubling Wealth: Halving Resource Use*, London: Earthscan Publications, 1997.
47 Ehrenfield, 'Industrial ecology'; B. Szerszynski, S. Lash and B. Wynne, 'Introduction', in S. Lash, B. Szerszynski and B. Wynne (eds), *Risk, Environment and Modernity*, London: Sage Publications, 1996, pp. 1–26.
48 W. Sachs, 'Global ecology and the shadow of development', in Sachs (ed.) *Global Ecology*; Shiva, 'Greening of the global reach'.
49 R. Goodin, *Green Political Theory*, Cambridge: Polity Press, 1992.
50 A. Dobson, 'Ecologism', in R. Eatwell and A. Wright, *Contemporary Political Ideologies*, London: Pinter, 1999, pp. 231–54.
51 Murphy and Bendell, 'Getting engaged'.
52 S. Benn, interview with Professor G. Molenkamp, Manager Environmental Consulting, KPMG, The Hague, 4 February 2002.
53 Murphy and Bendell, 'Getting engaged'.
54 S. Benn, interview with B. Scarsbrick, CEO Landcare Australia Limited, Chatswood, Sydney, 23 May 2001.
55 S. Lewis, 'The precautionary principle and corporate disclosure', in C. Raffensperger and J. Tickner, *Protecting Public Health and the Environment*, Washington, D.C.: Island Press, 1999, pp. 241–51.

56 S. Sagawa and E. Segal, 'Common interest, common good: creating value through business and social sector relationships', *California Management Review*, 2000, 42(2), 105–23.

57 B. Beuermann and B. Burdick, 'The German response to the sustainability transition', in T. O'Riordan and H. Voisey, *The Transition to Sustainability*, London: Earthscan Publications, 1998.

58 Planet Ark Environmental News, Interview, 'Sustainable development group aims to aid miners', at http://planetark.org/dailynewsstory.cfm/newsid/12485/story.htm (accessed 25 September 2001).

59 *The Financial Times*, 2 June 2000, quoted in L. Preston, 'Sustainability at Hewlett-Packard'.

60 S. Greenhouse, 'Nike shoe plant in Vietnam is called unsafe for workers', *New York Times*, 8 November 1997, 1.

61 D. O'Rourke, 'Monitoring the monitors: a critique of PriceWaterhouseCoopers labor monitoring', at http://web.mit.edu/dorourke/www/PDF/pwc.pdf (accessed 23 March 2002); NikeWatch News at http://www.caa.org.au/campaigns/nike/news/ (accessed 23 March 2002).

62 F. Grey, *Sustainable Business Forum*, at http://www.csp.uts.edu.au/csn/sbfjuly01.html (accessed 18 January 2002).

63 T. Clarke, 'Balancing the triple bottom line', *Journal of General Management*, 2001, 26(4), 16–27.

64 T. Wallace, 'A quiet move to ethical investment', *Australian Financial Review*, 27 February 2002.

65 Ibid.

66 Information from Greenbiz.com at http//www.greenbiz.com/ news/news_third.cfm?NewsID=11320 (accessed 21 June 2001).

67 S. Benn, 'The EHCA 1985 (NSW): a historical perspective on issues arising in the control of toxic chemicals', *Australian Journal of Political Science*, 1997, 32, 49–64.

68 A. Hoffman, *Competitive Environmental Strategy*, Washington, D.C.: Island Press, 2000.

69 Benn, 'The EHCA 1985 (NSW): a historical perspective on issues arising in the control of toxic chemicals'.

70 Beder, *Global Spin*.

71 U. Beck, *Risk Society: Towards a New Modernity*, London: Sage, 1992.

72 O'Riordan and Voisey, *Transition to Sustainability*.

73 P. Fray, 'Change is in the air as Britain rethinks energy policy', *Sydney Morning Herald*, 9–10 March 2002, 19.

74 M. Porter and C. van der Linde, 'Towards a new conception of the environment–competitiveness relationship', *Journal of Economic Perspectives*, 1995, 9(4), 97–118.

75 Ibid.

76 Institute for Environmental Management (WIMM), Amsterdam, *KPMG International Survey of Environmental Reporting 1999*, KPMG, The Netherlands, 1999.

77 D. Matten, 'Enforcing sustainable development by legislation: entrepreneurial consequences of the new German Waste Management Act', *Sustainable Development*, 1996, 4(3), 111–66.

78 US EPA, Environmental News, Press Release, 11 May 2000.

79 Porter and van der Linde, 'Towards a new conception of the environment–competitiveness relationship', p. 114.

80 J. Dryzek, *The Politics of the Earth*, Oxford: Oxford University Press, 1997.

81 A. Mol, 'Ecological modernisation: industrial transformations and environmental reform', in M. Redclift and G. Woodgate (eds) *The International Handbook of Environmental Sociology*, Cheltenham: Edward Elgar, 1997, pp. 138–49.

82 M. Mason, *Environmental Democracy*, London: Earthscan Publications, 1999.

83 M. Wallstrom, European Commissioner for the Environment, 'Database on eco-industries in the European Union', at http://europe.eu.int/comm/environment/ecoindus/intro.htm (accessed 19 January 2002).

84 A.D. Little and Associates, 1998, quoted in A.B. and L. Lovins and P. Hawken, 'A road map for natural capitalism', in R. Starkey and R. Welford (eds) *Business and Sustainable Development*, London: Earthscan Publications, 2001, pp. 288–312.

85 Manufacturers Alliance and National Association of Manufacturers Joint Survey, at http://www.nam.org/DOCS/ResourcesEnvironmental (accessed 24 May 2001).

86 http://www.abc.net/news (accessed on 19 February 2002).

87 A. Osborn, 'Vitamin Inc fined $1.4 bn for price-fix', *Sydney Morning Herald*, 23 November 2001, 14.

88 P. Gregory and M. Shaw, 'Mapping the journey', *Sydney Morning Herald*, 31 July 2001, 3.

89 J. McDonald, 'APEC and ESD: turning sustained economic growth into ESD', in P. Leadbeter, N. Gunningham and B. Boer, *Environmental Outlook No 3: Law and Policy*, Annandale: Federation Press, 1998.

90 E. Gallagher, UK Environment Agency Chief Executive, AGM UK Environment Agency, at http://www.edie.net/news/Archive/3220.html (accessed 23 January 2002).

91 L. Fitzgibbon, 'Is industry really ready to implement strategic environmental management?', *Strategic Environmental Management*, 1998, 1(1), 1–4 April, 5–7.

92 Survey of Manufacturers, 'Encouraging findings', *Industry Week*, 19 January 1998.

93 Wilkinson *et al.*, 'The sustainability debate'.
94 M. Anderson, 'Does the market value sustainability?', *Sustainable Business Forum*, Sydney, at http://www.csp.uts.edu.au/csn/sbfjuly01.html (accessed 18 January 2002).
95 M. Brinded, 'Perception versus analysis: how to handle risk', speech to the Royal Academy of Engineering, London, 31 May 2000.
96 Ibid.
97 Ibid.
98 F. Reinhardt, 'Bringing the environment down to earth', in R. Starkey and R. Welford (eds) *Business and Sustainable Development*, London: Earthscan Publications, 2000, pp. 53–64 at p. 62.
99 J. Collins and J. Porras, *Built to Last: Successful Habits of Visionary Companies*, New York: HarperCollins, 1997; B. Hirsh and P. Sheldrake, *Inclusive Leadership*, Melbourne: Information Australia, 2000.
100 Collins and Porras, *Built to Last*.
101 Wilkinson *et al.*, 'The sustainability debate'.
102 Sagawa and Segal, 'Common interest, common good'.
103 Ibid., 106.
104 Daily and Huang, 'Achieving sustainability . . .'.
105 A.B. and L. Lovins and Hawken, 'Road map for natural capitalism'.
106 Ehrenfeld, 'Industrial ecology', p. 226.
107 Preston, 'Sustainability at Hewlett-Packard'.
108 Ibid., 29.
109 R. Orssatto, 'The ecological competence of organisations: competing for sustainability', paper presented to the 16th EGOS Colloquium, Helsinki, Finland, 1–4 July 2000.
110 Reinhardt, 'Bringing the environment down to earth'.
111 M. Hajer, 'Ecological modernisation in cultural politics', in Lash *et al.* (eds), *Risk, Environment and Modernity*.
112 Ehrenfield, 'Industrial ecology'.

3 The sustaining corporation

- Generating a future reality
- The third wave
- Putting the jigsaw together
- Conclusion

Generating a future reality

In this chapter we aim to present a vivid image of the 'sustaining corporation', that is, the corporation which fully incorporates the tenets of human and ecological sustainability into its own operations and which also works actively to support the application of sustainability principles throughout the rest of the society.

We freely admit that there are few if any organizations today that fully embody this socio- and eco-centric ideal. To date the ones most cited, such as Ben and Jerry's, Patagonia and Interface, have not been public companies but are relatively small and privately owned. And they have not always been able to maintain the advances they have made, particularly through the transitions of takeover or CEO succession. The challenge is to learn from these early adventures in sustainability and extend that learning to larger public corporations. There is, however, another source of learning. Many larger companies have experimented successfully with aspects of sustainability and we illustrate the ideal with case examples of what some of these organizations have achieved. None of these organizations yet meets the ideal, but collectively they help us create an image of how a fully committed organization would operate. The future is emerging around us, if we have eyes to see it, as innovative companies explore sustainability practices in a range of operations. The analogy is to constructing a jigsaw puzzle – we assemble one piece from one organization, another piece from another organization, until we have an overall image of the organization of the future which is modelling sustainability in its own operations and supporting the wider sustainability movement. The sustaining organization is not only sustainable itself but is also promoting and supporting the further development of sustainability principles throughout society.

This image may seem a dream. It is. Managerial leadership is increasingly about having ambitious dreams and then ensuring that these dreams are realized. Dreams are only reality waiting to happen.

> At Honda, we turn the dreams of tomorrow into realities.
> *Source*: Honda website[1]

The internet was once a dream – until it was put in place and revolutionized the economy and society. Our argument here is that transformational social change is now happening at incredible speed and that the onset of the 'third wave' will make achieving corporate sustainability a political, economic and social priority. The challenge is to turn dreams into corporate visions and visions into concrete, practical actions:

> It is simply ridiculous that we allow businesses to continue to destroy our planet. The bottom line is now simple – people are dying because of environmental degradation, people are forced into working for subsistence wages because companies need to increase their profitability, those who resist the progress of capitalism are subjected to torture and even murdered by the state because they have campaigned for human rights. Yet business still operates in concert with the institutions and governments which cause such suffering and people still buy their products. Doing business in countries which abuse human rights and torture citizens means that you accept that practice. Not protesting when your opponents are hanged is tantamount to killing them yourself. To buy the products of such a company is to agree with its actions.[2]

These are strong statements, but we are moving to a society where more people will support these views and act on them. As we write these words, a Global Greens conference held in the Australian capital, Canberra, has called for a world-wide boycott of oil companies, such as Exxon Mobil, for their contribution to President Bush's decision to dump the Kyoto convention on climate change.[3] These small gestures are amplifying into powerful collective action. More ethical investment funds are being created around the world and the capital invested in these funds is growing every day. At first glance, it seems strange that radical green activists and conservative financial institutions are now working together to ensure that corporations act responsibly, but this is a regular occurrence now. We have examined the way that powerful drivers of change are converging to change the ground rules for corporate activity. The result is that old-style companies face increasing pressure from social and environmental activists and can no longer assume that they will be supported even by financial institutions. The future lies with those organizations that anticipate changes such as this and take the lead as the changes unfold.

The third wave

So we go on to outline the nature of the third wave. The third wave sees society moving into a new paradigm where complexity and interconnectedness are central, where transformational change is more widespread and occurs over shorter time periods, where direction and momentum are achieved through alliances, shared commitment to common goals, high levels of innovation and loose coupling. In this world there will be an increase in the number of temporary organizations formed for specific purposes. Whether long-lasting or temporary, these organizations of the future will be strongly value driven. They will be responding to an emerging shift in global values that is already becoming evident in a number of ways:

- increasing support for green political parties, already a significant political force in countries such as Germany, Italy, Australia and New Zealand, to date regularly achieving between 5 per cent and 8 per cent of the popular vote in elections in these countries;
- international co-operation between governments, corporations and environmental groups to protect the environment;
- growing scientific consensus and concern about the looming environmental crisis;
- development of international regulatory agreements to promote social justice and protect the environment;
- increasing questioning of the value of the dominant neo-liberal economic model accompanied by the rise of ecological economics as an alternative;
- increasing use of the precautionary principle as a policy tool;

- the rise of post-modern philosophy questioning the association between positivist science and materialistic views of progress, and rejecting social and environmental exploitation in favour of care for all humans, other species and the natural world.[4]

This last point represents a re-emphasis on spirituality and the emergence of a new way of conducting science so that it is embedded in values that affirm biodiversity and social justice.[5] Happily this is taking place as professional scientists set up ethics committees and sign public statements about critical issues of sustainability such as environmental warming.

The most successful of these sustaining organizations will act both locally and globally, will put a premium on speedily repositioning themselves strategically to take advantage of new market opportunities and will add value through providing new levels of customized service. In this regard, they are acting strategically. For these organizations, sustainability is central to their corporate strategies and a vital ingredient in how they assess their effectiveness. They see success as dependent on developing active stakeholder relationships with a variety of community groups – they build 'stakeholder capital'. They regard their success as dependent also on the 'intellectual and skill capital' of their workforce. Therefore they systematically develop the skills of those in the core workforce and contribute to skill development in the workforces of suppliers and alliance partners. They are consciously committed to actions that increase the human capability base of society and that maintain and restore the biosphere. For those who contribute to the leadership of these organizations, the corporation is a vital link in the ecology itself and in the inter-generational continuity of society. They are 'sustaining organizations'.

We contrast this world with the world of the first wave, where organizations were discrete and enduring entities with clear boundaries, were primarily cost driven, emphasized hierarchy and control and maintained traditional ways of doing things, resisting change unless the traditional ways were clearly failing. We also contrast the third wave world with the second wave, where organizations sought to establish radically new levels of efficiency and to develop more forward-looking business strategies to ensure their futures – we discuss this further in Chapters 4 and 5.

First-wave organizations largely took the ecological and social environment for granted. At worst, some actively opposed (and still do) moves to protect the biosphere from destructive exploitation or pressure for their active involvement in community development. Typically they argued that business exists simply to make a profit. Or they ignored sustainability issues, concentrating on a narrowly defined business concept, and treating the natural and social environment as a 'free good' or a regrettable source of cost. At best, they emphasized compliance with legal restraints (health and safety regulations, waste treatment) and pursued positive sustainability policies only when these measures reduced costs or provided a clear competitive advantage. Both first wave and early second wave organizations tended to ignore the wider issues of ecological and social responsibility, generally failing to recognize and measure the negative impacts of their activities on communities and on the ecological carrying capacity of the environment (unless public reaction compelled them to do so). Issues of social and environmental responsibility were, at best, regarded as marginal to the core business of the company and to its business strategies. They emphasized the goods and services they provided and conveniently ignored the 'bads' and 'disservices' they contributed. This, however, undergoes a significant change as organizations move into Phase 5: strategic proactivity.

> The basic development patterns of the industrial era are not sustainable.
> *Source*: P. Senge, in *Sloan Management Review*[6]

If we are to turn around the serious social and environmental degradation we have created, there must be a radical departure from past practices. We argue for a reinterpretation of the role of the corporation in society and for a reintegration of the economy into the ecology and the global community. Economics cannot be separate from issues of species survival, social justice and spirituality. Similarly science and technology cannot operate without regard to the risks they create for survival, health and human happiness. And businesses cannot ignore the costs, to future generations, of operations that outrun the rate of resource replacement. However, currently most corporations do use accounting practices that ignore the social and environmental costs of their business practices. We are all part of a living system that is dependent on a delicate balance of gases in the atmosphere and a thin residue of soil created over millennia. Our activities must preserve and enrich this precious life support system, not degrade it.

Similarly, we all come into this world as helpless infants and depend for our subsequent development as mature human beings on a society that provides caring relationships, socialization and education. Traditional economics tends to ignore these functions, for example, of parents caring for their children in the home. The proper function of the economy is to support a healthy biosphere and quality of social life for the earth's human population. Consequently the sustaining organization will create a social and ethical balance sheet and be accountable for it. An important part of this approach is the increasing interest in the study of collaborative relationships rather than the past obsession with competition, 'winners' and 'winning' which still characterize US business ideology in particular.

The Rabobank group, a large Dutch co-operative bank, is one organization that has demonstrated, for many years, a collaborative commitment to human and ecological sustainability. The bank was founded as a co-operative in 1888 and has expanded to rank thirty-second of banks globally. Rabobank's stated aim is to pursue the goals of 'profit, people and the planet'. Rabobank regards sustainability as central to its business activities.[7] It is strongly involved in several national and international business forums that exchange information and best practice and which engage in public advocacy for sustainability. In 1999 it launched the RG Sustainable Equity Fund which invests in companies chosen for their ethical approach to social and environmental issues. In the first eleven months, 'the fund achieved a return of 59 percent compared to 45 percent for its benchmark The Morgan Stanley Capital Index'.[8]

Putting the jigsaw together

What then are the characteristics of the sustaining corporation?

A new social contract

We begin with the corporation's connection with its key stakeholders and the notion of a social and ecological contract negotiated by management with these stakeholders or their representatives. This social contract provides the rationale for the corporation's continued existence for it defines the mutually valuable exchanges that will sustain the firm's ongoing network of relationships. It also defines the organization's mission and legitimizes the organization's right to operate, to produce valued goods and services and its responsibility not to produce 'bads' (pollution, waste and so on) and 'disservices' (socially or ecologically destructive processes). Concomitant with this is the development of a stakeholder accountability process that emphasizes transparency and openness in reporting on delivery to stakeholder expectations. For example, over fifty global corporations now produce comprehensive annual social reports that deal with their impacts on society. These companies have well known names such as BP, Amoco, Nike, Shell, Renault and Hewlett-Packard.

But all this begs the question: Who are the stakeholders? There is now a substantial body of work delineating stakeholder theory.[9] There are differences of opinion expressed in this literature about whether to confine the definition of stakeholder to those individuals and groups who are vital to the survival of the firm or to expand it to a wider set of groups whose interests are affected by the firm's actions. These views correspond to the two major uses of the word sustainability, which cause considerable confusion in the field: (a) the firm's ability to sustain itself versus (b) its impact on the sustainability of its social and ecological environment.

Both definitions are useful and Factor suggests that we distinguish between 'primary' and 'secondary' stakeholders.[10] Primary stakeholders are those engaged in some transactions with the firm and without whom the firm would cease to exist. Secondary stakeholders are those who are not essential for the firm's survival but who can influence the firm or who are influenced by the firm (or both). The distinction makes it clear that, to pursue its own immediate self-interest, the firm must concern itself with the expectations of primary stakeholders; however, it also has ethical responsibilities to secondary stakeholders.

The potential list of stakeholders includes shareholders and owners, suppliers, customers, government, the community, future generations and the rest of nature: that is, all 20 million or so species on earth. Each organization must decide which are primary and which secondary. We argue for a broad definition of the potential range of stakeholders – one that includes future generations, the good of society as a whole and the natural world. As Carl Anderson has noted:

> Over the last fifteen years, many managers have defined the market force doctrine in the narrowest way, as self-interest exploited through

laissez-faire economics. In the most extreme cases, using ethical principles in decision-making is seen as a sure path to ruin in the Darwinian fight for survival. Competing within an open system is stressed, but preserving the competitive system itself is not. Businessmen and businesswomen have a stake in analyzing systems as a whole, thinking about the overall good of the society in which we are to live. Stakeholder analysis, reasonableness, and enlightened self-interest force decision-makers to consider the situation of the worst off in society as well as of the owners who are obvious targets of attention.[11]

The social contract that emerges out of a company's interaction with its stakeholders has its visible form in clear, written policies and principles that relate to human resource development, community relations and the ecological environment. It is evident also in the firm's core business strategies and in the way they are interpreted in the process of day-to-day decision making. It is clear that the commitment to sustainability matters because it shows up in decisions about what the corporation both does and does not do. It does not exploit its workforce or pollute the planet with its products or emissions. It does work collaboratively with a variety of community bodies to solve social and environmental problems and to identify and take up opportunities that build community. It does actively help workforce members develop their personal and professional capabilities; it works actively to foster a healthy biosphere.

Already many companies world-wide have significantly modified their traditional approach of measuring the effectiveness of their operations through financial measures alone. Some firms, for example, have adopted the 'Balanced Scorecard' concept. This approach was developed in the 1990s by the Boston-based Nolan Norton Institute, a research arm of KPMG Peat Marwick. Its most comprehensive exposition is by Kaplan and Norton.[12] The Balanced Scorecard uses a wider set of indicators to represent future economic value. Some of the world's leading companies, including Du Pont, General Electric, Hewlett-Packard, EDS, Cigna and American Standard, have adopted this approach.[13] Ensuring that performance measures include ethical concerns, and engaging in dialogue around these concerns, keeps the firm in touch with the more fundamental concerns of those groups that can affect its future. It assists the firm to co-evolve with its life companions in the way that birds have co-evolved with trees or beetles with flowers.[14]

A focus on human sustainability

We move on now to the issue of how the corporation handles human sustainability. In this area the organization accepts responsibility for the process of contributing to and upgrading human knowledge and skill formation within the organization itself. It acts this way because it makes good business sense to develop the intellectual and social capital of the workforce, particularly in areas relevant to the organization's mission.[15] This upgrading is also valuable for its own sake and reflects the organization's commitment to treating people as having value in their own right. It also contributes to a society where human capabilities are enhanced rather than degraded and this process of continuous upskilling improves the quality of life in society as a whole.

> Everything in this firm works because of social capital.
> *Source*: Hobson Brown Jnr, President and CEO, Russell Reynolds[16]

Capability enhancement includes developing the organization's capacity for reshaping itself; that is, its ability to identify future strategic opportunities and to initiate action which effectively repositions particular products or services, repositions the organization as a whole to take advantage of changing markets, or proactively redefines the industry or a significant segment of it. There is an intimate connection between creating the capacity for organizational and for individual change. Flexible organizations need and develop proactive, flexible individuals who take responsibility for their own personal, professional and spiritual growth. In turn, they are able to raise the level of organizational innovation. Today we find more examples of organizations progressing human sustainability in 'hi-tech' companies in IT, software development, the arts and the service sector.

Consistent with this emphasis on innovation is strong support for a policy of workplace diversity, participation in decision making, gender equity and work–life balance. In addition, the organizational architecture reflects the emphasis on adaptability, flexibility, innovation and speed of response. It is a non-hierarchical, continuously evolving net of interrelated groups and individuals. For example, the Danish maker of hearing aids, Oticon, abandoned all formal structures, supervisory positions, job descriptions, budgets and policies in its head office, established a true paperless office, encouraged any and all of its head office employees, including its R&D staff, to form themselves on their own initiative into working groups around innovative projects, and made all information on its IT system (except trade secrets) available to all employees. Their multistory office building was reorganized to encourage people to communicate informally. After an initial period of disorientation, the result was a significant improvement in the company's market position. This resulted from doubling the rate at which new products were developed, halving new product lead time and growing sales at 20 per cent per annum when global markets were shrinking.[17] These results were achieved under the leadership of Lars Kolnid, CEO from 1988 to 1998. His successor, Niels Jacobson, received the prestigious Employee Empowerment Pioneer Award in New York in 1998 on behalf of Oticon, and stated: 'Our goal is to do business in a manner that positively contributes to society in every country where we do business. We support the principle that industry has a responsibility to society and that we have a collective responsibility to the environment.'[18]

One critical challenge for the company of the future will be to attract and retain highly talented people, either as 'permanent employees' or contract workers. There are some managers who imagine that, because there is significant unemployment in most societies, building and retaining a skilled workforce is not problematical. But there is intense competition for highly talented professionals and success is increasingly dependent on attracting, developing and retaining such people. Many executives are responding to this perceived need by trying to define their company as 'the employer of choice'. The fact is that talented professionals are highly mobile, in many cases define the world as their sphere of activity, and take for granted that they will be well paid. The deciding factor in choosing an employer is the opportunity that an organization provides for meaningful work, autonomy and professional development. Consequently human resource management strategies become critical for building a high performance culture that provides challenge, work satisfaction and effective career development. The success of companies such as Hewlett-Packard and Ericsson comes in part from their development of comprehensive human resource policies that recognize this.

Human sustainability also has an external as well as an internal focus. It involves adopting a strong and clearly defined corporate ethical position based on multiple stakeholder perspectives. It identifies key stakeholders with interests in human sustainability, builds positive relationships with them or their representatives, listens to their concerns, identifies their needs, and communicates the organization's mission and strategies to them. This ethical commitment also makes good business sense in that it provides, for example, an up-to-date customer knowledge base which signals previously unidentified customer needs or emerging interests – these represent potential future business opportunities. It also builds customer loyalty. Customers and other key stakeholders ask: 'Why would we go elsewhere when our needs are being identified and met so effectively here?'

Cultural diversity

We recognize and value our multi-cultural background as a company. We draw on the wealth of diversity as a unique strength to preserve, promote and protect the rich cult character of countries, communities and local regions. We value the variety of our diversity content, which represents our heritage and the world's cultural diversity and we strive to deliver competitively superior services to our local markets.

Source: Vivendi Universal website[19]

The sustaining organization seeks to exert influence on stakeholders, other industry participants and society in general to pursue human welfare, equitable and just social practices and to create the social circumstances that contribute to the fulfilment of human potential in all citizens. The concern here is global and multigenerational: 'citizens' includes citizens of other countries as well as our own and future generations. Sustaining organizations are aiming to use their influence to create a generative society. This is not considered an 'add on' to the organization's activities, as a charitable exercise, but as a demonstration of the organization's integrity as a responsible corporate citizen. We like the story of the organization which always keeps an empty chair at the table when the board meets to consider the organization's strategies. The chair represents unborn generations; it stands as a constant reminder to consider seriously the long-term impact of decisions on the future.

Patagonia is one company that has consistently acted on this principle. Patagonia manufactures sports clothing and gear and has built a strong reputation for quality and innovation. The company's environmental commitment is evidenced, for example, by its use of recycled materials and its decision to convert its entire sportswear line to 100 per cent organically grown cotton fibre even though this incurs higher costs. Despite the sportswear being more expensive, sales have grown, showing that there is public support for environmentally responsible action of this kind.[20]

The acceptance of these principles has an observable impact on the way the corporation operates. It is strongly and proactively committed to traditional occupational health and safety measures, ensuring that the workplace is safe and healthy. It is also strongly committed to equal opportunity and proactive in recruiting from minority groups and ensuring career progression for women and minorities. It adopts family friendly policies. But it goes beyond these concerns to place importance on the design of work for job satisfaction, personal and professional development and on creating a learning environment. It also actively encourages all members of the organization to be involved in community activities in which they contribute in their own right and as members of the organization.

Purposive, value-based action

Sustaining corporations are value based and attract members who are strongly committed to the same values – people who want to make a difference. In such organizations people feel that their work is meaningful and the process of innovation and strategy implementation flows more readily because of the basic alignment between the values of the organization and the majority of those working there. They want to see innovations with positive environmental impact and they are keen to make the developing environmental strategy work.

The sustaining corporation has a codified set of company values – a corporate value statement or credo – that is used as a reference point in decision making at all levels of the organization. This is actively workshopped and discussed throughout the organization and, where appropriate, modified so that it attracts widespread commitment. The company specifies guidelines for how the company will treat its members, the community and the environment. An external body is chosen to collaborate in conducting an independent ethical audit of the company's internal and external relations and their report forms an integral part of the company's annual report published on the company website. All this demands much more disclosure, transparency and accountability than has been the practice in the traditional firm.

The range of activities emphasized in sustaining organizations means that different capabilities and skills are developed within the organization

– the organization generally needs a broader range of skills than a traditional organization and the emphasis is on process skills. In particular, members develop higher-order skills of personal resilience, self-confidence, adaptation and learning, empathy, communication and influence, coaching, negotiation and conflict resolution. Chapter 9 discusses how leadership becomes increasingly diffused throughout the organization and how leaders develop these qualities.

Some sustaining organizations are not-for-profit and we are confident that, as third-wave thinking spreads, we shall see more organizations of this kind emerging, committed to social ideals other than profitability. One such organization in Australia is the Smith Family. It is enterprising, innovative and has active partnerships around community development issues with private sector organizations such BHP Biliton, Colgate-Palmolive, Cisco Systems and Bi-Lo. One of its programmes, *Learning for Life*, has 16,000 disadvantaged students receiving financial assistance and coaching in their school studies by trained volunteers. Their CEO, Elaine Henry, is committed to delineating and offsetting the growing inequality in Australian society.[21]

As more third-wave organizations develop, they will begin to bring pressure to bear on politicians to support the development of third-wave economies, that is, economies which value people and use resources to develop their capabilities, invest in environmental renewal and redefine progress in ways that are more meaningful than GNP. They will lobby governments to withdraw subsidies from unsustainable industries, to invest in social capital, to encourage innovation and the innovative industries of the future. They will also form alliances with like-minded companies whose activities are complementary to their own. In some cases the organizations in these alliances will co-locate their production facilities to form what are known as 'industrial clusters' or 'industrial ecosystems'. In these clusters, materials flow in closed loops. As Tibbs points out, this has the potential to create a massive increase in the efficiency of materials use because 'about 95 percent of all the materials we use end up as waste before the finished product is even purchased'.[22] Imagine the productivity increase possible if this material were fully utilized and recycled! The evidence is that focused industrial clusters like this can be highly productive in business terms and support a healthy environment and society. This brings us to the issue of ecological sustainability.

Focus on ecological sustainability

[handwritten annotation]

In the area of ecological sustainability, the sustaining organization seeks to define itself as an integral part of the ecology: like an earthworm, it takes up resources from the environment, processes them and, in returning them to the earth, ensures its own growth and enriches the environment. The sustaining organization ensures that resources are economically recycled or returned to the environment in a form which is not destructive of environmental value or actually helps restore and enrich the environment where it has been damaged. This is in contrast to most current industrial processes whose major output is waste.

> At Hewlett-Packard, our goal is to provide our customers with products and services that are environmentally sound throughout their life cycles and to conduct our business worldwide in a responsible manner.
> *Source*: Hewlett-Packard, *Commitment to the Environment*[23]

In the sustaining organization, environmental best practice is espoused and enacted because it is the responsible thing to do. The organization becomes an active promoter of ecological sustainability values and seeks to influence key participants in the industry and society in general. It is prepared to use its influence to promote positive sustainability policies on the part of governments, the restructuring of markets and the development of community values to facilitate the emergence of a *[handwritten: Level 19]* sustainable society. The environment is treated as integral to a viable global economy that is sustainable into the future for the benefit of generations to come as well as those alive today.

This has some important consequences for how firms with a material production process can operate in the future. They will be far more concerned about the initial design of products than with their ultimate disposal. Much of the problem of pollution and waste can be eliminated at the design stage by the choice of environmentally friendly, non-polluting materials and designing out waste. In natural systems there is no waste and our material production processes can increasingly emulate natural processes.

In 1992, Hewlett-Packard initiated a product stewardship programme:

> Under this program, Hewlett-Packard strives to prevent or minimize any negative impacts to human health or safety, or to the ecosystem,

that may occur at any point in the life of an HP product – from when it is designed until it is no longer used.[24]

The programme guidelines outline four key principles in their attempt to design environmentally friendly products:

- Minimize the energy consumption of our products, fewer raw materials, and increase our use of recyclable materials.
- Reduce waste and emissions from our manufacturing processes.
- Use less material overall and more recyclable material in our packaging.
- Develop products that are easier to reuse or recycle.[25]

Hewlett-Packard regularly reports progress against these guidelines.

Sustaining organizations conduct a life-cycle assessment for all products. They are concerned with the full production flow from extraction of raw materials to their disposal, even where their own operation may control only one link in the total chain. Where this is the case, they will actively negotiate collaborative solutions to social and environmental problems with other firms in the chain. In this way they build voluntary partnerships committed to working to raise their awareness of key interdependencies and to eliminate the, often unintended, negative impacts of the production process on the community or the ecology. Collectively, they view themselves as stewards of the resources they use: they either continue to recycle them or return them to the earth in a form that feeds the earth.

Such alliances can expand even further. In 1997 a Zero Waste New Zealand Trust was established with a vision for New Zealand to become the first country in the world to adopt a national zero waste strategy and a target of zero waste to landfill. Currently twenty-five local councils participate in the project, committing themselves to a target of zero waste to landfill by 2015, and the number participating continues to expand steadily. The Trust helps them research, develop and implement waste reduction strategies and connects them with best practice around the world. It also provides financial support.

This approach may also mean a reversal of the trend to create short-term, disposable products in favour of creating products that are used for lengthy periods and have lasting value. Sustaining organizations ensure that, all the way along the production chain, manufacturing processes are sustainable, the technology is the best possible from an environmental viewpoint and material and energy use is minimized. Where there is a choice of suppliers, they prefer to buy from those whose production processes are environmentally friendly.

In 1998, Xerox introduced its first fully digitized copier, the Document Centre 265, which is more than 90 percent remanufacturable and 97 percent recyclable. The product has only about 200 parts, an order of magnitude less than its predecessor. Its sales have exceeded forecasts. According to *Fortune*, remanufacturing and waste reduction saved Xerox US$250 million in 1998.

Source: P. Senge, *Sloan Management Review*[26]

An integral part of the life-cycle assessment is the reduction of packaging, the use of recyclable materials where packaging is necessary and the reuse of packaging and pallets where feasible. Staff at all levels are actively involved in finding innovative ways to improve the sustainability of throughput and innovations are widely diffused, communicated and recognized.

They also carefully consider the location of any new operations in terms of potential environmental impact; and they design the site to respect the natural values of the area, preferring to retain natural features and native vegetation where possible. New buildings maximize the use of natural rather than artificial lighting, use energy-efficient designs that make use of the sun's heat for warmth and natural materials such as rock and earth for cooling. 'Waste' water is purified to an appropriate level and recycled through the plant or used for maintaining the green environment.

A striking example of a major building project of this kind is the Olympic Village constructed for the Sydney Olympics 2000 by the partnership of Mirvac and Lend Lease: the Mirvac Lend Lease Village Consortium. This village, now a new Sydney suburb, consists of around 2,000 homes. The village was constructed on degraded land 15 kilometres from the Central Business District (CBD). The village exemplifies a set of clearly formulated environmental principles aimed at renewing the local environment and increasing biodiversity in the area. Life-cycle assessments were also made of all materials before the major building material types were selected. All power for the village is created by photovoltaic technology with excess power delivered to the local grid. The redesign of the site was carried out with participation of key interest groups, including environmentalists, and all site workers received environmental skills and diligence awareness training.[27]

The sustaining organization seeks partnerships with relevant 'green' groups, actively supports their involvement in assessing the firm's environmental performance and works collaboratively with them to develop improved environmental practices. It goes beyond compliance to develop and update a knowledge base relevant to its core production processes (for example, a register of chemical pollutants), to build a general awareness of environmental issues within its workforce and a commitment to progressive elimination of pollutants, product redesign for improved environmental impact and support for the 'dematerialization' of physical processes. It does not conduct animal testing for any of its products unless these are pharmaceuticals designed to improve human and animal health. It collaborates with an external 'green' group to conduct an externally verified environmental audit of its operations and publishes this as an integral part of its annual report and on its web page.

Frankel argues that there are four principles which companies must adopt to make genuine progress towards ecological sustainability.[28] The first is '*towards zero waste*': rather than reducing waste, every company must eliminate it entirely. One plant that has succeeded in doing this is the Nagoya plant of the Kirin Brewing Group in Japan which reached zero emissions in 1997.[29] Examples of other major corporations committed to achieving zero emissions are Ogihara and Chichibu Cement in Japan and DuPont in the USA.

The second principle is '*whole system thinking*' which fosters the reinvention rather than redesign of industrial processes. The third principle is '*look outward*' which means that companies have to go beyond cleaning up their own operations by helping smaller companies with fewer resources to put their houses in order. It also means working in concert with other companies to create symbiotic cycles of industrial ecology, that is, capitalizing on the notion that one company's waste is another's resource. And in addition it means creating alliances to capitalize on large-scale business opportunities in the greening process.

Principle four is '*remember sustainable development*'. Businesses need to think more broadly than the ecological environment. As we have pointed out above, sustainable development involves social issues as well as ecological ones. Because these issues are integral to the core strategies of the organization, they are not considered to be the sole responsibility of an environmental manager or a human resource manager. There may be an environmental manager and a human resource manager but they are regarded as technical experts who are there to provide the specialized input other senior executives need to implement sustainability strategies.

At any one time there will be a range of environmental initiatives being run on a project basis; all of these will also have human resource implications. As a consequence, lateral co-ordination is at least as important as vertical.

What are the advantages for the firm of pursuing ecologically sustaining policies with such commitment? We argue that, as the ecological crisis deepens and the third wave moves the values of society towards this ideal, it will be the bold but foolish organization that persists in environmentally destructive practices. As the conditions of the 'risk society'[30] emerge, there will be increasing pressure on firms to be 'squeaky clean' environmentally if they are to continue to have a 'licence to operate'.[31] But proactive policies in particular can provide a comparative advantage in the market place as consumers, investors and governments increasingly discriminate in favour of firms that are ethical in their approach to their people, their community and the natural world.

Nuon Energy is the second largest energy supplier in the Netherlands. Nuon employs 6,500 staff in its traditional divisions of water, gas and energy and 3,500 staff in its newer divisions responsible for green energy (wind and sun) and relationships with other companies. Nuon's mission is to become a leading company in Europe, including a leading company in sustainable energy supply. Currently, only 5–6 per cent of the energy they generate comes from wind and sun but the proportion is growing. Nuon's strategic long-term vision is based on the fact that eventually all energy must be supplied from renewable resources. Nuon is also working in partnership with NGOs in other parts of the less-developed world such as Mali, the Sudan and Albania to develop their use of renewable energy sources.[32]

As in the social arena, we are also witnessing a trend to the development of more not-for-profit organizations devoted to environmental protection and renewal. One well-known organization of this kind is Greenpeace which operates globally and has had a powerful influence on international, national and enterprise level environmental policies. But there is a plethora of such organizations and we are confident that we shall see many more. In addition, a range of new jobs, such as 'environmental manager', is being established in organizations. Tricia Casswell, executive director of RMIT University's Global Sustainability Unit in Melbourne, Australia, has recently identified ninety-eight different kinds of environmental jobs in the private and public sectors – her own job is one example.[33]

The sustaining corporation is currently a visionary ideal – but it is one that we illustrate with partial case examples to show that there are firms moving towards the ideal. Its visionary nature raises the issue of how the transition can be managed for those corporations that wish to move in this direction. We refer the reader to Chapters 7, 8 and 9 where we deal with the process of managing change, particularly to our discussion in Chapters 7 and 8 of the need for both incremental and transformative change processes. The transition to the third wave represents a significant value shift. Therefore the core of the transformative process which will bring about third wave organizations has to be culture change. We deal here with some of the characteristics of culture change but refer the reader forward to Chapters 7 and 8 where culture change is dealt with in more detail.

Building strategy into the culture

Many standard texts on strategic management describe it as a process that is logical, rational and non-problematical. Empirical studies of strategic management show that in reality strategic management differs substantially from this model. Strategy is created in a political environment where stakeholders have differing and sometimes conflicting interests. Within the organization itself, executives are seldom in full agreement about an appropriate strategy and sometimes in active conflict. This is not surprising because they face differing environments (for example, customers versus suppliers) and have differing career interests. There is, in fact, no single shared environment for the firm: there is a multitude of environments changing at different rates; there are too many factors to consider and there are legitimate differences of opinion about which are important signals of future trends. When we expand this confusing reality to the organization as a whole, we can conceive of the organization as a constellation of groups all perceiving differing environments, having differing interests and having close relationships with some groups but seldom or never relating to others.

In addition strategic planning is not only a rational process. Any attempt to define a future rouses strong emotions. People care about the future, as Mark Twain remarked, because it is where they will spend the rest of their lives. Strategic planning is an attempt to envision a desirable future and to take action to bring that future into being. Even where the senior executive team reaches consensus on a strategic plan, there is no assurance that the plan will be implemented as conceived. It relies for its implementation on the actions of other members of the organization, all of whom have interests at stake. Large-scale strategic shifts necessarily involve transforming the established culture (or cultures) of the organization and integrating strategic reorientation and sustainability into the corporate culture itself.

> A shift from environmental management to environmental strategy requires a concurrent and supporting shift in organizational culture, structure, reward systems, and job responsibilities.
> *Source*: A. Hoffman, *Competitive Environmental Strategy*, 2000[34]

But what exactly is corporate culture and why is it so important?

Organizational culture is usually defined as 'the way we do business around here'. Organizational culture consists of the basic assumptions, values and norms, symbols, myths and 'wisdom' that define the collective approach to day-to-day decision making and action. Culture centres on the creation and continuity of meaning for organizational members. Much of it may be unreflective and unarticulated – it is the 'world taken for granted' – often more visible to visitors than to inmates. One of the most powerful ways to create organizational change is to confront, develop or remould the core cultural values of an organization so that people experience a profound change in their understanding and purpose and, as a result, act differently. Leaders play a major role in this because they can embody a new cultural profile in their speech and action and become catalysts for cultural change.

In their book, *Blown to Bits*, Evans and Wurster discuss the forces that are massively reorganizing global and local markets and challenging our understanding of what corporations are and how they should do business.[35] They emphasize that the leader's first task is to create a culture and the second task is to develop a strategy. They then search for a way to define the core identity of the corporation of the future. They conclude:

> Theorists have variously seen the corporation as a set of physical assets, a set of property rights, or a body of core competencies. Those can all be deconstructed. What *resists* deconstruction is the idea of the corporation as defined by its culture and its strategy. The corporation as *purposeful community*. And if all else fades, perhaps purposeful

community becomes the essence of identity, of management, of leadership. In a world of impersonal, technical change, that is a refreshingly human thought.[36]

To move to the sustaining organization involves members of the organization at all levels internalizing the values of sustainability so that these values become a core theme in their work as a purposeful community. This does not mean that there will necessarily be unanimity about the solutions to be sought to emergent sustainability issues. However, it does mean the development over time of a strong and pervasive shared ideology. The members of the organization derive meaning from their ability to create useful goods and/or services that contribute to the community's quality of life and sustain the natural environment. In reality this is reflected in the fact that all members of the organization, as well as its subcontractors and suppliers, make day-to-day decisions on the basis of a deeply held, internalized commitment to sustainability values. This ideology does not negate the value of work in providing financially for the needs of the workforce or running a profitable enterprise. But it does define financial returns to organizational members and shareholders as the appropriate exchange for providing something of real value to society and the environment.

Culture is the glue which holds the pieces of the jigsaw puzzle firmly together so it cannot fall apart. A positive culture blends human and ecological sustainability seamlessly.

Proactive leadership

Critical to this culture-building process is proactive leadership consciously developed and practised at all levels of the organization. Ideally this starts with a fully committed executive team which has reached agreement that sustainability is central to the firm's ongoing strategy or strategic reorientation. The executive team emphasizes creating a strong corporate identity around sustainability values and creates shared experiences and reward systems which reinforce the emerging values. Culture is not created by fiat; rather it grows organically from the experience of working together successfully on meaningful tasks. Leaders are the shapers of the corporate culture and they must embody the core cultural values of sustainability in their actions.

Culture change involves creating an ongoing drama in which the members of the organization are both actors and audience. It is a drama in which heroes and heroic groups emerge who forge new meaning for themselves and others and whose success is embodied in powerful stories and myths. Leaders become attractors and role models, inspiring others to move in the same direction, so multiplying the momentum of change. This surge of human energy and meaning making is the matrix from which the new culture arises, is invigorated, and becomes a powerful shaper of the work-related behaviour of all organizational members. The process of continuing cultural innovation is an organizational endeavour to support and renew, rather than exploit and degrade, the world, the community and the planet. It is a process which restores a fuller meaning to human work than the accumulation of capital and material goods.

> I fully expect that we'll no longer be talking about economic, environmental and societal values as being distinctly different, but see them as integral and interlocking aspects of every business process and activity.
> *Source*: Paul Tebo, Vice President for Safety, Health and the Environment, E. I du Pont de Nemours[37]

Conclusion

Corporations are the fundamental cells of the modern economy. If we are to transform our economy to make it sustainable and sustaining, then we must make significant changes to the way corporations operate. Corporations also control most of the resources of our global society; if we are to have effective leadership of the sustainability movement, then much of that leadership must come from the corporate sector. Building sustainable organizations requires a fundamental shift of mindset from traditional mainstream business thought and practice. In the future, the corporation will remain profitable by becoming an active partner in the ongoing renewal of global society and of the earth's biosphere.

However, the path to creating the sustaining organization is not travelled quickly and easily. Having sketched the ultimate goal in this chapter, we now trace the major staging points along the way. In our next chapter we begin with compliance (Phase 3), which is the first positive move organizations need to make in leaving behind active opposition to sustainability, rejection (Phase 1) or indifference/non-responsiveness (Phase 2). Achieving compliance is the launch platform for further

progress towards the fully sustainable organization and this is the issue
we address in Chapter 4.

 Phase 6: The sustaining corporation

Human sustainability (HS6)

The organization accepts responsibility
for contributing to the process of
renewing and upgrading human
knowledge and skill formation in the
community and society generally and is
a strong promoter of equal opportunity,
workplace diversity and work–life
balance as workplace principles. It
adopts a strong and clearly defined
corporate ethical position based on
multiple stakeholder perspectives and
seeks to exert influence on the key
participants in the industry and in
society in general to pursue human
welfare, equitable and just social
practices and the fulfilment of human
potential of all. People are seen as
valuable in their own right.

Ecological sustainability (ES6)

The organization becomes an active
promoter of ecological sustainability
values and seeks to influence key
participants in the industry and society
in general. Environmental best practice
is espoused and enacted because it is the
responsible thing to do. The organization
tries to assist society to be ecologically
sustainable and uses its entire range of
products and services to this end. The
organization is prepared to use its
influence to promote positive
sustainability policies on the part of
governments, the restructuring of
markets and the development of
community values to facilitate the
emergence of a sustainable society.
Nature is valued for its own sake.

Notes

1 http://www.hondacorporate.com (accessed 6 February 2002).
2 R. Welford, *Hijacking Environmentalism: Corporate Responses to
Sustainable Development*, London: Earthscan Publications, 1997,
p. xi.
3 *Sydney Morning Herald*, Tuesday, 17 April 2001, News 6.
4 W. Fox, cited in J. Dryzek, *The Politics of the Earth: Environmental
Discourses*, Oxford: Oxford University Press, 1997, p. 156; M. Fox, *The
Reinvention of Work: A New Vision of Livelihood for Our Time*, San
Francisco: Harper, 1994.
5 R. Welford, 'Rediscovering the spiritual dimension of environmentalism',
in R. Welford, *Hijacking Environmentalism: Corporate Responses to
Sustainable Development*, London: Earthscan Publications, 1997,

pp. 211–27; K. Wilber, *The Marriage of Sense and Soul: Integrating Science and Religion*, Melbourne: Hill of Content Publishing, 1998.

6 P. Senge, 'Innovating our way to the next industrial revolution', *Sloan Management Review*, 2001, Winter, 2.

7 G.J.I. Schrama, 'Sustainability banking at the Rabobank', in K. Green, P. Groenewegen and P.S. Hofman (eds) *Ahead of the Curve: Cases of Innovation in Environmental Management*, Dordrecht, The Netherlands: Kluwer Academic Publishers, 2001, pp. 77–91, this quote p. 85.

8 Ibid.

9 R.E. Freeman, *Strategic Management: A Stakeholder Approach*, Boston, Mass.: Pitman, c.1984; R. Mitchell, B.R. Agle, D. Wood, 'Toward a theory of stakeholder identification and salience: defining the principle of who and what really counts', *Academy of Management Review*, 1997, 22(4), 853–86; M. Clarkson, 'A risk based model of stakeholder theory', paper presented for the Second Toronto Conference on Stakeholder Theory, Toronto: Centre for Corporate Social Performance and Ethics, University of Toronto, 1994; L.K. Trevino and G.R. Weaver, 'The stakeholder research tradition: converging theorists not convergent theory', *Academy of Management Review*, 1999, 24(2), 222–7; A. Factor, 'Barriers and catalysts associated with environmental initiatives within small and medium-sized enterprises, unpublished doctoral thesis proposal, Department of Organization and Management, Aarhus School of Business, Aarhus, Denmark, May 2000; D. Goldblatt (ed.), *The Stakeholding Society: Writings on Politics and Economics*, Oxford: Polity Press, 1999.

10 A. Factor, 'Barriers and catalysts associated with environmental initiatives within small and medium-sized enterprises', doctoral thesis proposal, Department of Organization and Management, Aarhus School of Business, Aarhus, Denmark, May 2000, p. 7.

11 C. Anderson, 'Values-based management', *Academy of Management Executive*, 1997, 11(4), 25.

12 R.S. Kaplan and D.P. Norton, *The Balanced Scorecard: Translating Strategy into Action*, Boston, Mass.: Harvard Business School Press, 1996.

13 W.G. Wilson and D.R. Sasseville, *Sustaining Environmental Management Success: Best Business Practices from Industry Leaders*, New York: John Wiley, 1999, pp. 208–13.

14 C. Kaesuk Yoon, 'A taste for flowers helped beetles conquer the world', *New York Times*, 28 July 1998, Science Times section, C1.

15 For a comprehensive review of the concept of social capital and its implications for managers, see P.S. Alder and S.W. Kwon, 'Social capital: prospects for a new concept', *Academy of Management Review*, 2002, 27(1), 17–40.

16 Hobson Brown Jr, President and CEO, Russell Reynolds, quoted in L. Prusack and D. Cohen, 'How to invest in social capital', *Harvard Business Review*, 2001, June, 93.

17 Personal observation and on-site interviews, D. Dunphy, 1995; B. Burnes, Case Study 1 'Oticon – the disorganized organization', in B. Burnes, *Managing Change: A Strategic Approach to Organizational Dynamics*, 3rd edn, London: Financial Times/Prentice Hall, 2000, pp. 319–28.

18 Ibid., p. 327.

19 Extract from 'Our Values' statement, Vivendi Universal Website, http://www.vivendiuniversal.com/vu2/en/who-we-are.cfm (accessed 6 February 2002).

20 Corporate Essay, 'Global alliance for the 21st century', Special Advertising Section, 'The Next Bottom Line', *Business Week*, Asian Edition, 3 May 1999, 45–96.

21 Personal communication, The Smith Family, 5 June 2002.

22 'H. Tibbs, 'The technology strategy of the sustainable corporation', in D. Dunphy, J. Benveniste, A. Griffiths and P. Sutton (eds) *Sustainability: The Corporate Challenge of the 21st Century*, Sydney: Allen and Unwin, 2000, pp. 191–216.

23 From Hewlett-Packard's 'Commitment to the Environment', Hewlett-Packard Co., USA, 1998, p. 1.

24 Ibid.

25 Ibid.

26 P. Senge, 'Innovating our way to the next industrial revolution', *Sloan Management Review*, 2001, Winter, 2.

27 Case example 9, 'Lend Lease – The Olympic Village', in B. Hirsch and P. Sheldrake, *Inclusive Leadership: Rethinking the World of Business to Generate the Dynamics of Lasting Success*, Melbourne: Information Australia, 2001, pp. 121–40. Note, however, that some environmentalists remain critical of remediation measures for the site: see S. Bader, *Global Spin*, Carlton North, Victoria, Australia: Scribe Publications, 2000.

28 C. Frankel, 'Into the fourth era', in *In Earth's Company: Business, Environment and the Challenge of Sustainability*, Canada: New Society Publishers, 1998, pp. 81–94.

29 M. Ota, 'Cutting edge: the zero emissions challenge', *Aichi Voice*, 1998, 9; 9.http://www.pref.aichi.jp/voice/9_cutting-edge.html.

30 U. Beck, *The Risk Society: Towards a New Modernity*, London: Sage, 1992.

31 J. Elkington, *Cannibals with Forks: The Triple Bottom Line of 21st Century Business*, Oxford: Capstone, 1997.

32 From an interview by S. Benn with Hans Nooter, Human Resource Management, Nuon Energy at Hardewijk, The Netherlands, 7 February 2002.

33 'The greening of life', *Sydney Morning Herald*, weekend edition, 12–13 May 2001, section 8, 1, My Career.

34 A. Hoffman, *Competitive Environmental Strategy*, Washington, D.C.: Island Press, 2000, p. 163.

35 P. Evans and T.S. Wurster, *Blown to Bits: How the New Economies of Information Transforms Strategy*, Boston, Mass.: Harvard Business School Press, 2000.

36 Ibid., p. 229.

37 A. Spencer-Cooke, 'Hero of zero', Environmental Leadership Award 2000, *Tomorrow*, Nov./Dec. 2000, 10–16, this quote p. 10.

Part II
Managing the persistent past: dealing with first wave corporations

4 Compliance and beyond

- Changing expectations of corporate behaviour
- Making the structural changes needed for compliance
- Moving to 'compliance plus'
- Phases in the development of compliance

Changing expectations of corporate behaviour

> The belief that companies will pick up on profitable opportunities
> without a regulatory push makes a false assumption about corporate
> reality – namely, that all profitable opportunities for innovation have
> already been discovered, that all managers have perfect information
> about them, and that organizational incentives are aligned with
> innovating.[1]

So states Michael Porter, in a controversial article in which he and his
co-author, Claus van der Linde, outline a strong case that government
regulation can encourage firms to pursue innovation strategies, resource
productivity and competitiveness. In this chapter, we agree with Porter
and argue that firms actually benefit from focusing first on compliance.
By doing this, they gain initial understandings, tools, techniques and
capabilities that are valuable in themselves but also form a base from
which they can engage more proactively with other sustainability issues
and reap further benefits in the future.

Changing attitudes to compliance

Changing attitudes towards corporate regulation and compliance are
shaping a new role for corporations in society. For more than a decade
after the Second World War, OECD governments allowed business

development to go largely unchallenged. Any government regulations were regarded as an unnecessary burden and to go beyond compliance with such regulations was anathema. Indeed, in 1970 the widely known economist Milton Friedman claimed that a company spending more money on pollution control measures than required by law was practising 'pure and unadulterated socialism'.[2]

However, in the latter part of the last century governments increased their regulatory control over the potential impact of corporations on society. New measures have included compulsory employer contributions to supplant universal pensions, anti-discrimination laws, forms of industrial democracy and an increasing variety of environmental requirements. Many governments have also developed occupational health and safety (OH&S) legislation, often as a result of tripartite agreements between unions, government and industry associations. New legislation means that the employer can be held vicariously liable for the negligence of the employee.

Over the last fifteen years, industry representatives have generally shifted their position on regulation and compliance. The managers of many companies actively contribute to rule-making and are shifting to more proactive strategies. They pre-empt policy changes and adopt precautionary measures before being required to do so. In this way, compliance becomes enabling for organizations such as INCO. They can progress human and ecological sustainability measures, enhance their reputation and take moral leadership in order to increase competitiveness.

Precautionary measures at INCO

The close relationship between the nickel manufacturer INCO, in South Wales, UK, and the regulatory agency illustrates this approach. The Environmental Officer of this Environment Award-winning nickel processing plant negotiates standards with the agency so that high achievement in one area can be traded off against poor results in another. For instance, INCO's management is currently looking at improving their stack emissions. The firm is pre-empting expected legislative changes, looking at new dust pollution measures now. According to INCO's Environmental Officer: 'It's better to be ahead of the change and perhaps even influence the direction of legislation. Our emphasis is on a very transparent, negotiated relationship with the regulator.'[3]

We are now forty years on from the first wave of these legislative reforms and a great deal of experience has accumulated. So in this chapter we give an outline of the organizational strategies that have proved most effective in achieving compliance with the broad range of social and environmental legislation. We then examine the management initiatives required to reach 'compliance plus', a more proactive and voluntary form of compliance with standards set by corporations themselves, by non-government organizations or by coalitions of corporations.[4] 'Compliance plus' goes beyond conformity to legislation to voluntary action on the part of the corporation designed to meet the actual and anticipated demands of the firm's stakeholders.

So what is compliance?

Compliance is doing what you are required or expected to do. What this means for a particular organization depends on the country the company is operating in, the company structure and its market sector. In most developed countries, environmental legislation now covers such areas as use of land, discharge of substances into air or water, construction of buildings, taking and use of water, entry into conservation areas and the sale of certain products.[5]

Legislative requirements concerning *social* performance have also increased dramatically. Many countries now require compulsory reporting of charitable donations, employment of the disabled, employee share ownership schemes, reporting of general employment data and provisions for worker health and safety.[6] Most recently, socially responsible disclosure legislation has been passed in Germany, Switzerland and the Netherlands requiring fund management institutions to state in writing to all investors how they take into account social, ethical and environmental concerns. The legislation also now applies to pension funds in the UK and to the management funds industry in Australia.

A multinational, or a company which contracts outside a national legal system, has a different set of challenges and responsibilities to a company operating within a single country. For example, its managers need to know exactly who its suppliers are and where their factories are located. Otherwise the company may be targeted or sued for failure to comply with local legislation. The company must also have systems in place which can inform management if and when the firm falls short of compliance on human rights and environmental issues so that remedial action can be taken before penalties are imposed on the organization.

The maze of legal statutes and the general trend towards litigation and class action suits mean that large firms operating in sectors such as chemicals, mining, construction and manufacturing generally employ in-house lawyers. Other companies ensure that regular contact is maintained with legal professionals. In many instances, particularly in relation to environmental law, certain activities may be prohibited. They may be termed 'unlawful', an 'offence', 'subject to penalty' or described in some similar fashion. These provisions are usually qualified by licensing arrangements (sometimes termed 'permits', 'consents' or 'approvals'). Licences themselves refer to the relevant legislation and usually require holders to update information to the regulator at set intervals. Keeping abreast of such a range of proliferating regulatory measures requires professional advice.

The range of matters subject to environmental and social controls is already very wide and will increase further as the public demand for corporate accountability grows. There are good reasons for the public's increased concern about the potential impacts of corporate activity on the natural environment and society, as the ongoing story of Minamata Bay shows.

Costs of non-compliance: the ongoing story of Minamata Bay

Thirty years after the poisoning of Minamata Bay by an organic compound of mercury, thousands of claimants are pressing the Japanese government to be compensated for having Minamata Disease, a nerve disorder caused by eating seafood from the Bay. Symptoms of the disease appeared in the 1950s, but were discounted until 1968 when the government blamed the Chisso chemical company for pumping wastewater containing the mercury from its acetaldehyde plant into the Bay. More than 900 victims died, babies were born deformed and thousands of others suffered impaired sight, hearing, smell, taste and touch. The plant was belatedly shut down in 1968.

Only now is it being recognized by a research team from a university in Japan that damage occurs when mercury is present at just 10 parts per million in hair and umbilical cords, five times lower than the officially recognized safe level. The researchers have found that the effects of the mercury lasted 10 years longer and spread much further than had originally been recognized. The government, accused by environmentalists of colluding with the Chisso corporation, is now being pressured to certify that another 18,000 claimants should obtain compensation from Chisso. The firm is currently paying compensation at the rate of approximately US$2,000 per month per claimant.[7]

National variations in compliance

Lester Thurow in his book *Head to Head*, published in 1992, argued that the twenty-first century would see an economic battle between the 'communitarian' capitalism of Japan and Germany with the individualistic values aspired to by governments and corporations in Britain, the USA and other countries such as Australia.[8] While the growing influence of stakeholder theory on both sides of the Atlantic has lessened these differences in national approaches, the analysis remains a useful means to understand the quite different approaches to compliance by governments and corporations in different cultural traditions.

National and cultural differences reflect different institutional settings, different understandings of risk and different opinions on the appropriate systems that should be instituted to control risk. In the USA, the UK and Australia, for instance, an individualist understanding of capitalism dominates government and corporate policy making. In the USA, there is an adversarial tradition of policy making. The regulatory agency and the corporation are seen as opponents, partly reflecting the social activist movements of the 1960s and the expansion of social rights. The US tradition is grounded in scientific risk assessments, standards and guidelines that are developed and administered by regulatory agencies. Governments typically make reporting mandatory to ensure that industries act responsibly. The US Toxic Release Inventory is an excellent example of this approach and Yencken argues it has had more effect than any other government intervention in changing business behaviour.[9]

In Northern Europe, a more consensus-based approach prevails. There is bargaining between political actors to set compliance requirements acceptable to both industry and government. In Germany, in particular, governments have set demanding environmental standards which have resulted in business shifting direction towards eco-efficiency and the development of new eco-technologies. The UK relies on the principles of 'sound science' in environmental protection, leading to an emphasis on accumulating data, building models and careful monitoring. In Australia, the development of precautionary legislation has been a controversial topic.[10] Australia has rich and diverse ecosystems and substantial mineral and biological resources, recently valued by the Australian Bureau of Statistics at A$117 billion. This has resulted in an ongoing struggle between environmentalists and mining and other industry sector lobbyists about whether governments should implement ecologically sustainable development principles more strongly.[11]

Despite such national differences, the general trend in developed countries has been towards adopting a more precautionary approach to environmental compliance. The idea is to minimize risk. Measures include the rigorous monitoring of early impacts from emissions and wastes or health and safety provisions requiring industry to avoid risks wherever reasonably practicable. Manufacturer's liability has become an increasing concern to industry.[12]

The move to develop universal global standards

Despite national differences and preoccupations, there are also emerging global pressures for companies to achieve compliance to internationally set standards. For instance, corporate responsibility for the health of workers throughout the world has been addressed by various international workplace conventions developed by the International Labour Organization (ILO). The ILO standards are the universally accepted benchmark for human work conditions and are set by the International Labour Conference. They are not universally applied but they do affect practice, particularly in large multinational companies.

These conventions are based on the premise that the corporation is an integral part of society, not somehow insulated in its own domain. ILO conventions address benzene pollution of the air (1971), the hazards of carcinogenic chemicals (1974), air pollution, noise and vibration (1977), general occupational health and safety (1981), asbestos use (1986), and workplace chemicals (1990).[13] Standards soon to be under consideration include maternity protection and OH&S for agricultural workers.

Global watchdogs for human rights and ecological sustainability

The events of 11 September 2001 have been a harsh reminder to governments and multinationals that many in the developing world associate global deregulated capitalism with corporate aggression, colonization and greed. In the developed countries themselves, the massive expansion of information technology has led to a growing awareness of corporate irresponsibility and antagonism to the idea that multinational corporations can somehow act autonomously, accountable only to shareholders.

More informed consumers have pushed corporations into a new arena of competing for reputation and for access to the benefits of social capital, such as relationship building with other corporations, suppliers, clients and NGOs. NGOs such as Amnesty International, Greenpeace, WWF and Human Rights Watch act as monitors of environmental and social standards across the world and have had a major impact on how corporations perceive compliance. Corporations failing to comply with standards set by these alert watchdogs can be targeted and their transgressions given huge publicity. As the Human Rights Watch Executive Director Kenneth Roth said recently: 'I think there is broad recognition that no business concerned with its brand name can afford to be indifferent to social issues.'[14]

For instance, after publicity revealing that an illicit trade in diamonds had funded at least three African wars, the International Diamond Manufacturers Association endorsed a radical set of rules in 2001. Among other measures, the Association banned for life anyone dealing in diamonds where the proceeds of the sale went to fund conflict.[15] But perhaps the most powerful force for change has been the pressure placed by large corporations on firms in their supply chain. For instance, the airline KLM has opened an environmental dialogue with a major supplier of aircraft parts and intends to formulate a new policy in 2002 concerning the purchasing of wood and paper from sustainable sources.[16] KLM also has a purchasing policy which requires human rights issues to be included in contract considerations.

Lawyers representing NGOs are forcing disclosure by governments as well as corporations. In a recent decision by US District Court in Washington, the judge ordered the US Energy Department to release thousands of documents which allegedly contain the names of energy industry executives who assisted the Bush administration develop the US government's energy policy. The release of the documents follows requests by the Natural Resources Defence Council under Freedom of Information legislation.[17] Lawyers for Greenpeace, WWF and the Natural Resources Defence Council are currently investigating the possibility of winning damages for islands in the South Pacific against corporations and governments which contribute to global warming.[18]

Global watchdogs in action

Human Rights Watch has recently publicized the involvement of the energy industry in human rights violations around the world and questioned the effectiveness of the monitoring and compliance programmes implemented by the US and European apparel and footwear industry. They include the White House-sponsored Fair Labor Association (FLA), the Council on Economic Priorities (CEP) Social Accountability 8000 programme (SA-8000), and the new Workers' Rights Consortium (WRC). Litigation against apparel companies has commenced in US courts as garment workers filed class action suits against twenty-two companies for violations of the Fair Labor Standards Act and accused them of conspiracy under the Racketeering Influenced Corrupt Organizations Act.[19]

Amnesty International has also established a working checklist of human rights principles for companies and developed a set of business principles for companies operating in China that respect basic labour standards as defined by the ILO and the UN Universal Declaration of Human Rights as well as China's national laws.[20]

Another international campaign was mounted against the ING Group, a Dutch investment company, because of their investment in palm oil plantations in areas of tropical rain forest. After a vigorous campaign by Greenpeace and Friends of the Earth, the ING Group revised their policy on financing these plantations and other sectors with sensitive sustainability issues such as coal energy, mining, life sciences and fur. The ING Group is now the Dow Jones Sustainability Index leader for the banking/ investment sector. According to Pieter Kroon, Head of Public Affairs for the ING Group:

> Managing our products according to sustainability requirements outside the Netherlands can raise difficult questions. We now take precautions and take each industry as a special consideration. Reputation is really important. Your products have to be socially accepted. The Board is vigilant in trying to avoid a repeat of the Brent Spar episode. For instance, the ING Group closed its representative office in Burma because of the repressive political system.[21]

The need to build and sustain reputation works along the supply chain. As KLM's Environmental Manager, Udeke Huiskamp, puts it: 'The ING Group is one of our stakeholders and they give investment preference to sustainability.'[22]

The case for moving to compliance

The previous sections outlined a broad case for corporations to adopt a proactive approach to compliance. In summary, the reasons are:

- the emergence of more widespread and increasingly sophisticated forms of government regulation;
- increasing scrutiny by NGOs,
- public access to information technology and the risks to corporate reputation of public perception of poor corporate citizenship;
- the opportunities provided by achieving compliance to improve the firm's competitive situation;
- the benefits of building co-operative relationship with regulators;
- the risks associated with delays in achieving compliance. While rejection or non-responsiveness to regulation may delay costs and assessments, they can end up resulting in much higher costs being paid for non-compliance and in more negative assessments by the law and the public.

In the remainder of this chapter we take up issues relating to the move to compliance and 'compliance plus'. We concentrate on substantive issues in the move, that is, what to do. In Chapters 7 and 8, issues of process (how to do it) will be addressed in more detail.

Making the structural changes needed for compliance

Making the initial changes

Moving to compliance involves important changes such as an increased emphasis on training, top-level commitment, and guidance from skilled change agents. Moving towards compliance does not necessarily require major restructuring, but it does require management to identify roles and responsibilities more clearly in relationship to all legislative requirements. Take, for example, the case of a manufacturing company which has traditionally opposed governmental regulation of its activities and is non-compliant in several key areas such as plant safety and pollution of ground water. A new CEO is appointed and discovers that the firm is non-compliant and in a high risk situation. What can the CEO do?

In the area of human sustainability, the CEO needs to focus on those compliance aspects which will give the firm the status of a 'decent employer'. How is this achieved? He or she may decide to begin moving, in the area of human sustainability, from the rejection phase towards compliance by selecting change agents who initiate ad hoc incremental changes. The place to start is with areas that represent the major risks of non-compliance. These have to be identified first. The culture and vision of the company can then be gradually adjusted by assigning staff the responsibility for more systematic improvement to areas such as industrial relations, worker health and safety, and equal employment opportunities (EEO). Human resource requirements for training, the introduction of Total Quality Management (TQM) and organization development can be addressed while the organization is moving towards a more systematic integration of these measures into an overall plan. New quality standards can also be introduced before an overall strategy is delineated.

In the area of ecological sustainability, 'compliance officers' need to be allocated responsibilities for environmental management. For some manufacturing sectors, firms must also comply with requirements to establish a community liaison committee and an identified member of staff who can communicate readily with community representatives. At the INCO nickel manufacturing plant in South Wales, UK, for instance, the Environmental Officer has the responsibility of contacting local residents concerning community liaison committee meetings. In keeping with INCO's proactive strategy, not only is the community advised of any expected changes in noise or chemical emissions, but the Environmental Officer makes sure he goes to see community members on a regular basis to identify areas of potential complaint.[23]

New technical solutions or programmes may be implemented to enable cleaner production techniques and improved worker health and safety. These often include operating within 'consents' or specified standards, eliminating hazardous operations, waste disposal, water quality and planning requirements for new developments.

Employee empowerment is a key aspect of these initial changes. For instance, if technological developments are to lead to a more sustainable workplace, employees with low standards of qualification must still be able to succeed in the company. The case of Portugal Telecom SA provides an example of the sort of employee support measures which may be required in association with technological changes.

Portugal Telecom SA: preventing social and professional exclusion

As a result of a merger, Portugal Telecom was faced with a situation requiring major technological improvements. It established a training programme designed for employees with low educational standards. The programme was voluntary, took place after worktime and was accredited according to government standards. Those who completed it gained a certificate showing equivalence to external programmes.[24]

Developing a more systematic approach

There is a limit to what can be achieved by an ad hoc approach to compliance. A more systematic approach usually involves making structural changes and developing new co-ordinating mechanisms to create a systematic, integrated compliance framework. The usual framework for environmental compliance is an Environment Management System (EMS), supported by a range of human resource and community development tools or techniques. These techniques focus on two areas: the management and operation of facilities, and the design, manufacture and delivery of products or services.[25] For the latter, various laws such as those concerned with the emissions of toxic substances (such as the Toxic Substances Control Act in the USA) must be complied with.

At this stage, strong adherence to codes of occupational health and safety and well-advertised workplace safety precautions are leading areas of change for human sustainability. Progressing this requires an occupational health and safety (OH&S) policy and an OH&S committee with equal representation from employees and managers. A process designed to upgrade safety performance, for example, could commence with a safety audit by a third-party safety professional. Other steps typically include establishing bookkeeping arrangements, such as keeping required records of emissions, or required training to satisfy OH&S regulations, and monitoring the implementation and effectiveness of OH&S programmes. Governments may blacklist firms from receiving government contracts unless they are compliant with human rights, environmental, tax and antitrust standards. Such legislation was passed in the USA under the Clinton administration but later repealed by Bush. However, it is in force in many other countries.

For multinational organizations, the CSR Starter Pack, developed by the Corporate Social Responsibility Network, has useful suggestions that assist an organization ensure that the supply chain is moving to compliance with human rights legislation.[26] These include:

- knowing which issues are likely to be significant in a particular country or sector;
- requiring suppliers to certify their compliance with environment or employment legislation;
- using all opportunities to monitor performance; and
- working collaboratively to foster changes.

The next step towards compliance is the implementation of environmental and human resource reviews. The reviews require management to formulate a strategy which anticipates and scopes future issues and intended impacts of company operations, products and services.[27] A stakeholder analysis which defines roles and responsibilities, including those of senior management, is a key aspect of the review. For instance, the Dutch investment bank, the ING Group, has identified its core stakeholders as employees, clients, shareholders and society. In order to ensure compliance, it has established a Code of Conduct and Business Principles as internal regulations applicable to these stakeholders. A compliance organization has been created within ING and an executive board member serves as Head of Group Compliance. The Royal Dutch/Shell Group has a set of General Business Principles with which all Group companies, partners and contractors are expected to comply.

For compliance to be effective, each organization must develop policies for the environment, for community development and for employee training and development. These can be developed in parallel. Together they give a vision of what management wants to achieve, set out goals, objectives and strategies, and outline how success will be measured. To be comprehensive, the environment policy should align with community relations policies and with human resource policies covering industrial relations, safety and workplace standards and worker protection. Systems such as TQM assist in ensuring that the workplace compliance system, once established, is maintained.

Mobilizing change units and agents

Change units and change agents are business units and staff charged with the specific responsibility for organizational change. Sustainability initiatives are typically taken by change agents who are concerned individuals, but not necessarily privy to a technological overview or part of the senior executive group; for one reason or another, they have the personal or professional capacity to influence a limited area of organizational activity. Initiatives of this kind can provide an initial impetus and a heightened awareness that can be expanded and systematized in the next phase. Managers can encourage such personal initiatives by communicating widely throughout the organization that they welcome sustainability initiatives and will provide resources where appropriate.

Ad hoc initiatives are important but systematic progress needs competent, qualified professional change agents. Developing a specific sustainability change unit and a cadre of change agents enables attitudinal change, the building, managing and accounting for social as well as environmental capital and fosters the innovation needed for significant corporate change. Simple measures can send powerful signals to employees that corporate behaviour should be modified according to environmental and social responsibilities. Structural reforms that enable organization-wide reforms include:

- creating functional positions responsible for compliance that report to the CEO and the Board of Directors;
- requiring training and experience in the management of environmental, human resource and community relations for 'fast-tracking' careers in management and professional areas;
- creating audit committees that report to the board or are represented on the board.[28]

While important in many situations, technical solutions are not the basis for ensuring compliance. Organizations are human constructs, and human needs, attitudes and responses are ambiguous more often than they are clearly specified and predictable. Change agents need to develop a tolerance for ambiguous situations. This skill development and the processes of change are dependent upon the firm's human resource function. The resources available need to be sufficiently adequate to provide for training in interactive skills, team building, benchmarking, brainstorming and consensus building.[29]

Within a traditional hierarchical organization, the structural requirements are relatively clear-cut and the 'environmental manager' and HR managers can play separate and effective roles in enabling compliance. But they will only achieve the required changes if strongly supported by senior management. Traditional hierarchical organizations often handle cultural change ineffectively and this may offset the apparent advantage of a command structure in developing corporate compliance.

Assessing and measuring the change

Denmark became the first country to implement legislation on public environmental reporting in 1996. Major strides have been made since then in the techniques of environmental assessment and reporting. Many countries have established mandatory environmental assessment and reporting. In the USA, the Toxic Release Inventory requires companies with more than ten employees to submit data on specified toxic chemicals to the Environment Protection Authority. The EU, Norway and Australia all have comparable environmental reporting policies.

The performance of operational and review systems is critical in the shift to compliance. Auditing is a key tool and can be established at multiple entry points. Audits of the operations of newly acquired plant, other environmental auditing and verification of systems should be conducted at regular intervals. Failures of new initiatives may be due to inappropriate organizational structuring. For instance, creating a new staff function may be seen as the way to achieve an Environment Management System (EMS) or to devise a human resources plan. However, if this function has no authority over other staff, it will be marginalized and ineffective.

The trend towards flatter organizational structures, more participative management styles and the implementation of self-managed teams, task forces and project groups can make compliance monitoring more difficult. Consequently, monitoring by external organizations becomes more important in ensuring that compliance is maintained. Every three years KPMG carries out a survey of over 100 companies. The most recent KPMG survey showed that, of the top 100 companies in the Netherlands, 37 per cent have a non-financial corporate report or a sustainability report. As George Molenkamp, of KPMG Environmental Consulting, puts it: 'The reporting is not greenwash – a lot of energy is required to implement a policy of reporting for complex organizations with thousands of employees. It is a real challenge to get the data and do proper reporting.'[30]

External verification can establish system weaknesses and often results in recommendations to improve reporting procedures. Multinationals operating across a variety of cultures need to organize external verification locally, due to different expectations and regulations in each locality. As a result, external verification of reporting is increasing. In 1995 no Dutch companies were verifying corporate social responsibility reports externally; in 2000 the figure was 30 per cent. Twenty per cent of reports now have codes of conduct for business principles, taking in wider issues of business ethics. According to Molenkamp: 'The two big issues for reporting are climate change and EEO. Other key issues are community involvement and stakeholder dialogue.'[31]

The recent spate of corporate and auditor self-examination in the wake of the Enron collapse has highlighted the need for the audit committee to take a central and more strategic role in the organization. Broad-based reporting on anything questionable not only attests to compliance but facilitates best-practice governance.[32]

In sum, establishing a structured, systematic response to compliance requirements depends on implementing learning strategies and appointing change agents or specific change units, such as compliance committees, environmental management committees, human resource and environmental health and safety units to gatekeep information. But for more effective compliance these responsibilities need to move from the periphery into the core function of the firm.[33] They should be integrated into such departments as marketing and product and process design. Importantly, these reforms will succeed only if employees recognize that they create value for them. Employee ownership of the changes takes us into the area of cultural change.

Moving to 'compliance plus'

The *Exxon Valdez*

Most managers would have a broad recollection of the 1989 *Exxon Valdez* spill of 10.8 million gallons of crude oil into Prince William Sound and along 1,000 miles of beach in South Central Alaska. They could probably recall the sad scenes of the deaths of 250,00 birds, 2,800 sea otters and 300 harbour seals. They may not realize the extent of the fines and damage claims faced by Exxon, some of which are still unresolved.

continued

Exxon was fined $150 million, the largest fine ever imposed for an environmental crime in the USA. Although the court forgave $125 million of that fine in recognition of Exxon's co-operation in cleaning up the spill and paying certain private claims, Exxon has argued that the clean-up cost to the firm exceeded $2 billion. As restitution for the injuries caused to the fish, wildlife and lands of the spill region, Exxon agreed to pay $100 million. This money was divided evenly between the federal and state governments. The civil settlement took the form of an agreement for Exxon to pay $900 million with annual payments stretched over a 10-year period. Although the final payment was received in September 2001, the settlement contains a 'reopener window' between 1 September 2002 and 1 September 2006, during which the governments may make a claim for up to $100 million in addition in order to restore resources that suffered loss or decline as a result of the oil spill, the injuries to which could not have been known or anticipated at the time of the settlement in 1991. As of March 2002, claims by private parties are still before the courts. In 1994, a jury awarded the plaintiffs $5 billion in punitive damages as well as $287 million for compensatory damages. Exxon appealed and the issue remains unresolved.[34]

While many managers may argue that 'it could never happen to us', the issue of liability and risk stands out as a powerful leverage point for organizations to change course on sustainability issues before they become the subject of the next crisis of confidence.[35]

Adding further weight to the high-profile cases are other pressures, as managers of corporations across the world face consumer boycotts, public scrutiny, regulatory monitoring and even fines over their seemingly casual approach to sustainability issues. It prompts a simple question: Is there a better way of doing business that enables organizations to achieve sustainability and economic outcomes?

Corporations are now being called on to meet tougher standards set by industry associations and a range of other internal and external stakeholders. An organization which does not take responsibility for current or future environmental impacts or for the health, welfare and future career prospects of employees, and rejects community concerns, is now under pressure from across society to change. Initiatives such as green taxes on emissions and products, supply chain requirements and consumer pressure all place demands on corporations to move along the sustainability spectrum from rejection and indifference to compliance and to 'compliance plus'.[36]

The 'risk society' in action

The Association of British Insurers (ABI) has recently announced new guidelines on disclosure under which all public companies are now expected to report on the management and verification policies they use to identify and mitigate any risks associated with their environmental or social performance. The importance of these guidelines lies in the fact that the 400 member companies of the ABI control 20–25 per cent of all public equity in the UK. The publication of the guidelines follows ABI research showing that companies which take their social responsibilities seriously are successful companies.[37]

When managers are working to create the compliant organization, they often only place importance on the perceived 'primary' stakeholders, such as a regulatory agency, or perhaps the immediate neighbours of a manufacturing site. But as government legislation shifts in the direction of systems of co-regulation, different strategies are required. For example, a government agency may set the standards and the industry may do its own monitoring of emissions. Other stakeholders assume a new importance, too. These new stakeholders may be employees as well as others external to the firm. Managers are now recognizing that human and intellectual capital are critical to the firm's competitiveness in a knowledge-based economy and need to be sustained.[38] Externally, stakeholders such as environmental and human rights organizations, industry associations and other non-government organizations are setting new and higher standards for compliance. Different strategies are required to meet the expectations of these different groups.

Companies are increasingly driven by an urgent need to achieve immediate legitimacy in the face of new and potent forces policing compliance and driving the shift to 'compliance plus'.[39] The effects of these protests are now evident at top government and corporate levels. At the 2002 World Economic Forum in New York, for instance, they included a more inclusive participant list (corporate representation reduced to 40 per cent), a massive donation from Bill Gates to prevent the spread of HIV-AIDS in Africa, and workshops on 'Understanding Global Anger' headed by McDonald's chief, Jack Greenberg.[40]

Many corporations now market themselves as compliant according to standards set by governments, by co-regulatory arrangements between government, industry and non-government associations, or by a range of other non-government associations. The leadership for this change is also coming from managers who recognize the benefits for the firm from participating in the new co-regulatory system. That is, they see rewards for the firm in voluntarily working towards social and environmental standards which are not enforced by government. For instance, measuring performance according to the triple bottom line approach draws the attention of employees, the community and other stakeholders to the fact that the organization's managers are acting responsibly and seeking to improve progressively the organization's contribution to social and environmental sustainability. Corporations now voluntarily report on their performance in energy saving, consumer protection, community involvement, redundancies and employee training, and display their mission and value-added statements for public perusal.

In the post-industrial era, companies are reconceptualizing their strategies to preserve long-term value in the face of shortened product life cycles for every industry.[41] Developments such as the information revolution, the increased complexity of large heterogeneous organizations and expanded external and internal stakeholder influences may seem to be only loosely coupled. Yet their combined effect has highlighted the failure of traditional command and control systems to effectively evaluate, record and monitor corporate performance.

Developing inter-organizational relations for 'compliance plus'

'Compliance plus' reflects more general trends in corporate strategic thinking. Inter-organizational relations are now seen as more important factors in achieving success than internal structure or technology.[42] In a more complex global world, industry-sector organizations, inter-sector alliances, networks, communities of practice, community consultation committees and other collaborative structures provide a 'licence to operate' and a 'licence to grow'.[43]

Other collaborative management initiatives include agreements with regulatory agencies or community organizations to improve sustainability management, including community representatives in compliance committees and appointing NGO representatives as compliance monitors. Voluntary initiatives can be unilateral actions taken by a single firm, private codes designed by industry associations, NGOs or standards organizations, such as the International Standards Organization (ISO) code, or participation in government-sponsored programmes. These codes do not mandate and are not prescriptive but encourage change. ISO 14001 was published in 1996 to add standards relating to the natural environment to the 8,000 or more internationally accepted ISO standards already in existence. The environmental standards share many common principles with ISO 9000, the international standards for quality control. Unlike other ISO standards, the 14000 series go beyond accepted business or commercial practice to more exploratory areas for management. They include standards for eco-labelling, environmental auditing, life-cycle assessment, environmental performance evaluation and environmental aspects in product standards.

In an example of an industry-sector initiative, Europe's public telecom operators have recently launched a voluntary code: the European Telecommunications Network Operators Charter. Although in some ways a low-impact industry, telecommunications uses large amounts of energy and employs large and growing numbers of people. The goal of the Charter is to engender commitment to a set of industry-based principles and to develop indicators against which individual companies can benchmark.

In another example, such forms of relationship management are clearly of great importance to the global financial group, the ING Group. The ING Group is a member of the World Business Council for Sustainable Development; it represents the Dutch branch of the International Chamber of Commerce (ICC) by participating in a working group on the role of business and sustainability; and it is a member of the Round Table on Business and Human Rights in the Netherlands and of the Environmental Affairs Committee of the Netherlands Bankers Association, as well as of the Committee of Sustainable Development of the Dutch Association of Insurers.[44] These community links signal that the firm is going well beyond regulatory compliance.

Moving to a culture of 'compliance plus'

Organizational structure, policy formation and technical systems are the 'hard-wired variables' of change. The 'soft' variables are those that involve people and the transformation of meaning. While these are usually labelled 'soft', they are in fact more difficult to manage effectively. An integrated approach to 'compliance plus' is needed to create the consistent achievement of compliance goals that is only possible with ongoing employee commitment. This normally requires cultural change. Hence moving to compliance from the rejection or non-responsiveness phases is dependent on managing both soft and hard variables of change. The human resource function becomes a critical element in such a transition: a matter we take up in more detail in Chapters 7 and 8.

As surveillance at all levels of the corporation is not possible, compliance requires the internalization of new standards by people at all levels of the organization. Major litigation costs, for example, are often a result of employee carelessness. So attitudinal change is essential to ensure respect for legislative requirements. It is a major cultural shift to move from ignoring issues of wider social responsibility and community concern to meeting even minimal community expectations.

Compliance is not just a matter of changing policies and values: it involves capturing the hearts and minds of all employees and building practical procedures which everyone in the organization can understand. As Udeke Huiskamp, Environmental Manager of KLM, puts it: 'New ideas need to come from the bottom up. We have developed an awareness-raising course and are thinking of having a regular information day. Some employees see the environment as a technical issue and difficult to understand.'[45]

Values and attitudinal changes are required where employees have not been aware of their legal responsibilities as members of the organization. If the collective assumption within the organization has been that exploitation of community groups, employees or the environment is justified by economic benefits to the corporation, the cultural values of the organization are in need of reformulation. Such cultural change cannot be enforced – it only evolves with leadership and over time. Structural change underpins and provides some of the social organization needed for the shift to compliance. But the enthusiasm and commitment of the workforce at all levels has to be generated. In effect, both top-down and bottom-up approaches are needed, neither being sufficient on its own.[46] At Shell UK, for instance, the firm's managers have recognized that their actions must always reinforce their words if they are to get across the message of the importance of safety over profit. According to Malcolm Brinded, Chairman of Shell UK, words alone cannot change the culture. Regular deeds are the answer.[47]

Ensuring senior managers are committed and that their roles and responsibilities are defined is crucial to the cultural change involved in ongoing and full compliance. At KLM, the first airline to obtain ISO 14000 for all departments, senior managers have remained committed to sustainability, despite the pressures on the airline industry since 11 September. According to KLM's Environmental Manager:

> Since September 11, insurance costs have increased and more money is being spent on IT systems. But the Board has said that we do not want to change ambitions. We have a lot of support from the Board of Directors – it is important to have their leadership.[48]

The role each employee must play in the compliance agenda and the purpose of the compliance initiative should be workshopped and discussed in team meetings and other forms of workplace interaction. Increasingly, compliance also involves participation by the wider community. Community consultative committees can facilitate the internal and external cultural changes required. Placing employees in face-to-face situations with those who will be most affected by their work activity can have a powerful impact on attitudes.

The emergence of newer structural forms such as networks and strategic business units bring new challenges for the implementation of the cultural shift.[49] Employee participation in decision making through work groups or quality circles is commonly used as a strategy to improve organizational performance, motivation and commitment in these situations.[50]

Integrating sustainability agendas

Planning a fully integrated approach to the broad agenda of human and ecological sustainability requires an even more profound change in organizational culture. The change should be set in the context of an overall sustainability plan. The organizational change strategy developed to achieve the sustainability plan must be selected to suit the mission and context of the firm. Too often environmental managers and human resource managers move in different worlds from strategic business managers. The environmental manager is technically focused and often unaware of business objectives, except in the broadest sense. Similarly the human resource manager's interest may be in training and other intra-organizational needs. As a result, sustainability issues may be marginalized or moved off to agendas unrelated to the firm's core business. As a counter to this, human and ecological compliance policies are usually integrated into an overall sustainability policy which is an integral part of the firm's business policy.

Integration is a key concept for both successful business and sustainability. It points to the need for cross-functional relationships and the building of trust between areas of business that have previously been regarded by managers as only loosely connected.[51] Active relationships can be fostered between line managers and sustainability experts, so that the issues of human and ecological sustainability are not perceived by employees as an add-on, irrelevant to the core priorities of management. For instance, at KLM, line managers all have sustainability action points and targets.[52]

Limiting staff training to the technical training required for compliance is an add-on approach, not likely to bring about either attitudinal changes or allow the development of a culture capable of adopting self-regulation. Restricting skills development to a few key individuals can also lead to disaster, particularly in some industries where toxic chemicals or dangerous technologies are used by others in the corporation. The global banking, insurance and investment company, the ING Group, has attempted to avoid these problems by developing an e-learning compliance course in order to familiarize its 7,000 employees in eleven countries with compliance principles.

Sharing knowledge across the institution and developing an integrated policy according to the triple bottom line of social, environmental and economic objectives requires more co-ordination between internal elements of the firm.[53] A significant step along this road is the merging of human and ecological sustainability policies through the explicit recognition by management of the need for a comprehensive sustainability strategy. Nuon Energy, for instance, the second largest energy producer and largest producer of green energy in the Netherlands, has an Environmental Knowledge Centre which is part of a larger section, Human Relations Management.[54]

Steps that organizations can take to bring about a more integrated vision include the following.

Step 1: getting started

- Establish sustainability indicators and keep senior management informed on the progressive development of human capabilities, community relations and environmental initiatives. Measures of sustainability have been developed that combine social, economic and environmental indicators and which demonstrate links between and among them. The triple bottom line approach, for instance, requires establishing key performance indicators for social, environmental and economic performance and auditing against these indicators.

- Establish working groups and project teams that can assist in the internalizing of sustainability norms.[55] Liaison roles can be developed within these groups to take the findings of the groups deeper into the organization. These don't need to be authority roles, but rather to act more as information conduits and thus motivators.[56] While these liaison roles may be part-time positions, there may also be a need for a special 'risk communicator' to act as an integrator.

- Develop the informal links across the organization required for the shift to an integrated position on sustainability. This can be achieved by encouraging the development of the informal roles that enable inter-unit collaboration. Examples of these roles include the champion, the gatekeeper, the idea generator and the sponsor.[57] These informal roles can become ineffective if formalized, but thrive when those in them are good networkers and strongly committed to the core value of sustainability.

At the INCO nickel plant in South Wales, for example, the company doctor acts as the 'champion' and represents the company at international conferences and forums. The Environmental Officer acts as the 'idea generator'. He attends meetings of business units on a regular basis, negotiates standards with the regulatory agency and ensures that employees are trained according to ISO 14001 requirements. The role of 'gatekeeper' is played by some senior people who are also trained as auditors for ISO 14001. The 'sponsor' is the plant manager whose idea it was to start the plant down the road to ISO 14000 and who gives 'very decisive leadership'.[58]

New roles to alleviate harassment: the listeners scheme at Royal Mail

The UK organization Royal Mail has demonstrated how such informal links can help in ensuring compliance as well as developing a more cohesive workplace. At Royal Mail, volunteers are sought from among employees to become listeners assisting in the counselling system provided for women, the disabled, ethnic and other minorities who

continued

are harassed in the workplace. The volunteers provide a superior support system to those being harassed. The service also limits the escalation of equal opportunity and harassment issues and assists in building morale. Selected volunteers then go on to have further training in the skills required. Royal Mail has also found it essential for managers and union representatives to be involved in the scheme.

The results of this programme include compliance with EEO legislation, organization-wide communication of EEO and harassment policies, and improved staff morale.[59]

Systems thinking is vital, as it provides an impetus to move the organization towards the next phases of efficiency and strategic sustainability. Everything the firm produces should be regarded as an output to the society and the environment. Human impacts such as the provision of employment and the social consequences of restructuring are included. When goods and services are increasingly made more environmentally friendly and any deleterious effects eliminated, employees become more committed and the company enjoys more community support. At Nuon Energy, for example:

> We regard sustainability as part of our being. It is a strategic longterm vision but also is a policy designed in response to the fact that we have to develop sustainable sources with the end of non-renewable sources of energy. Sustainability is also applied to an understanding of employee priorities – the use of the intranet for education, for instance. In terms of community relations, Nuon has some partnerships in developing countries such as one concerned with knowledge development and sustainable water use in Mali. Another relationship is with various organizations in Albania, where the staff can use some of the company's time to work on various projects. These projects also try to bring in sustainability, in the sense of helping and developing to achieve more equitable outcomes.[60]

Step 2: winning staff support

Results of a recent survey of 5,000 employees carried out by a Sydney recruitment agency indicate that worker loyalty is fostered by 'mutual respect' (48 per cent of respondents), 'open and honest communication' (46 per cent of respondents), and by a 'pat on the back' (2 per cent). Only 3.7 per cent said more money would make any difference.[61] As Gollan points out, employee consultation, participation and feedback are crucial if the organization is to move towards an integrated position on sustainability compliance and beyond.[62]

Through the implementation of quality schemes, companies can raise compliance levels and ensure continued compliance with legal requirements such as safety and workplace standards. A more meaningful integrated compliance system develops through the active participation of the workforce in developing the documented procedures. A coercive culture and bureaucratic administration are not appropriate for an organization moving to integrate sustainability principles into the organization for the long term. Participative processes may take longer initially but they result in more genuine internalization of the new norms.

Lowering business risk through compliance demands a trained workforce. Enabling cultures which concentrate on staff training and ongoing participation have more capacity to achieve and maintain an internalized commitment to compliance than coercive cultures. Performance benefits are more likely if this training is contextual, based on collaborative learning principles and provided by supervisors in an ongoing fashion.[63]

Step 3: assessing for 'compliance plus'

The 'compliance plus' stage involves increased disclosure and generally introduces codes of conduct such as ISO 14000. Implementing systems according to the internationally set standards of ISO 14000 and ISO 9000 helps identify priorities for improvement programmes. The Responsible Care code provides the basis of a broad new ethic for business management in the chemicals industry. This code states that every research and development, manufacturing, storage, distribution and waste management site will have an active community awareness and emergency response programme in place. The differences between the old ethic and the new ethic fostered by Responsible Care are summarized in Table 4.1.[64]

The Global Reporting Initiative (GRI) provides an outstanding example of benchmarks for 'compliance plus' set by external organizations. The GRI consists of three tools: a set of core metrics applicable to all business enterprises; sets of sector-specific metrics customized to specific types of enterprises; and a uniform format for reporting these metrics and related information integral to a company's sustainability performance. The GRI also aims to create a permanent institutional 'home' to monitor, advocate

Table 4.1 *Old and new ethics*

Old ethic	New ethic
Do the minimum the law requires	Do the right thing
Keep a low profile	Show you are doing the right thing
Limit product obligations to the minimum	Exercise life-cycle stewardship
Downplay public concerns	Seek to identify and address public concerns
Make decisions on the bottom line and laws alone	Integrate all the above into decision making
Ignore or fight advocates	Seek advocates' inputs
Act on the belief that it is 'every company for itself'	Work collaboratively with industry associations to set standards; collaborate with stakeholders
Provide hazard information only if necessary	Accept the public and employees' right to be informed of all risks
Assume product 'innocence' unless others produce contrary evidence	Operate according to a risk-based precautionary principle

Source: Adapted from Canadian Chemical Producers Association, *Codes of Practice*

and continually upgrade the practice of standardized reporting world-wide. Institutions which have followed the GRI format for sustainability reporting include Fuji Xerox (Japan), KLM Royal Dutch Airlines (Netherlands), Konica (Japan), Nissan (Japan), Ricoh (Japan), Saint-Gobain (France) and Suncor Energy (Canada).[65]

The Sustainability SMART© tool has been developed by the Sydney-based consultancy Worthwhile Projects to assist organizations in evaluating their progress to sustainability and point to directions for improvement.[66] The tool draws from the internationally recognized Global Reporting Initiative (GRI) and the Standards of Corporate Social Responsibility developed by the USA-based Social Venture Network.

Table 4.2 describes an indicative set of twenty sustainability elements appropriate for, say, a manufacturing company.[67] The sample Sustainability SMART© element shown at Table 4.3 describes the sustainability features for specific business aspects and enables users to select the stage of development or progress relevant to their organization or business unit.[68] The numerical score for sustainability status for each

Table 4.2 *Sustainability elements*

Corporate and business unit management	1.1	Scope of commitment
	1.2	Management systems
	1.3	Accountability
	1.4	**Risk management**
	1.5	Compliance review and reporting
	1.6	Continuous improvement
	1.7	Supply chain and outsourcing
Financial planning	2.1	Budgeting
	2.2	Investor relations
	2.3	Cost controls
Human resources	3.1	Communications
	3.2	Employee relations
	3.3	Health and safety
Social responsibility	4.1	Community relations
	4.2	Business ethics
Environment	5.1	Land protection, remediation and rehabilitation
	5.2	Environment protection
	5.3	Waste management, recycling and reuse
	5.4	Energy conservation and climate change
	5.5	Water management

element is then applied using the rating ruler. A weighting can be applied to individual elements if desired – this provides the opportunity to give extra importance to certain sustainability elements as required.

Step 4: building corporate credibility

The scandal associated with the financial collapse of Enron in the USA shows that reputation, communications, disclosure, transparency and trust are interconnected issues for organizations. If any one of these factors fails, all others are affected and the path back to rebuilding them is a long one at the very least. Nike's experience also shows this: after a series of reputational problems, Nike has endorsed the Environmental Code of Conduct of the Coalition for Environmentally Responsible Economics

Table 4.3 Sustainability SMART© sample: risk management element

1 Corporate and business management	1.4 Risk management – new business and/or new development, plant, equipment			
Not applicable	Level 1	Level 2	Level 3	Level 4	Importance	Notes
Not applicable	**Regulatory processes are followed** during the development approval/permitting process for new equipment/operations. The company **responds to government or customer pressure** to modify or introduce products, services and/or operations in order to prevent serious impacts on the community or the environment.	Systems are in place to **identify potentially serious or irreversible environmental or community impacts** that may arise from products or operations. Processes are in place to identify feasible alternatives and appropriate changes to practices.	The company actively supports development of improved processes to reduce risk. **Integrated approach to identification, analysis and implementation of improvements** in the way products and services are made, delivered and used. Design and marketing strategies respond to changes in a coordinated manner. Products and services are analysed for long term impacts and decisions taken on a **precautionary principle approach.**	Cross-functional teams co-ordinate efforts to **reduce direct and indirect impacts from products and services** on the environment and communities. System for implementing changes is monitored, evaluated and changed to ensure that **aspects of importance to the community and the environment are not degraded.** Engagement with internal and external sources is co-ordinated and integrated with business units.		

N/A	0	0.5	1	1.5	2	2.5	3	3.5	4	SCORE
☐	☐	☐	☐	☐	☐	☐	☐	☐	☐	(Level × Importance) ☐

(CERES). While this does not mean that CERES endorses Nike's practices, it does mean that Nike will communicate with CERES members. CERES comprises members from citizen and community groups, as well as from investors, advisers and analysts representing over $300 billion in invested capital, more than fifty large companies and many small and medium-sized companies. Hence Nike has addressed its credibility problems by voluntarily committing time and resources to collecting information and participating in the sustainability-related activities of the CERES group of organizations.[69]

The chemicals industry: in the vanguard of 'compliance plus'

After 200 years of industrialization our lives are surrounded by synthetic chemicals. Yet it was not until the publication in 1962 of Rachel Carson's book *Silent Spring* that the risks associated with the vast array of new substances began to be recognized. Carson's book accused the chemicals industry of producing organochlorine pesticides which could enter the food chain and permanently disrupt the web of life. As a result of the publication of this now-famous book, the chemicals sector became the first to be targeted for more stringent regulatory compliance. In the 1960s and 1970s, incidents involving toxic chemicals were further triggers for national and international responses to corporate malpractice, at community and government levels.

But the most dramatic incident that triggered major action occurred in 1984. The spill of methyl isocyanate at the Union Carbide plant at Bhopal in India killed more than 3,000 and injured tens of thousands more. As a result, Union Carbide paid $470 million in compensation to the state. Eight officials of Union Carbide, including one American, remain before the Indian legal system, charged with negligence. Union Carbide itself has disappeared after the recent $7.3 billion takeover by Dow Chemical Co. In the history of corporate social and environmental responsibility, Bhopal marks a milestone. The public reaction was sufficient to push many companies to expand the notion of compliance beyond simply meeting government regulations to meeting the expectations of a wider range of stakeholders.

In the developed countries, Bhopal triggered an across-the-board shift in corporate accessibility and accountability. The first major response from government was the passage of the landmark Superfund legislation in the USA, requiring industry to report all pollution occurring at their plants. Dow Chemical became the focus of activism because of its association with the use of napalm during the Vietnam War. The response from Dow Chemical was to become the first industry advocate of stronger compliance measures in the form of self-regulation. Since the 1980s, Dow Chemical, for instance, has halved the amount of chlorine it stores at its Freeport facility – just one of many such measures.[70]

continued

But the reputation of the chemicals industry had been badly damaged, and by 1988 Monsanto had become the first corporation voluntarily to disclose its polluting emissions. This was an attempt to win back public favour. In 1990 the US Chemical Manufacturers Association initiated the Responsible Care Program. In many countries, Responsible Care goes well beyond compliance to the law to establish a set of industry standards which all members of the national chemicals associations must abide by.

Step 5: risk management through 'compliance plus'

Instituting a compliance-based management approach avoids the financial risk associated with non-compliance. But achieving compliance does not necessarily foster the continuous improvement required to minimize compliance costs, or reduce or eliminate all penalties. Consequently many firms are now moving to the 'compliance plus' stage in order to develop this capacity and thus achieve both flexibility and consistency.

Legislation is generally lagging behind leading-edge sustainability thinking and can makes some abrupt shifts particularly as governments move in and out of power. Companies which have developed and established a system of voluntary compliance are best prepared for this eventuality and may have already anticipated and acted on the new expectations; if not, they are still in a better position to respond rapidly. Hence, the move to 'compliance plus' also indicates a changing perception of the importance and nature of business risk. Risk management now involves more prediction than control.[71]

Step 6: establishing the learning organization

We have discussed the nature of the shift from (a) achieving compliance to the demands of external regulators to (b) voluntary compliance with internally generated or externally negotiated voluntary standards. This shift requires the whole organization to learn. The development of flexible mental models is the basis of effective organizational change.[72] When a firm makes the move beyond compliance, some 'old ways' may still be appropriate if they help the organization achieve compliance with regulatory standards efficiently and effectively. The processes upon which a structured compliance have been built do not necessarily need to be discarded. What must go is the 'machine' metaphor of the closed and highly regulated system. If a structured EMS has been adopted, for instance, it now needs to be reassessed for its value in delivering the negotiated understandings of 'co-regulation'. With the firm now partly responsible for instigating and monitoring compliance, institutionalizing reflection and implementing feedback becomes a priority. The whole organization needs to emerge from a legalistic understanding of regulation and begin to support what may seem less tangible ends, such as the capacity of employees to examine their own attitudes towards change.

For example, many managers are recognizing that learning capacity is the true capital of the firm. Dealing effectively with such issues as risk liability is dependent on this capacity. According to de Geus, the successful company encourages the development of a culture which is sensitive to its general environment.[73] Ongoing compliance is assured because the organization becomes an open system, capable of learning through interaction among employees and between employees and the wide range of stakeholders. These stakeholders include not only customers, competitors and suppliers but the environment and society.[74] In an organization of this kind, compliance simply becomes an integral aspect of the way people conduct business.

Step 7: developing trust

More organizations are moving into the new structural forms which will characterize the third millennium, such as networks, 'spider-webs', the 'infinitely flat' organization, alliances and the virtual organization. In this new order, fewer interactions within the organization involve hierarchical relations and more depend on trust. Bureaucratic implementation of procedures will still remain important for some regulatory requirements. But increasingly, managers gain credibility from their ability to put in place voluntary codes for healthy human and ecological relations.

Managers are increasingly required to expand the knowledge base of the workforce and institute high performance management practices. Studies demonstrate that these practices (such as reduction of status differences, sharing information and extensive training) can build commitment.[75] In other words, a culture of voluntarism can only be developed through a shared sense of identity. However, this is increasingly difficult to create given that career paths are ill-defined and unpredictable and more employment is contractual and part time rather than permanent and full time. Managers need high-level skills in team-building, empowerment and the development of trust.[76] Because a certain proportion of expert knowledge is tacit, working in self-managed teams requires trust, otherwise the critical knowledge needed to make the new systems work will not be exchanged.[77]

The ongoing challenge

In 1991, a McKinsey's survey of 100 business executives confirmed that the environment would be the central corporate issue of the twenty-first century.[78] In the same year, a senior official of Union Carbide (USA) and Director of Occupational Health and Product Safety of the Chemical Manufacturers Association (USA) said: 'We are not just trying to stay with regulation, we are trying to go beyond it.'[79]

A decade later, the major challenge for organizations, as they attempt to systematize compliance requirements and move towards 'compliance plus', is for organizational learning. What will be the role of knowledge management, including both tacit and expert systems? How can managers look beyond the quick technical fix and create effective learning systems that combine compliance with innovation and flexibility?

A strong human resource-based approach to an integrated concept of sustainability facilitates learning of this kind. This approach accords with current perspectives on corporate behaviour. Rather than doctrinaire systems or constant surveillance, commitment to a clearly articulated sustainability policy is the key element in a system of compliance that can be sustained.

Sustained compliance in both ecological and human domains is more likely to be attained if more co-operative approaches to problem solving are followed and if these approaches are supported by the application of systems thinking. An organizational culture which exhorts intra-organizational competition, or enforces a mechanistic structure, is less likely to develop the sense of ownership of problems and the organizational learning which enables sustained compliance and the shift to 'compliance plus'.[80]

The introduction of an array of voluntary mechanisms for compliance has underpinned a shift in the concept of compliance. It is now seen as a broad agenda going beyond the implementation of clean technology techniques to the redesign of organizational structure and systems that support further initiatives in sustainability.

Future trends in compliance

More stringent demands for company reporting through the application of company law are likely in the near future. In the UK, a recent company law review recommended a raft of statutory requirements concerning items for inclusion in annual reports. Mandatory items will be company policy on creditors, employment practices, disability and non-discrimination, compliance with international labour conventions, environmental policies and performance, and policies and performance on community, social, ethical and reputational issues.[81] In 2003, the EU will introduce the European Pollutant Emission Register which is expected to shame Europe's worst polluters into reducing their emissions. More than 20,000 industrial facilities in the EU will be required to report on emissions of more than fifty pollutants. Governments will be able to use the data to monitor environmental targets set in place in national or international agreements.

All these trends signal that governments and communities are now taking seriously their responsibility to issue a 'licence to operate' only to organizations that meet satisfactory basic standards of responsibility to the environment and society.[82]

Moving along the sustainability spectrum to the efficiency phase

Developing compliance systems requires building a baseline level of human and technical competence. Moving towards 'compliance plus' enables change flexibility as the internal corporate system is modified to address the requirements of external stakeholders. However, voluntary initiatives alone often lack rigorous performance criteria and specific objectives. To ensure rigour, the voluntary phase should be tied firmly to efficiency and strategic objectives. In the shift to the next stage of efficiency, human resource management becomes resource management.[83] Specific targets include how to identify cost inefficiencies and how to develop natural capitalism by increasing resource productivity and operational efficiency.

We have seen that for an organization to move from rejection to compliance requires incremental organizational learning in the form of gradual shifts in culture and structure. However, the organization at the compliance stage remains in a defensive position on sustainability.

It is not directly targeting sustainability in order to operate more efficiently or to gear the organization to benefit in a strategic sense from these reforms. To achieve this shift in organizational thinking requires transformative learning. The next chapter explores this process.

Phases in the development of compliance

 Phase 1: Rejection

Human sustainability (HS1)

Employees and subcontractors are regarded as a resource to be exploited. Health and safety features are ignored or given 'lip service'. Disadvantages stemming from ethnicity, gender, social class, intellectual ability and language proficiency are systematically exploited to advantage the organization and further disadvantage employees and subcontractors. Force, threats of force and abuse are used to maintain compliance and workforce subjection. Training costs are kept to a minimum necessary to operate the business; expenditure on personal and professional development is avoided. The organization does not take responsibility for the health, welfare and future career prospects of its employees nor for the community in which is a part. Community concerns are rejected outright.

Ecological sustainability (ES1)

The environment is regarded as a 'free good' to be exploited. Owners/managers are hostile to environmental activists and to pressures from government, other corporations, or community groups aimed at achieving ecological sustainability. Pro-environmental action is seen as a threat to the organization. Physical resource extraction and production processes are used which directly destroy future productive capacity and/or damage the ecosystem. Polluting by-products are discharged into the biosphere causing damage and threatening living processes. The organization does not take responsibility for the environmental impact of its ongoing operations nor does it modify its operations to lessen future ecological degradation.

Phase 2: Non-responsiveness

Human sustainability (HS2)

Financial and technological factors dominate business strategies to the exclusion of most aspects of human resource management. 'Industrial relations' (IR) or 'Employee relations' (ER) strategies dominate the human agenda with 'labour' viewed as a cost to be minimized. Apart from cost minimization, IR/ER strategies are directed at developing a compliant workforce responsive to managerial control. The training agenda, if there is one, centres on technical and supervisory training. Broader human resource strategies and policies are ignored, as are issues of wider social responsibility and community concern.

Ecological sustainability (ES2)

The ecological environment is not considered to be a relevant factor in strategic or operational decisions. Financial and technological factors dominate business strategies to the exclusion of environmental concerns. Traditional approaches to efficiency dominate the production process and the environment is taken for granted. Environmental resources which are free or subsidized (air, water and so on) are wasted and little regard is given to environmental degradation resulting from the organization's activities. Environmental risks, costs, opportunities and imperatives are seen as irrelevant or not perceived at all.

 ## Phase 3: Compliance

Human sustainability (HS3)

Financial and technological factors still dominate business strategies but senior management views the firm as a 'decent employer'. The emphasis is on compliance with legal requirements in industrial relations, safety, workplace standards and so on. Human resource functions such as training, IR, organization development, TQM are instituted but there is little integration between them. Basically the organization pursues a

Ecological sustainability (ES3)

Financial and technological factors still dominate business strategies but senior management seeks to comply with environmental laws and to minimize the firm's potential liabilities from actions that might have an adverse impact on the environment. The most obvious environmental abuses are eliminated, particularly those that could lead to litigation or strong community action directed against the firm. Other environmental issues, which policy of benevolent paternalism with the expectation of employee loyalty in response. Community concerns are addressed only when the company faces risk of prosecution or where negative publicity may have a damaging impact on the company's financial bottom line. Compliance is undertaken mainly as a risk-reduction exercise.

are unlikely to attract litigation or strong community action, are ignored.

Notes

1 M. Porter and C. van der Linde, 'Green and competitive: ending the stalemate', *Harvard Business Review*, September–October 1995, 120–33.

2 Milton Friedman cited in A. Hoffman, *From Heresy to Dogma*, San Francisco: New Lexington Press, 1997, p. 3.

3 S. Benn, interview with R. Savage, Environment Officer, INCO, Swansea, Wales, 14 February 2002.

4 N. Roome, 'Developing environmental management strategies', *Business Strategy and the Environment*, 1992, 1, 11–24.

5 R. Ramsey and G. Rowe, *Environmental Law and Policy in Australia*, Sydney: Butterworths, 1995.

6 T. Clarke, 'Balancing the triple bottom line', *Journal of General Management*, 2001, 26(4), 16–27.

7 J. Watts, 'Minamata mercury horror worse than thought', *Sydney Morning Herald*, 17 October 2001, 13.

8 L. Thurow, *Head to Head*, London: Nicholas Brealey, 1992.

9 D. Yencken, 'Investing in sustainable futures', *Dissent*, no. 6, Spring 2001.

10 R. Harding and E. Fisher (eds) *Perspectives on the Precautionary Principle*, Annandale: Federation Press, 1999.

11 S. Beder, *The Nature of Sustainable Development*, 2nd edn, Newham: Scribe Publications, 1996; S. Benn, 'The EHCA 1985 (NSW): a historical perspective on issues arising in the control of toxic chemicals', *Australian Journal of Political Science*, 1997, 32, 49–64.

12 Harding and Fisher, *Perspectives on the Precautionary Principle*.

13 Ramsey and Rowe, *Environment Law and Policy in Australia*.

14 P. Kelly, 'Business forced to examine its ledger', *Australian*, 6 February 2002, 10.

15 A. Osborn, 'Dealers to outlaw "conflict diamonds"', *Guardian Weekly*, 20–26 July 2000, 1.

16 S. Benn, interview with U. Huiskamp, Environment Manager, KLM Airlines, Schipol, The Netherlands, 6 February 2002.

17 D. Van Natta, 'Judge orders energy files released', *Sydney Morning Herald*, 1 March 2002, 10.

18 K. Seelye, 'Greenhouse offenders to be targeted in lawsuits', *Sydney Morning Herald*, 7 September 2001, 13.

19 Human Rights Watch, at http://www.hrw.org/ (accessed 10 April 2001).

20 Amnesty International, at http://wwwamnestyusa.org/business/ (accessed 10 April 2001).

21 S. Benn, interview with P. Kroon, Head of Public Affairs, ING Group, Amsterdam, 5 February 2002.

22 Benn, interview with U. Huiskamp.

23 Benn, interview with R. Savage.

24 Business Best Practice Case Study: Portugal Telecom SA, http://www.business-impact.org, (accessed 10 November 2001).

25 J. Fava, 'A flexible framework to select and implement environmental strategies', *Strategic Environmental Management*, 1998, 1, 21–33.

26 CSR Starter Pack, http://www.business-impact.org (accessed 18 April 2002).

27 Roome, 'Developing environmental management strategies'.

28 S. Suthersen, 'Editorial', *Strategic Environmental Management*, 1998, 1(1), 1–4 April.

29 B. Daily and S. Huang, 'Achieving sustainability through attention to human resource factors in environmental management', *International Journal of Operations and Production Management*, 2001, 21(12), 1539–52.

30 S. Benn, interview with Professor G. Molenkamp, KPMG, The Hague, The Netherlands, 4 February 2002.

31 Ibid.

32 S. Bartholomeusz, 'Time to redefine the audit', *Sydney Morning Herald*, 12 February 2002, 19.

33 Hoffman, *From Heresy to Dogma*.

34 Exxon Valdez Oil Spill Trustee Council, http://www.oilspill.state.ak.us/facts/qanda.html (accessed 18 April 2002).

35 J. Elkington, *The Chrysalis Economy*, Oxford: Capstone, 2001.

36 Roome, 'Developing environmental management strategies'.

37 ABI website, http://www.abi.org.uk/ (accessed 10 May 2001).

38 Clarke, 'Balancing the triple bottom line'.

39 B. Paton, 'Voluntary environmental initiatives and sustainable industry', *Business Strategy and the Environment*, 2000, 9, 328–38.

40 J. Barrett, 'Global anger tops forum agenda', Newsweek Web, http://www.snbc.com/news (accessed 5 June 2002).

41 N. Adler and M. Tushman, *Competing by Design: The Power of Organizational Architecture*, Oxford: Oxford University Press, 1997.

42 S. Clegg and C. Hardy, 'Introduction: organizations, organization and organizing', in S. Clegg, C. Hardy and W. Nord (eds) *Handbook of Organizational Studies*, London: Sage, 1996.

43 J. Elkington, *Cannibal with Forks*, Oxford: Capstone, 1999.

44 ING Group, *ING in Society 2000*, The Netherlands, 2000, also available at http://www.ing.com.

45 Benn, interview with U. Huiskamp.

46 D. Stace and D. Dunphy, *Beyond the Boundaries*, Roseville: McGraw Hill, 2001.

47 M. Brinded, 'Perception versus analysis: how to handle risk', speech to the Royal Academy of Engineering, London, 31 May 2000.

48 Benn, interview with U. Huiskamp.

49 Stace and Dunphy, *Beyond the Boundaries*.

50 P. Gollan, 'Human resources, capabilities and sustainability', in D. Dunphy, J. Benveniste, A. Griffiths and P. Sutton (eds) *Sustainability: the Corporate Challenge of the 21st Century*, Sydney: Angus and Robertson, 2000.

51 B. Piasecki, *Corporate Environmental Strategy: The Avalanche of Change since Bhopal*, New York: John Wiley, 1995.

52 Benn, interview with U. Huiskamp.

53 Elkington, *Cannibal with Forks*.

54 S. Benn, interview with Hans Nooter, Nuon Energy, Hardewijk, The Netherlands, 7 February 2002.

55 A. Griffiths, 'New organizational architectures: creating and retrofitting for sustainability', in Dunphy *et al.* (eds) *Sustainability*.

56 Adler and Tushman, *Competing by Design*.

57 Ibid.

58 Benn, interview with R. Savage.

59 Business Best Practice Case Study, CSR, at http://www.business-impact.org.

60 Benn, interview with Hans Nooter.

61 J. Huxley, 'For richer, for poorer: devoted to the boss', *Sydney Morning Herald*, 16 October 2001.

62 Gollan, 'Human resources, capabilities and sustainability'.

63 P.S. Adler, 'Building better bureaucracies', *Academy of Management Executive*, 1999, 3, 36–46.

64 Canadian Chemical Producers Association, *Codes of Practice*, at http://www.ccpa.ca/english/who/rc/Codes/statement.html (accessed 18 April 2002).

65 Information from the GRI website http://www.globalreporting.org (accessed 18 April 2002).

66 Frank Hubbard, Director, Worthwhile Projects Pty Ltd, Sydney, Australia, Environment, Safety and Sustainability Management Consultants, Info@WorthwhileProjects.com

67 Ibid.

68 Ibid.

69 Fava, 'A flexible framework . . .'.

70 Hoffman, *From Heresy to Dogma*.

71 Piasecki, *Corporate Environmental Strategy*.

72 P. Senge, *The Fifth Discipline: The Art and Practice of the Learning Organization*, Sydney: Random House, 1992.

73 A. de Geus, 'The living company', *Harvard Business Review*, 1997, 75, 51–9.

74 C. Laszlo and J. Laugel, *Large-scale Organizational Change*, Boston, Mass.: Butterworth-Heinemann, 2000.

75 J. Pfeffer and J. Veiga, 'Putting people first for organizational success', *Academy of Management Executive*, 1999, 13, 37–48.

76 I. Palmer and R. Dunford, 'Organizing for hyper-competition: new organizational forms for a new age?', *New Zealand Strategic Management*, Summer 1997, 38–45.

77 Pfeffer and Veiga, 'Putting people first . . .'.

78 Winsemius and Guntram, 1992, quoted in N. Gunningham, 'Beyond compliance: management of environmental risk', in B. Boer, R. Fowler and N. Gunningham, *Environmental Outlook*, Annandale: Federation Press, 1994.

79 Ibid., p. 254.

80 Roome, 'Developing environmental management strategies'.

81 Company Law Review Steering Group cited in Clarke, 'Balancing the triple bottom line'.

82 Elkington, *Cannibal with Forks*.

83 Gollan, 'Human resources, capabilities and sustainability'.

Part III

The dominant current reality: understanding and reconstructing second wave corporations

5 Achieving sustainable efficiencies

Beyond low-hanging fruit

'Picking the low-hanging fruit' is an expression that managers use to describe the easily achieved efficiency gains made within their corporations. However, once all the low-hanging fruit is picked, where are new efficiency gains to be achieved? This chapter takes the search for efficiency beyond the obvious cost reduction exercise. We identify three paths to efficiency:

- efficiencies via cost reduction;
- efficiencies through value adding; and
- efficiencies through innovation and flexibility.

These are not mutually exclusive paths to efficiency. Together, they represent a radical shift in the way that corporations approach efficiency – both human and ecological.

The Scandic hotel chain provides insights into how organizations can capitalize on these three paths to efficiency. Today, Scandic is the dominant operator of full-service 3–4 star hotels in Scandinavia and one of the major hotel chains in Europe.[1] However, this was not the case in 1992, when the hotel chain was in crisis. The newly appointed CEO, Roland Nilsson, instigated a major turnaround project that lasted two years. The successes achieved in the turnaround enabled the corporation to shift its focus from crisis management to future strategy. Central to this achievement was a change in values and philosophy. The company adopted 'profound caring' as its value statement. This reflected a commitment to care for all major stakeholders: customers, employees, shareholders, communities and the environment.

Environmental responsibility became a central focus of the organization. A corporate-wide programme, The Natural Step, was instigated to instil the new values approach throughout the corporation. Nilsson viewed The Natural Step as a powerful tool for communicating the importance of achieving sustainable outcomes. All managers and employees were exposed to the ideas of The Natural Step through workshops. Scandic managers and employees then sought to translate the principles of The Natural Step into concrete actions that would reduce the 'ecological footprint' of the corporation and simultaneously harness efficiencies to deliver in a practical way on the commitment of 'profound caring'.

The first efficiency impacts at Scandic were felt almost immediately. Employees identified many 'low-hanging fruit', ripe for picking. For instance, the overall amount of soap and shampoo used was reduced by 25 tons and refuse by 8.5 tons annually. This was achieved by the introduction of recyclable soap and shampoo and the elimination of waste by the use of refillable containers. The implementation of ideas such as these continues to generate cost efficiencies for Scandic.[2]

Second, Scandic moved towards efficiency gains through the adoption of value-adding activities. In order to generate value-adding outputs, the company had first to build the capability of its employees. Anticipated efficiency gains were shared with employees by investing in their skills. Emphasis was placed on developing and training employees (enhancing human capital) to identify value-adding opportunities. Employees developed and used a range of metrics such as environmental barometers (quarterly benchmarking reports) and an environmental index. In addition a resource hunt was initiated to gain resource efficiencies in energy, water, waste and dematerialization. In its first year, average energy consumption in its Nordic hotels was reduced by 7 per cent, water consumption by 4 per cent and unsorted waste by 15 per cent. This resulted in estimated financial benefits of US$800,000.[3] Through investment in such value-adding activities, Scandic built on its initial cost-cutting approach to deliver more fundamental efficiency improvements in resource utilization. This strategy is now being applied to Scandic's supply chain and procurement practices.

Finally, at Scandic innovation has become another means of gaining further sustainable efficiencies. Renewing and refurnishing are major investment activities in hotels. One major innovation Scandic has developed is the 97 per cent recyclable 'eco-room'. Rooms are designed and built for disassembly and all components that cannot be reused or recycled are sold: 'Approximately 2,000 rooms are being refurbished each year with an estimated decrease per year of plastics by 90 tons, metals by 15 tons and mercury by 50 per cent.'[4] Innovation – a change in mindset – has led to huge cost savings, reduced ecological impacts and enhanced the reputation of the corporation with its customers.

The Scandic case reinforces two important messages contained in this chapter. First, the move to efficiency often starts with an emphasis on using cost measures to capture short-term efficiencies. However, to achieve sustainable longer-term gains, the appropriate human systems and cultural values must be built to support value adding and innovation. Second, in a world where population is still increasing, the stewardship of natural and social resources is critical. An economy made up of efficient organizations may simply devastate the natural and social world more efficiently by, for example, using up natural resources at a greater rate or generating a larger pool of unemployed. Efficiency is a contestable term that can only be defined by reference to values. At Scandic Corporation, efficiency gains are shared with employees and a broader set of stakeholders, as well as being used to build internal competencies and the reputational capital of the firm. These strategies create a virtuous circle of steadily increasing efficiencies.

In this chapter we detail these three approaches to efficiency: cost reduction, value adding and innovation. While we discuss all three, we emphasize the importance of the latter two in creating positive benefits for the natural and social world. We refer to these as the high road to sustainability. Cost reduction alone is not necessarily a positive achievement for the organization, society or the environment. However, it can become a significant first step on the journey towards achieving sustainable competitive advantages and benefiting society and the environment.

What is efficiency?

Efficiency is a concept that means different things to different people. So what is efficiency? How can efficiency contribute to creating a more sustainable world? Who owns the increased efficiency? And how is the pay-off shared?

The search for corporate efficiencies has a long history that provides a useful framework for understanding current approaches. As organizations became larger and more complex in the late nineteenth century, a movement emerged focused on controlling the complexities that had arisen in these new factories. Frederick Taylor, the father of scientific management, was one leader who responded to this challenge. He involved himself in studying the new factories and trying to improve their productive efficiency. Taylor aimed to tame organizational complexity through the systematization of work and to increase organizational profitability through incremental improvements to the efficiency with which work was performed. Taylor's scientific management was only one historical source of traditional bureaucratic attempts to improve the efficiency of organizations. A comparable European source was the work of Henri Fayol. Both Taylor and Fayol had visions of more-productive organizations which they and their followers were able to implement in the real world.[5] Their ideas on what constitutes efficiency were, however, limited in scope and unrelated to issues of sustainability.

The principles generated by these approaches were simply an extension of Newtonian science. Success in scientific endeavour had been achieved by breaking the whole into duplicate parts with highly specialized functions and making these parts interchangeable. Scientific management extended these principles to the creation of a logical, linear workflow, the selection of applicants best suited to the job, training workers in the skills needed, measuring output and motivating workers by suitable rewards for performance. One result was the assembly line which dominated manufacturing through most of last century.

The systematizing of work that Taylor captured in his *Principles of Scientific Management* still remains an influential concept in much work redesign. Many of the principles embodied in Taylor's work were later taken up by industrial engineers and incorporated in operations management: the application of mathematical and technical solutions to solving managerial problems.

More recently, business process re-engineering (BPR) has built on these earlier incremental approaches to creating corporate efficiencies. It has attempted to do this by designing organizational transformations which 'bust silos'; that is, break down the boundaries between functional management areas such as marketing, manufacturing and sales. The aim is to reorganize corporations into discrete lateral process and/ or product flows.[6] Re-engineering can result in positive benefits such as a reduction in the number of levels in the organizational hierarchies, a refocusing of activities and resources on the core business, elimination of non-value added activities, the outsourcing of non-core businesses and simplification of workflows that cross traditional functional boundaries. This in turn requires the devolution of authority and in some cases the introduction of team-based work.[7] With BPR, efficiency moved from being treated as simply an operational issue to being a corporate-wide performance improvement strategy. However, issues of social responsibility, the systematic building of human capability in the workforce and environmental regeneration were largely ignored by BPR specialists.

So how do we understand corporate performance? Hilmer identified three factors affecting organizational performance: cost, value and flexibility.[8] We shall deal with each of these potential components of performance in turn.

If they are working within a conventional business perspective, corporations seeking efficiency are primarily concerned with the first factor – cost. If a firm is to compete against other firms producing similar products or services on price alone, then cost becomes the vital factor in success, and the search for ongoing cost reductions is the way to sustain success. This may include reducing the costs of inputs, redesigning work, product and process flows to generate internal efficiencies, reducing labour inputs and creating better utilization of company resources (see Figure 5.1). Most firms compete on cost to some extent, but cost is less

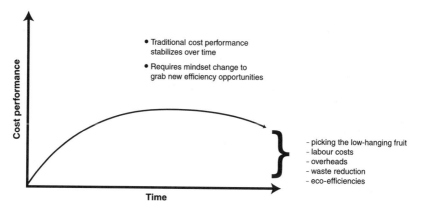

Figure 5.1 *Traditional cost efficiencies*

likely to be the most important factor in success where the firm has developed a unique product, service or production process. In other words, many cost advantages are shortlived. As one manager put it: 'Anything engineered can be de-engineered, copied, mass produced. Any advantage gained will have both value and cost components.'

A second approach to performance improvement comes from improving the quality of the product or service through adding value of some kind. Innovation around adding value is a potential source of performance improvement. Being an innovator is a strategic choice, with very different implications from competing primarily on cost, because adding value usually incurs extra costs, such as those associated with research and development and new product design.

Environmental performance at SC Johnson

SC Johnson is a family owned company, established in 1886. Its headquarters are located in the United States but the company operates in over sixty countries. SC Johnson is a leading manufacturer of household products for floor, furniture, air care and insect control. The firm has a long history of philanthropy and corporate social responsibility. When faced with increasing consumer awareness and a resulting pressure for regulatory compliance, the management of the company initiated an eco-efficiency approach to improve the environmental performance of its manufacturing operations. Rowledge *et al.* point out that, initially: 'it was not a particularly explicit or integrated strategy designed to carefully position itself in customer minds . . . it was clear that there were business benefits to be won from reducing waste, improving efficiency and minimising liabilities'.[9]

SC Johnson's strategy at first focused on improving operational efficiencies by finding engineering and technical solutions in the areas of waste management, filtering, recycling and in some cases the use of gas from landfill to produce steam power.[10] However, as the programme of change continued, its success became more reliant on company-wide educational programmes, eco-efficiency workshops, communication strategies and developing the capabilities of its people. The experiences of this company highlight a central theme of this book: that it is important to make a start somewhere, where at least small wins may be readily made. But where a company ends up may be very different from what management envisaged in the beginning. SC Johnson's initial endeavours were devoted solely to the capturing of eco-efficiencies and reducing risk by removing noxious chemicals. But now the emphasis has changed and the company is asking: 'How can we create products without any chemicals at all?' Eco-efficiency often starts with the idea of improving the environmental performance of existing operations. However, its inherent logic carries those involved into a more substantial change process.

Source: Rowledge *et al.*, 1999[11]

A third approach to performance improvement comes from increasing flexibility through innovation; that is, maintaining the ability to monitor, respond to or even anticipate changing market demands. The key to success here is to move in speedily with appropriate products or services to meet emerging demands. Innovation, speed to market and organizational flexibility become key components of success in this approach to creating a high-performance organization.[12] The emphasis is placed on competing by developing unique bundles of competencies and organizational capabilities, particularly those involved with reshaping the organization.[13]

The efficiency approach to sustainability is therefore not only a way of reducing costs to ensure competitive advantage but also an approach that can involve investments in value-adding and innovation-based activities. When managers apply efficiency approaches to ecological issues, for example, they initially recognize that poor environmental practice may result in fines, boycotts or expensive clean-up operations. Product or service redesign may eliminate these risks, which are avoidable costs. On the human sustainability side, efficiency-driven organizations regard employees as a necessary resource required to make returns to the corporation, but a significant source of expenditure. Reducing employee numbers by process redesign can minimize these costs. But this is only one way to achieve this end. In addition they are a denominator-driven approach. Another way to increase profitability is to make better use of the workforce to increase the numerator. Adding value through more effective use of employees is another approach to efficiency.

Efficiency approaches to sustainability are a recognition of the scarcity of organizational resources and are about finding efficiency improvements through changing the resource mix or through better utilization of resources. We argue that these latter two approaches to efficiency require significant mindset changes within organizations.

How can the search for efficiency contribute to sustainability?

Efficiency rests on value judgements – particularly about whose interests will be served by the changes. For instance, there is 'efficiency for the firm on the cheap'. It is relatively easy to increase the efficiency of any subunit of an organization or of society by externalizing costs to others. A simple example from managing a household economy is to throw the garbage over the neighbour's fence or on to the commons. All this does is transfer the costs to someone else. While efficient in the short term, we do not see it as leading to sustainability. Similarly we may reduce household costs in the short term by chopping up the floorboards for heating and selling off basic facilities like the refrigerator and stove. In this case we have externalized costs to the future. So when we are evaluating efficiencies, we cannot evaluate them solely on whether they benefit the organization: we also have to look at their impact on the environment and society.

In many cases the efficiency approach to sustainability is a natural extension of an organization's engagement in compliance activities. Compliance involves reviewing and monitoring organizational performance in order to identify inefficiencies. Efficiency approaches to sustainability have been particularly popular with organizations engaged in activities that significantly impact on the environment such as those operating in the resource extraction industries, in manufacturing and in petrochemicals.[14] Companies in these industries have typically moved over time beyond compliance activities towards the adoption of efficiency approaches to sustainability. In other words, the new lens of sustainability helps management and others see current organizational activities in a fresh light so that new opportunities to make efficiency improvements become apparent.

The message is simple: the efficiency approach represents a natural move towards sustainability because it builds on existing operational and technical capabilities and is a natural extension of installing compliance systems. However, efficiency defined solely as cost reduction and the simplification of product, process and service flows is insufficient to achieve fully sustainable communities and a sustainable world. In addition, such efficiencies will only provide limited competitive advantages for the organization, as efficiencies of these kinds are readily copied by competitors. Nevertheless the cost efficiency paradigm can help organizations lay the foundation for a more comprehensive approach to becoming a strategically sustainable organization.

We argue that a radical rethink of efficiency is required. The Scandic case highlights this in practical terms. The Scandic change programme started with a cost-cutting focus but went on to initiate value-adding and innovation approaches. In *Factor Four* and *Natural Capitalism*, Lovins *et al.* provide many detailed examples of efficiency and resource gains to be made in organizations and societies as they engage seriously with protecting the natural environment.[15] The examples they give demonstrate the need for a mind shift in how managers look at and value natural resources. Similarly, Hardin Tibbs argues that a paradigm shift in thinking on resource usage is required:

> At the moment, the industrial system is less a system than a collection of linear flows. Industry draws materials from the earth's crust and the biosphere, processes them with fossil energy to derive transient economic value and dumps the residue back into nature. For every 1 kilogram of finished goods we buy, about 20 kilograms of waste have been created during production, and within six months 0.5 kilograms of our average purchase is already waste.[16]

In other words, if close to 95 per cent of the material used in the production process doesn't make it into the final product, then there must be dramatic opportunities for more efficient use of the waste and for major productivity increases. There is a need to replace the current 'extract and dump' mindset with one that seeks to create virtuous cycles of resource usage and utilization.[17] For instance, this can be achieved through developing an industrial ecology where we begin with the principle of maximizing overall benefit to the total system. Efficiency based on value adding places the full cost of disposing of anything dangerous or not used (waste) on the producer. This leads the producer to initiate a search for 'beginning of pipe' design solutions to eliminate pollution and waste, to maximize use of all resources and to recycle material output. This in turn can lead to the creation of new industries which use waste as valuable inputs to further production. Such industries represent new strategic opportunities.

We represent this diagrammatically as designing organizations – that is production and service systems – as a series of concentric loops (see Figure 5.2). The search for value-adding efficiencies can be represented as a single loop where the reconstituted value chain of an organization becomes a value loop, incorporating everyone from suppliers through to customers.[18] The traditional value chain flows from resources/suppliers to the manufacturers of a product or service and then on to customers. However, an innovation approach to efficiency creates another potential loop where data about product or service performance are collected from clients or customers in the external environment and then fed back into the design of that product or service. The result of this is an improvement in the original value loop. This creates further innovations and new forms of organizational learning. This is the case at Fuji Xerox Eco Manufacturing plant in Sydney, where data about customers' preferences and product performance data are fed back into the redesign and production process to create more environmentally friendly and efficient office machines. They also significantly redefined and expanded their business in doing this.

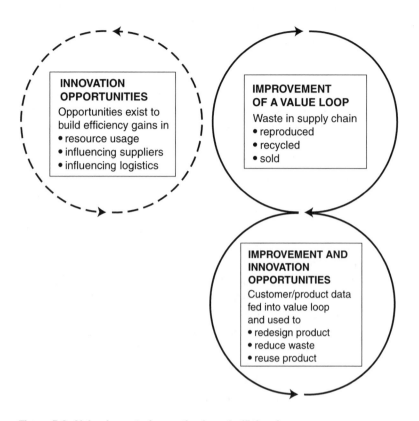

Figure 5.2 *Value loops to innovation-based efficiencies*

These latter two approaches are a radical departure from the traditional short-term cost cutting approaches to efficiency. While technologies are important in generating new efficiencies, fundamental shifts in mindsets are also required to maximize the value of new technologies so that they contribute towards value-adding and innovation-based approaches to efficiency.

As the Scandic case highlights, human capabilities are crucial in creating and capitalizing on these higher-level efficiencies. In a rapidly changing world, marked by unforeseen discontinuities, the capability for flexible response, the ability to change and to reshape the organization to meet new challenges is vital. Therefore it is false to imagine that anything that reduces this capacity to create higher-level efficiencies is itself an efficiency. It is easy to cut costs in the short term by putting off skilled and experienced staff and cutting back on investing in capabilities and competencies. But these human capacities are crucial to generating long-term competitiveness. Roland Nilsson, CEO of Scandic, has the last word here when discussing their decision to invest in people and the environment: 'So we can accept a higher investment today, because it will lower the cost in the future. It hasn't cost us anything. No one can claim that this has cost us more money.'[19]

Potential benefits of efficiency

There are potential benefits to the organization, society and the ecosystem from adoption of efficiency initiatives that build on compliance activities. First, efficiency approaches to ecological sustainability are the front line of action on sustainability for the majority of organizations today. Efficiency initiatives of this kind usually take place within the functional 'silos' of these organizations. These ecological initiatives can be relatively isolated and limited interventions such as the implementation of 'end of pipe' filtering systems and the use of programmes such as total quality environmental management or waste elimination. Alternatively they can be much more comprehensive interventions such as the development of fully integrated industrial ecosystems. Central to the successful adoption and utilization of such programmes is the development of a high degree of engineering and technical competence and the use of compliance-based monitoring systems to drive on-going business performance. The benefits for the organization of the development of such programmes are:

- the building of technical capabilities;
- the development of integrated human resource management systems;
- cost savings through waste reduction;
- the development of corporate specific knowledge on product design, process and service layouts that can result in future competitive advantages.

There can also be societal benefits from the application of efficiency approaches to sustainability. These include the more efficient use of scarce natural resources and the development of industrial ecosystems that protect and promote healthy communities by recycling and reusing industrial waste. Similarly there may be some forms of community involvement – such as the funding of public programmes or the establishment of community consultative committees.

Efficiency improvements to organizations, such as business process re-engineering and socio-technical systems redesigns, can flow from better use of people, that is, investment in 'human capital'. By destroying traditional boundaries within organizations, opportunities emerge for new forms of work organization dependent on high skill, teamwork and delegation of authority. This can generate process and product efficiencies, improve internal competency development and enhance the organization's reputation as a desirable employer. It can also make the organization an excellent investment prospect and lay the foundation for future competitive advantage.

Finally, efficiency approaches can have positive benefits for the natural environment. Lovins *et al.* (1999) provide several examples of how organizations, by changing the way that they approached efficiency – looking through the lens of sustainability – have not only garnered cost savings themselves but have also benefited the environment. Consider the case of the Center for Holistic Management in Albuquerque, New Mexico. The members of this community have introduced more efficient ways of range feeding cattle based on the 'natural' methods used by the moving herds of native grazing animals.[20] As Lovins *et al.* point out: 'It turns out that changing industrial processes so that they actually replenish and magnify the stock of natural capital can prove especially profitable because nature does the production; people just need step back and let life flourish.'[21] The full range of potential benefits of efficiency can only be realized when efficiency is maximized simultaneously for the organization, society and the environment.

Efficiency choices: high or low paths to competitive advantage?

Efficiency is the dominant concern of many organizations today; so the key issues here are understanding what efficiency is and making it happen. The drive towards enhanced corporate performance through efficiency gains diverges in two directions: the first path is based primarily on the search for internal efficiencies and cost reductions, and is related to competition on cost alone. The second path leads to the development of specific capabilities and strategies that can add value – a major feature of high-performance organizations. Organizations can often choose the direction they take. If they follow the first path, they run the risk of creating only temporary competitive advantages that are ultimately easy to imitate so that the immediate advantage can be leap-frogged by more strategically focused organizations. If they follow the innovation and flexibility path, new opportunities for business growth and sustainability emerge.[22]

In Australia, for instance, whole industry sectors – such as the resource-based meat industry – have formulated their strategies on low-cost factor endowments. For most of the industry's history, they have used the low-cost production of range-fed cattle to compete in export markets. Institutional arrangements, government policies and corporate strategies created an industry environment based on low-quality inputs. This caused significant environmental damage to semi-arid lands and made the industry vulnerable to other low-cost competitors. An alternative scenario can be found in Denmark: there competition is based on adding value to cattle production. Significant research and development has been put into technologies and production processes and the industry has been used to leverage spin-off industries in biotechnology, cattle production, technology management and consultancy services. The high road to efficiency provides both organizations and societies with greater choices and significant added value.[23]

Sony and the high road to ecological efficiency

Sony provides us with an example of an organization that is attempting to pursue the high road to ecological sustainability. Sony is a leading Japanese multinational company involved in the development, design and provision of consumer and industrial electronic equipment and devices.[24] Sony's first attempts at ecological efficiency in the 1970s focused on the reduction of hazardous waste in the production process and the introduction of health and safety initiatives for its work-force. These initial efficiency approaches were 'production' orientated and focused on process improvements – much in the same vein as quality management. However, these production orientated approaches became the springboard from which the company launched and extended its efficiency approaches to ecological sustainability. For instance, the company has gone about implementing environmental management systems, furthering its work on process efficiencies, product redesign for the environment and product recycling.[25] In the case of its second generation TV, these programmes have reduced plastics by 52 per cent, increased recyclability to 99 per cent and reduced the costs of the cabinet by 30 per cent.[26] Sony Corporation is now moving beyond the production and cost efficiency basis of earlier initiatives to integrate environmental issues into its corporate strategy.[27]

Creating eco-efficiencies

In the previous chapter, the case for compliance was examined. Compliance-based companies focus primarily on the implementation of monitoring and performance-based systems and the early experimentation with programmes that bring the organization into alignment with external stakeholder demands. The major aim is to reduce the organization's exposure to liability and the risk of penalty, fines and loss of reputation. As we pointed out, the failure to do so by many organizations can be costly in terms of the loss of reputational and social capital and the organization's overall ability to develop internal competencies. However, we now discuss positive examples of organizations creating eco-efficiencies. We build on the distinction made earlier between low and high approaches to efficiency, concentrating on examples of corporations following the high road.

Some corporations can and will achieve short-term efficiencies by dumping their waste products. While cost effective for now, such practices are ultimately unsustainable and will increasingly create costs in future for the organizations that pursue this approach. By contrast, those that have built the competencies to eliminate waste will thrive. For instance, Energy Technology and Control, a small UK manufacturer, won the Queen's Environmental Award for the creation of a new technology that reduces emissions and costs by regulating electronically the amount of fuel and air pumped into combustion boilers. What is remarkable is how this system has become a source of export generation, with the company selling its systems across the world from Scandinavia to Malaysia.[28]

What is eco-efficiency? The World Business Council for Sustainable Development and the United Nations Environment Program (UNEP) define eco-efficiency in this way: 'Eco-efficiency is reached by the delivery of competitively priced goods and services that satisfy human needs and bring quality of life while progressively reducing ecological impacts and resource intensity, through the life-cycle, to a level at least equal with the Earth's estimated carrying capacity.'[29]

Eco-efficiency is about the more efficient use of environmental resources. The efficiencies, however, provide benefits both to the firm and to the environment. Lovins *et al.* refer to this as Natural Capitalism and recommend changes in four key areas:

- increase the productivity of natural resources through changes to the production design, layout and technologies of operations;

- use biologically inspired production models, that is, closed loop production systems;
- develop new business models based on value and service;
- reinvest in natural capital.[30]

The World Business Council for Sustainable Development and the United Nations Environment Program have also outlined what they regard as the major principles of eco-efficiency. These include:

- reducing material intensity of goods and services;
- reducing energy intensity of goods and services;
- reducing toxic dispersion;
- enhancing material recyclability;
- maximizing sustainable use of renewable resources;
- extending product durability;
- increasing the service intensity of goods and services.[31]

Organizations, particularly those based in the manufacturing sector, are increasingly using these principles to design their eco-efficiency programmes. This efficiency approach to ecological sustainability is driven primarily by technocultures associated with engineers and scientists. Eco-efficiency builds incrementally on the compliance approaches and revolves around the establishment of and commitment to environmental programmes and the introduction of technologies to capture these benefits. Xerox is an example of this.

Xerox environmental leadership programme

Eco-efficiency highlights:[32]

- 3R programme: reduce, reuse, recycle contributed savings of $45 million in 1998 alone.

- Waste-free factories programme achieved 90 per cent reduction in solid waste to landfill, 90 per cent reduction in hazardous waste, 25 per cent post-consumer recycled materials.

Eco-efficiency is characterized by a variety of programmes such as: total quality environmental management; industrial ecology; end of pipe solutions; design versus labelling; and environmental management systems. While these systems are primarily technological they also involve developing the human capabilities that enable the effective use of these systems. These capabilities include identifying, collecting and understanding information and taking action to implement these programmes.

Furthermore, it appears that several key issues drive corporations towards the pursuit of eco-efficiency. These include the degree of alignment between market opportunities and eco-efficiencies, the internal structure and culture of the company and pressure from external stakeholders demanding action.[33] We have discussed the full range of these pressures for change in Chapter 2.

Consider the case of the Canon Group. Facing increasing regulation over the use of toxins in their manufacturing operations and increasing consumer awareness, Canon instigated technical and cultural changes designed to deliver eco-efficiencies. Emura states that Canon's corporate philosophy is 'Kyoseri' – harmonious co-existence.[34] This has been interpreted as co-existence both within human communities and with the natural environment. As Emura points out: 'the pursuit of Q (quality), C (cost) and D (delivery) are allowable only under conditions that fulfil environmental protection and that businesses that cannot protect the environment have no right to manufacture products. Under the EQCD policy, the E (environment) must be given higher priority than management efficiency.'[35]

What are the strategies that Canon has employed to create a high-value road to eco-efficiency? The first initiative was to improve resource productivity, through efforts to reduce energy consumption, reduce waste and thereby save on resources and the removal of hazardous substances from production. In the second initiative, the environmental focus shifted from these product and process improvements to the issue of eco-design. Eco-design has involved the examination of the environmental impact of Canon's products and the introduction of environmental considerations in the initial stages of the product design process (see Table 5.1).

The third initiative in the Canon approach to eco-efficiency has been to reorganize the supply chain through the use of 'green' procurement policies and accreditation systems. Emura states: 'Canon requested 1200 suppliers in Japan . . . 200 suppliers in South East Asia and China and 100 suppliers in North America to supply environment-conscious products.'[36] In the 1960s and 1970s Japanese automotive producers introduced quality improvement and just-in-time (JIT) programmes to create lean production systems. Similarly today, Canon is using its

Table 5.1 *Characteristics of product eco-efficiency at Canon*

Resource conservation	Ease of recycling	Ease of disposal
Energy consumption	Energy conservation	Environmental preservation
Resources	Ease of assembly	Ease of disposal
Layout	Ease of sorting	
	Ease of reusing	

influence over the supply chain to set standards for 'green' products and provide suppliers with the capabilities to develop 'green' components.

The final initiative in the eco-efficiency strategy at Canon is inverse manufacturing – or product recycling (remanufacturing). Along with other companies such as Volvo and Fuji-Xerox, Canon realizes that eco-efficiency is a transition phase to strategic sustainability. The pursuit of eco-efficiency enables the firm to develop and build broad environmental management capabilities signified by EMS accreditation and environmental management information systems and environmental accounting systems that leverage this transition.[37] Canon sees that its environmental mission is to move the focus from internal company changes to broader societal changes requiring community co-operation, particularly through 'green' procurement, product recycling and environmental disclosure. The Canon experience aligns with that of other major companies. For instance Bristol-Myers, Squibb, IBM and Xerox encourage their suppliers to develop environmental management systems consistent with ISO 14001. Ford, General Motors and Toyota actually require their suppliers to obtain 14001 certification.[38]

Industrial ecology

Industrial ecology is another innovative form of eco-efficiency. This involves the clustering of different firms in which the wastes or by-products for one company are used as material, resources or energy for another.[39] These clusters are often known as industrial ecology parks; the focus is on waste reduction and the recycling of outputs to create closed-loop manufacturing systems. Eco-efficiency is gained by all firms in the park by forging strategic alliances and relationships so that waste products, for instance, are recycled through other firms rather than being sent to landfill. One of the most famous examples of industrial ecology is that of the Kalundborg Park in Denmark. The Park, completed in 1982, consists of: a plasterboard factory; a company that remediates polluted soil; a power station; an oil refinery; a plant that produces insulin and industrial enzymes; and a water recycling facility.[40] In one instance of eco-efficiency savings generated by this facility, participants reduced overall oil consumption by 19,000 tons. The gas released as a by-product from oil production was used to replace 90 per cent of the oil previously used to power the plasterboard factory.[41] The principles of industrial ecology highlight an important management capability in delivering eco-efficiencies, that is, the ability to manage and forge networks and alliances. Those firms that are able to create learning networks, such as those in industrial ecology clusters, seem best positioned to capitalize on eco-efficiencies. The collaborative relationships among alliance partners in the network stimulate collective learning as well as efficiency trade-offs.[42]

Key issues in creating eco-efficiency

What lessons can we draw from these examples of collective organizational attempts to become eco-efficient? The characteristics of a winning formula for the creation of eco-efficient organizations are:

- establishment of measurement systems to monitor performance in key areas of energy, waste and quality, for example, systems such as Life Cycle Assessment, Eco Productivity Index, or Design for Environment;[43]
- development of environmental programmes, similar to the quality management initiatives of the 1980s, that provide guidelines, tools and basic knowledge which can be diffused to line managers and employees alike or alternatively, rather than using such tools, development of an internally generated approach closely tailored to the needs of the particular organization. For example, Roome refers to a Canadian pulp and paper manufacturer where participative approaches were used to develop a vision for the future. This vision was then used to build a corporate culture that linked environmental issues with cost leadership;[44]
- building strong support of these initiatives by middle management (if the initiatives are isolated to functional or business units) and by senior management if these programmes are corporate wide. For instance, at Du Pont, Chad Holliday, Chairman and CEO has set stretch targets and

goals for 2010 that focus on reducing greenhouse gases and increasing the use of renewable resources;[45]

- systematically identifying significant inefficiencies, unnecessary steps in the production or service process, poor layout, physical waste, old technologies and wasteful procedures. In the process of addressing inefficiencies, managers at Portland Aluminium in Victoria, Australia, found that they were dumping 1,000 cubic metres of solid waste into landfill at a cost of A$1.3 million a year. They have now made a 60 per cent reduction in solid waste through selling much of it, such as carbon dust to cement manufacturers;[46]

- accessing the tools available to address these issues: TQEM; environmental management systems; new technologies; industrial ecology opportunities and eco-design. Off-the-shelf solutions are generally less useful than combinations of these approaches;

- using the tools identified above to introduce extensive value-adding activities such as eco-design, recycling of products and conversion of products into services;

- piloting initiatives in a variety of business units and then progressively integrating them across the organization;

- measuring and monitoring the costs of the improved systems using both 'hard' measures (financial improvements, waste reduction, production quality) and 'soft' measures (capability development, knowledge transfer, change agent development, consumer awareness and value changes in employees);[47]

- including external stakeholders in the sustainability/eco-efficiency process through adopting, for example, procurement and supply chain management practices that involve suppliers also adopting eco-efficiency approaches. For example, British Telecom (BT), one of the UK's largest single purchasing organizations, has implemented a stringent set of environmental criteria when assessing suppliers. The result has been a significant change in sustainability practices across a range of industries;[48]

- linking human capabilities and knowledge to generate new value-adding and innovation opportunities. For instance, Electrolux's environmental product line is more profitable than that of its conventional products. The development of this product line has involved investing in people capabilities and creating a culture of innovation. This is a learning process which then feeds back into the generation of new products.[49]

We have emphasized here both the technical elements of generating a winning formula for eco-efficiencies and the vital links that must be made to human sustainability to maximize gains for both the organization and society. As Tibbs states:

> Change in either values or in technology alone is not enough: the two must happen in conjunction. One of the reasons for this is that technology – and new technology in particular because it is more powerful – can either help provide solutions or make the situation worse. What makes the crucial difference is human intention.[50]

Proactive environmental management of ecological information

In an innovative study of six organizations pursuing ecological sustainability agendas, Fung found that those organizations that had moved beyond compliance were seeking to gain efficiencies through the use of environmental management programmes and tools. An important trigger for this orientation was the environmental managers' lack of certainty over the extent to which they had achieved compliance with regulatory regimes. Rather than run the risk of breaching regulations, some of these organizations instigated programmes such as TQEM and EMS and other reporting systems which ensured that the organization was in compliance. However, once such technical systems had been introduced, they 'had their own momentum' and pushed these organizations into the compliance-plus efficiency orientations. The success of these programmes also relied on the development of specific capabilities which enabled organizations not only to monitor their impact on the environment but also to develop the additional skills and knowledge base needed to act to change and deliver efficiency outcomes.

Fung found that these programmes were piecemeal, were only in the formative stages of being integrated into the organization and for the most part were made to fit the organization's existing values, structures and systems. Clearly it is uncommon for organizations pursuing environmental efficiency goals to develop a fully integrated human and ecological strategy. It is easier to solve the technical problems piecemeal than to develop the human and managerial capabilities needed to create an integrated high performance system. A key finding of this study was the central roles played by motivated environmental managers and their pursuit of organizational structural changes in contributing to enhanced organizational ecological responses. The study concludes by stating that the challenges for developing both ecological and human resources in companies and the future are daunting but feasible.[51]

Creating human efficiencies

We have all heard the mantra: 'People are an organization's most valued asset.' In many cases they are only its most valued asset until the organization experiences a crisis and then they are seen as disposable.

Even when the organization does not downsize, the stated value placed on people is often demonstrated by low pay and failure to invest in employee competency development or to use fully employees' knowledge and skills. Many corporations have been trading on rhetoric for decades and in the process they have been losing their intellectual capital and consequently the basis for competition in the knowledge economy:

> If employers do not bridge the current gap between their rhetoric and workplace reality, then the likely outcome will be an exodus of bright and enthusiastic people to organizations that do. For true corporate sustainability, an organization must recognize, value and promote the capability of its people. For human resource sustainability to be achieved, therefore, the HR policies and practices need to be integrated for sustained business performance and positive employee outcomes of equity, development and well being.[52]

Placer Dome and Scandic Hotels

The case of Placer Dome, a gold mining company, highlights the potential conflict between narrow and broader views of human sustainability. In the 1990s Placer Dome's human resource policies and strategies had a strong focus on employee development, training and safety and on valuing employee contributions to the company's sustainability efforts. A range of human sustainability initiatives were aimed at developing the capabilities of both employees and local communities affected by mining operations. However, a dramatic decline in the gold price caused a setback in the pursuit of sustainability. Their decision to downsize led to a substantial reduction in one area of their core capabilities: for instance, at the Marcopper mine site a retrenched employee was rehired to undertake negotiations with key stakeholders when executives realized that he was the only one in the company who had developed a strong and trusting relationship with the community stakeholders. This example is an instance of a managerial decision, made in the name of efficiency, which can threaten the corporate capabilities required for future competitive advantages.

The Placer Dome approach is similar to the approach initially adopted by Scandic Hotels during its period of crisis. However, after the implementation of turnaround management strategies which lasted two years, Scandic's CEO realized that the best way to deal with future problems was to develop the human capital and competencies of its people that would enable the corporation to adapt. Therefore investments were made in training people to deliver on the hotel chain's stated value of 'profound caring'. In the process Scandic rebuilt its reputational capital and shared the efficiency gains with a range of stakeholders.[53]

Corporations can achieve human efficiency by downsizing and retrenchments. While these policies provide short-term financial benefits and efficiency gains for companies, they provide few, if any, efficiency benefits for the societies in which they operate. Efficiency approaches dominated by such practices as cost-cutting through downsizing and poor work environments such as exist in many call centres may create short-term efficiencies for corporations. However, they may also create long-term inefficiencies for the company and significant inefficiencies for society as a whole.

For instance, in the USA, Marriott Hotels was finding it difficult to attract new recruits and to retain good managers. The company had a strong culture of 'face time', that is, managers stayed at their hotel and pretended to work even if they had completed their work! In the Marriott culture, having managers put in long hours at the hotel was regarded as a benefit for the corporation. But there were heavy hidden costs in increased turnover and difficulty in recruiting new managers. When these costs were identified, the senior executive team instigated a programme of 'flexible work' which encouraged managers to adopt a different approach. If they had a busy week and put in more hours at work, they were encouraged to work fewer hours in down times. So far, the pilot programme has proved successful and Marriott is reaping the rewards of these new efficiencies, as reflected in a reduction of management turnover.[54]

What then is human efficiency? The high road to human efficiency involves organizations making maximum use of their human capabilities; that is, efficiency for the organization is primarily about ensuring that the organization has the requisite number of people, the mix of skills to perform its goals effectively and a strong base for future development. In the drive towards efficiency through added value, the human resource function increasingly develops an integrated approach to the management of a corporation's human capital. This is evidenced through:

- the development of human resource information systems;
- the identification of core competencies;
- focused training and organization development initiatives to enhance managerial and supervisory skills or to create core competencies;
- introduction of displacement technologies;
- outsourcing of those areas identified as not cost efficient.

The development of well-organized corporate human resource capabilities makes a significant contribution to human efficiency. Furthermore, current research has identified a strong link between a company's investment in its workforce and its stock market performance.[55] In other words, companies that invest more in their employees, for example in training and development and knowledge creation, show increased profits and productivity improvements.[56] These are characteristics of the value-adding and innovation approaches to efficiency.

Aristocrat and the development of internal human capital

Aristocrat Leisure Industries is the world's second largest designer and manufacturer of gaming equipment. One of its key undertakings during the 1990s was the introduction of efficiency improvements to its production processes to control spiralling costs, reduce waste and promote the desire to manufacture to quality, speed and flexibility. The major change has involved the transformation of the production system from a push to a hybrid pull system reliant on just-in-time approaches. This has in turn required a change in management style from autocratic and controlling to one that is more inclusive and empowering. This led to: the up-skilling of employees; the shift from a culture of fear and mistrust to one of trust; linking people systems (teams) to the new process layouts; a focus on the creation of a group culture through teaming; and the involvement of employees in addressing quality issues. Aristocrat approached the capability building process of its people through the introduction of quality teams. This quality programme showed immediate improvements, increased production efficiencies and reduced waste across the plant. Over time the quality teams were turned into production-based teams focused on running 'mini-factories'. The social changes at Aristocrat lagged behind the technical changes. However, executives realized that an important prerequisite for increasing performance further was a significant investment in human capital designed to build on the production and process efficiency improvements. Consequently Aristocrat is now also adopting a high value-added approach to human sustainability.[57]

The Aristocrat case highlights an interesting dilemma in the creation of sustainable corporations. Aristocrat is pursuing an efficiency approach to sustainability. However, many would argue that their products (gaming equipment) can damage the social fabric of communities and most ethical investment groups avoid investment in gaming activities. Gaming corporations respond that they have initiated programmes on responsible gambling and have created community benefit funds. This debate illustrates the usefulness of our framework, which can point to the real contribution of a firm like Aristocrat in one area of human sustainability (employee relations) and raise issues about its impact in another – social responsibility.

The external stakeholder relations of the organization can also contribute significantly to efficiency because they are often strongly affected by the reputation of a company. There is an increasing realization of the value of reputational capital. Reputational capital takes years to build, cannot be bought but can be quickly and easily damaged. As Petrick *et al.* note, organizations that systematically build this aspect of intangible assets do so by demonstrating: trustworthiness to employees; credibility with investors (through profitability); reliability to customers and suppliers; and responsibility with communities for stewardship of community and natural resources.[58] The paybacks can be significant: 'The reputational capital of Coca Cola, for example, has been estimated at $52 billion, of Gillette, $12 billion, of Eastman Kodak, $11 billion'.[59] In other words these corporations have added value via their enhanced reputations and public profiles.

So how does reputational capital contribute to efficiency? As organizations gain cost efficiencies by picking the low-hanging fruit, that is, by using their resources more effectively, increased emphasis is placed on leveraging those fewer resources that the organization has to increase value. As McIntosh *et al.* state: 'As businesses have become leaner, tighter organizations with fewer staff, key relationships and brand image are the company's greatest assets and their management becomes more important.'[60] That is, organizations need to leverage the resources that they have more effectively, such as reputation, to gain further value-added outcomes.

Steps to the creation of reputational capital

Petrick *et al.* suggest four practical steps that managers can take to build reputational capital in the area of sustainability:

1 Provide leadership education to managers and all levels of the organization in the areas of stewardship, behavioural skills so that sustainability competencies become commonplace.
2 Create senior executive roles for co-ordination of stakeholder relations that impact on reputational capital.
3 Conduct an annual audit of global reputation.
4 Use competitions for various product, organizational, social and leadership rewards to develop and maintain reputational capital.[61]

For organizations that seek to compete on efficiency there is a clear choice. The challenge is to look beyond a simple-minded cost cutting approach – the low-cost path. The value-adding route to efficiency offers greater returns to the organization, the society and the natural world. In this approach, the organization continues to reinvest in technologies, in research and development, and in developing knowledge-based competition. This in turn involves a shift away from an unskilled or semiskilled workforce to a workforce with high skill levels and an extensive knowledge base. Organizations taking the added-value path have an efficiency focus in the present, but it is tempered by a future vision of adding value and innovating.

Hamel and Prahalad argue that building world class leadership may take five years or more and requires investment in core competencies today. For instance: 'Sony's unrelenting pursuit of leadership in miniaturization has given it access to a broad array of personal audio products . . .'. Furthermore, they state that: 'The commitment a firm makes to building a new core competence is a commitment to creating or further perfecting a class of customer benefits, not commitment to a single product-market opportunity.'[62]

As a result, companies that have a future vision of value adding do not cut costs in a way that would jeopardize the progressive development of a highly skilled, well-paid workforce and the customizing of products and services. This choice involves a fundamentally different way of leading and managing organizations: it demands new structural forms and flexible work systems for the organization, a transformed approach to work design and new cultural values that reflect the shift to a knowledge-based economy. Managers who locate their organizations within the paradigm of value-adding/innovation efficiency are in a prime position to move to the next phase of developing a strategic approach to sustainability.

Potential pitfalls in pursuing human efficiencies

Several key issues for organizations emerge in the pursuit of human efficiencies. First, human resource managers often find it difficult to convince senior management and line managers that their efficiency programmes work because of the intangible nature of the benefits of many HR programmes and also because of the longer time frame involved before the efficiency gains become apparent. The contrast is between short-term cost efficiencies but medium- to long-term negative impacts (as in the case of downsizing or re-engineering) versus short-term increased costs (such as in training and development) and medium- to long-term benefits. However, evidence has been accumulating over the

Table 5.2 *Human sustainability orientation*

Compliance	Cost efficiency	Value added/ innovation efficiency
Characteristics:	Characteristics:	Characteristics:
• Industrial relations emphasis on awards, legal agreements, formal negotiations	• Early capability development often subjected to cost cutting in times of crisis • Downsizing for realignment • Core values focus on short- to medium-term profitability and returns on investment	• Capability enhancement • Integration of sustainability programmes at all levels of the organization • Value added and flexibility enhancement are linked to long-term financial goals
Aims:	Aims:	Aims:
• Survival, 'licence to operate'	• Utilize resources to maximize financial returns from resources	• Increasing emphasis on employee rewards • Capability building • Adding value, cost minimization (without damaging capabilities and flexibility)

last thirty years showing that advanced human resource policies, procedures and practices do contribute to the performance and financial competitiveness of organizations. More recently, these case-based examples of advanced human resource performance are supported by surveys of large numbers of organizations.[63]

Second, efficiency alone will not deliver sufficient long-term competitive advantage in turbulent and competitive markets. Skinner has referred to 'the productivity paradox'. He found that organizations that were obsessed with increasing the productivity of labour capital and technology became locked in a vicious cycle of their own making and that this inhibited their ability to develop new ways of competing and enhancing their performance.[64] The relentless search for short-term productivity gains or efficiencies resulted in long-term decline. One danger of adopting a single-minded cost efficiency focus is that, in tough times, it can lead managers to cut programmes designed to up-skill the workforce and create positive corporate cultures, thereby reducing the organization's ability to pursue a value-adding path.

Hamel and Prahalad make a similar point in their discussion of the way management fervently embraced re-engineering. They argue that re-engineering focuses too much attention on immediate efficiencies and neglects the vision for future innovative strategies; so there are real limits to an organization's ability to develop a fully sustainable human and ecological approach based on cost-efficiency alone. Managers need to ensure that cost-cutting today lays the organizational basis for moving towards the next phase of sustainability, the adoption of the strategic paradigm, rather than undermining it.[65]

So how can an organization pursue efficiency goals in a way that lays the basis for adding value? Here are some guidelines:

- Shift the efficiency orientation of the organization away from cost towards value and innovation. This can be achieved by demonstrating the value of building human capital and by changing management reward systems to ensure that they do not encourage short-term cost-cutting measures that destroy human capabilities for enhanced performance in the medium and long term (see Figure 5.3 on building cost reducing, value adding and innovation cultures).
- Develop and implement systems which reflect increases in human capital, reputational capital and intangible assets at the corporate level. At the operational level demonstrate the value added contribution of HR programmes to operations.
- At the corporate level, develop integrated human resource information systems (HRIS) that enable the HR professional to identify the organization's existing core competencies so that they can provide informed advice to senior managers about human capital competency areas of the organization.
- Initiate and implement trials of high-performance work environments and practices such as multi-skilled teams, value-adding programmes, culture change programmes.
- Protect innovative units of the organization from cost-cutting initiatives until they have had a reasonable time to demonstrate the value of their innovations to the corporation.
- Diffuse demonstrably successful high-performance practices and experiment with new organizational structures such as virtual teams, networks and communities of practice.
- Give line managers responsibility for the human sustainability agenda, establish support networks which include line and staff innovators and use corporate HR as a centralized resource facility to encourage and inform value-adding initiatives.

- Recognize that not all areas of the organization will be value adding and develop appropriate policies to maintain cost efficiencies in these areas.
- Seek opportunities to build reputational capital and develop monitoring systems that measure the movement away from physical and financial assets to intangible assets.
- Ensure that the head of the HR function is included in senior management and board decisions regarding corporate strategy.

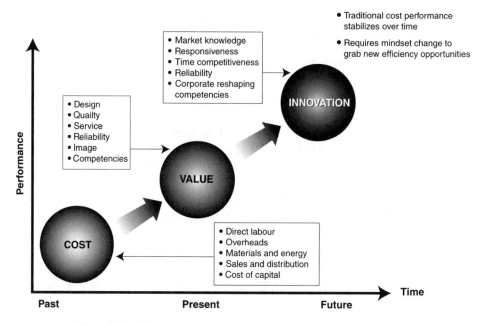

Figure 5.3 *The changing nature of performance*

The challenge: integrating human and ecological efficiency

Integrating the human and ecological approaches to efficiency is a key challenge at this stage of the journey to sustainability. Initially energies are often directed to one approach or the other, or initiatives are undertaken independently. It is only as these initiatives have been implemented that opportunities emerge to develop an integrated approach to efficiency. However, as organizations move further down the efficiency path, particularly in the development of eco-efficiencies, human capabilities become more important to the success of these programmes.[66]

In a recent study, Daily and Huang found that human sustainability factors, such as senior management support, environmental training, empowerment, teamwork and reward systems, were key elements in the implementation of environmental management systems.[67] The evidence suggests that the pursuit of value orientated eco-efficiencies is reliant upon the parallel development of human capabilities. However, the development of human capabilities is not reliant upon eco-efficiencies.

Who leads in the pursuit of eco and human efficiencies? The cases presented in this chapter show that senior managers play an important role in championing efficiency programmes. The case evidence also suggests that responsibility for making efficiency measures work belongs with line managers. They must take on the major responsibility for building future capabilities and for identifying future value-added opportunities. Efficiency approaches, by their very nature, are operational in focus and content. Efficiency programmes, whether human or eco-based, focus on such measures as the application of new technologies, the development of integrated and systematic information systems, cost and waste reduction and the effective utilization of a company's human, physical and resource assets. Line managers play an important stewardship function in addressing these issues: they must make the overall approach work.

Moving beyond efficiency approaches

In this chapter we have outlined a case for a radical rethinking of efficiency approaches to sustainability. We have argued that cost-reduction approaches are only one path corporations can use to achieve efficiency gains. For corporations to develop long-term competitive advantages and position themselves to make the leap to strategic sustainability, there is a need to invest in capabilities and competencies that capitalize on value-adding and innovation paths to efficiency.

The cases we have used demonstrate that once people become committed to developing human and ecological sustainability, the momentum builds. In the cases presented here, all organizations started with simple cost-reduction measures but went on to adopt a value-added/innovation approach to efficiency performance. In the process they found that this value-added approach unleashed a momentum of its own that led to the development of distinctive competencies. These competencies can be turned into competitive advantages. Technology initiatives are easily imitated; however, configurations of organizational capabilities – such as those found at Scandic or Canon – are harder to emulate. This is particularly so when these investments lead to and enhance the firm's reputational capital. Efficiency approaches based on adding value and innovation provide organizations with a strong impetus for moving into the next phase of achieving strategic sustainability. This is the subject of the next chapter.

 ## Phase 4: Efficiency

Human sustainability (HS4)

There is a systematic attempt to integrate human resource functions into a coherent HR system to reduce costs and increase efficiency. People are viewed as a significant source of expenditure to be used as productively as possible. Technical and supervisory training is augmented with human relations (interpersonal skills) training. The organization may institute programmes of teamwork around significant business functions and generally pursues a value adding rather than an exclusively cost reduction strategy. There is careful calculation of cost–benefit ratios for human resource expenditure to ensure that efficiencies are achieved. Community projects are undertaken where funds are available and where a cost benefit to the company can be demonstrated.

Ecological sustainability (ES4)

Poor environmental practice is seen as an important source of avoidable cost. Ecological issues that generate costs are systematically reviewed in an attempt to reduce costs and increase efficiencies by eliminating waste and by reviewing the procurement, production and distribution process. There may be active involvement in some systematic approach such as Total Quality Environmental Management (ISO 14001). Environmental issues are ignored if they are not seen as generating avoidable costs or increasing efficiencies.

Notes

1 B. Nattrass and M. Altomare, *The Natural Step for Business*, Gabriola Island: New Society Publishers, 1999, p. 75.
2 Ibid., p. 80.

3   Ibid., p. 92.
4   Ibid., p. 97.
5   D. Dunphy and A. Griffiths, *The Sustainable Corporation*, Sydney: Allen and Unwin, 1998.
6   M. Hammer and J. Champy, *Reengineering the Corporation*, London: Nicholas Brealey, 1990.
7   D. Stace and D. Dunphy, *Beyond the Boundaries*, Sydney: McGraw-Hill, 2001, p. 238.
8   F. Hilmer, *Coming to Grips with Competitiveness and Productivity*, Canberra: Economic Planning Advisory Council Paper 91/01, 1991; Stace and Dunphy, *Beyond the Boundaries*, p. 143.
9   L. Rowledge, R. Barton and K. Brady, *Mapping the Journey: Case Studies in Strategy and Action Towards Sustainable Development*, Sheffield: Greenleaf Publishing, 1999, p. 170.
10 Ibid.
11 Ibid.
12 Stace and Dunphy, *Beyond the Boundaries*.
13 D. Turner and M. Crawford, *Change Power: Capabilities that Drive Corporate Renewal*, Sydney: Business and Professional Publishing, 1998.
14 J. Keegan, 'Corporate environmentalism and market performance: an analysis of US corporate annual reports 1988–1999', honours dissertation, School of Management, Queensland University of Technology, 2002.
15 E. von Weizsacker, A. Lovins and L. Lovins, *Factor Four: Doubling Wealth – Halving Resource Use*, London: Earthscan Publications, 1998; P. Hawken, A. Lovins and L. Lovins, *Natural Capitalism: Creating the Next Industrial Revolution*, Boston, Mass.: Little Brown, 1999.
16 H. Tibbs, 'The technology strategy of the sustainable corporation', in D. Dunphy, J. Beneviste, A. Griffiths and P. Sutton (eds) *Sustainability: The Corporate Challenge of the 21st Century*, Sydney: Allen and Unwin, 2000, pp. 191–216, esp. pp. 202–3.
17 Ibid., p. 203.
18 Ibid., p. 210.
19 Nattrass and Altomare, *Natural Step for Business*, p. 80.
20 Example cited in A. Lovins, H. Lovins and P. Hawken, 'A road map for natural capitalism', *Harvard Business Review*, 2000, May–June, 145–58, esp. p. 156.
21 Ibid., p. 155.
22 R. Day, 'Beyond eco-efficiency: sustainability as a driver of innovation', *Sustainable Enterprise*, World Resources Institute: http://www.wri.org/meb/sei/beyond.html (accessed 15 September 1998).
23 A. Griffiths and R. Zammuto, 'Institutional governance systems and variations in national competitive advantage: an integrative model', Technology and Innovation Management Centre, University of Queensland, unpublished manuscript, 2002.

24 Rowledge *et al.*, *Mapping the Journey*, pp. 129–50.
25 Sony has also instigated new approaches to the collection, use and recycling of electrical goods. They have taken part in a pilot programme in Minnesota. See: 'US begins to wrestle more earnestly with electronic waste', *CutterEdge Environment*, environment@cutter.com.
26 Rowledge *et al.*, *Mapping the Journey*, p. 131.
27 Ibid., p. 134.
28 L. Boulton, 'Green at the margins', *The Financial Times*, 21 March 1998, 19.
29 World Business Council for Sustainable Development and the United Nations Environment Program (UNEP), *Cleaner Production and Eco-efficiency: Complementary Approaches to Sustainable Development*, 1992, p. 3.
30 Lovins *et al.*, 'Road map for natural capitalism', 145–58.
31 D. Buzzelli, 'The challenge of eco-efficiency', in P. Allen (ed.) *Metaphors for Change*, Sheffield: Greenleaf Publishing, 2001.
32 These figures are from J. Azar, 'Xerox environmental leadership program', in ibid., pp. 50–1.
33 J. Cramer, 'Environmental management from stretch to fit', *Business, Strategy and the Environment*, 1999, 7, 162–72.
34 Cited in Y. Emura, 'Environmental management of Canon group', in P. Allen (ed.), *Metaphors for Change*, Sheffield: Greenleaf Publishing, 2001, p. 57.
35 Ibid., p. 58.
36 Ibid., p. 60.
37 Ibid., p. 59.
38 Global Environmental Management Initiative, *New Paths to Business Value*, Washington, DC: GEMI. 2001, p. 7.
39 Cited in M. Kimura, 'Zero emissions', in P. Allen (ed.), *Metaphors for Change*, Sheffield: Greenleaf Publishing, 2001, p. 6.
40 Cited in E. Pedersen, 'Remarks', in ibid., p. 98.
41 Ibid., p. 99.
42 M. Blum-Kusterer and S. Husain, 'Innovation and corporate sustainability: an investigation into the process of change in the pharmaceuticals industry', *Business Strategy and the Environment*, 2001, 10, 300–16.
43 H. Pulm, 'Eco-performance evaluation', in J. Köhn, J. Gowdy and J. van der Straaten (eds), *Sustainability in Action*, Cheltenham: Edward Elgar, 2001.
44 K. Green, P. Groenewegen and P. Hofman, *Ahead of the Curve: Cases of Innovation in Environmental Management*, Dordrecht: Kluwer, 2001, p. 7.
45 C. Holliday, 'Sustainable growth the DuPont way', *Harvard Business Review*, 2001, September, 129–34.
46 B. Collis, 'Green bucks', *Qantas: The Australian Way*, 1999, 75, 23.
47 For sustainability indicators at the firm level, see D. Tyteca, 'Sustainability indicators at the firm level', *Journal of Industrial Ecology*, 1999, 2(4), 61–77.

48 M. Wright, 'The number you have dialed is green', *Tomorrow*, 2000, 10–11.
49 G. Hedstrom, S. Poltorzycki and P. Stroh, 'Sustainable development: the next generation of business opportunity', *Prism*, 1998, 4, 15.
50 Tibbs, 'Technology strategy of the sustainable corporation', p. 201.
51 V. Fung, 'The management of ecological information: understanding how organizations approach and structure sustainability issues', honours dissertation, School of Management, Queensland University of Technology, 2000.
52 A. Wilkinson, M. Hill and P. Gollan, 'The sustainability debate', *International Journal of Operations and Production Management*, 2001, 21(12), 1492.
53 J. Benveniste and D. Dunphy, *The Path Towards Sustainability: A Case Study of Placer Dome Asia Pacific*, Centre for Corporate Change, Australian Graduate School of Management, University of New South Wales, 1999.
54 B. Munck, 'Changing a culture of face time', *Harvard Business Review*, 2001, November, 125–54.
55 L. Bilmes, K. Wetzker and P. Xhonneux 'Value in human resources', *Financial Times*, 21 September 1997, 11.
56 P. Gollan, 'Training and the bottom line', Graduate School of Management, Macquarie University, Sydney, Australia, 1998.
57 A. Griffiths, A. Morgan and R. Waldersee, *The Implementation of World Class Manufacturing: The Case of Aristocrat Leisure Industries*, Case Study Series, Australian Centre in Strategic Management, Queensland University of Technology, 1998.
58 J. Petrick, R. Scherer, J. Brodzinski, J. Quinn and M. Fall Ainina, 'Global leadership skills and reputational capital: intangible resources for sustainable competitive advantage', *Academy of Management Executive*, 1999, 13(1), 60.
59 Ibid.
60 M. McIntosh, D. Leipziger, K. Jones and G. Coleman, *Corporate Citizenship*, London: Financial Times Management, 1998, p. 62.
61 Petrick *et al.*, 'Global leadership skills . . .', 60.
62 G. Hamel and C.K. Prahalad, *Competing for the Future*, Boston, Mass.: Harvard Business School Press, 1994, p. 219.
63 J. Pfeffer, *Competitive Advantage Through People*, Boston, Mass.: Harvard Business School Press, 1994.
64 W. Skinner, 'The productivity paradox', *Harvard Business Review*, 1986, July–August, 55–9.
65 Hamel and Prahalad, *Competing for the Future*.
66 A. Griffiths, J. Petrick and V. Fung, 'Proactive environmental management of ecological information', Technology and Innovation Management Centre, University of Queensland, unpublished manuscript, 2002.
67 B. Daily and S. Huang, 'Achieving sustainability through attention to human resource factors in environmental management', *International Journal of Operations and Production Management*, 2001, 21(12), 1539–52

6 Sustainability: the strategic advantage

Turning sustainability to advantage

> To avoid making the same mistakes, managers must start to recognize environmental improvement as an economic and competitive opportunity, not as an annoying cost or an inevitable threat. Instead of clinging to a perspective focused on regulatory compliance, companies need to ask questions such as What are we wasting? And how could we enhance customer value? The early movers – the companies that can see the opportunity first and embrace innovation based solutions – will reap major competitive benefits. . . .[1]

This quotation from the work of Porter and van der Linde, two of the world's leading strategy theorists and free market proponents, is a manifesto to managers and corporations alike: It is now time to link the firm's competitive advantage to environmental issues. Some firms have already responded to this emerging challenge and are developing corporate strategies that make sustainability a critical component of competitive success. The shift is a significant one, but those organizations that succeed in making the new integration will be the strategic leaders in the new economy.

The Royal Dutch/ Shell Group was a pioneer of workplace innovations in introducing teams and strategy formation in the 1960s and 1970s. It is now a corporate pioneer in integrating sustainability into its corporate strategy. In 1996, stung by critics over its handling of the decommissioning of the Brent Spar oil rig and alleged human rights abuses in Nigeria, the Shell group undertook a major review of its stakeholders' expectations. The review showed that Shell's reputation had suffered substantially as a result of these incidents. Rather than acting defensively and dismissing the review, senior management used it as a basis for transforming the business principles and strategy of the corporation.[2] As part of its strategic review process, Shell has since committed itself to:

- measuring and reporting its greenhouse gas emissions and reducing them through continuous improvement;
- using efficiencies in production processes to achieve these goals;
- working with governments and international bodies to find solutions to emission problems;
- promoting product innovations that are energy efficient and encouraging their use by consumers;
- developing alternative energy sources, including renewables.[3]

Managers at Shell see that future competitive advantages can be achieved by integrating three key elements: human and social capital, ecological sustainability and financial performance. They are now actively and successfully pursuing these strategies.

BP has adopted a similar strategic approach to sustainability. As one of the world's largest extractive resource-based companies and energy producers, BP has strategically repositioned itself to be seen as moving 'beyond petroleum'. Like Shell, BP has committed to:

- the development of alternative energy products and technologies;
- reduction in greenhouse gas emissions;
- the implementation of the Kyoto agreement;
- the pursuit of social and community sustainability by enhancing opportunities in local communities;

- the development of its internal human capital by enhancing the quality of life of employees.

BP has incorporated these goals into its corporate strategies in five broad areas of business policy: ethical conduct; employees; relationships; health, safety and environmental performance; and control and finance. BP executives have also decided that they need to develop core competencies in these areas if BP is to make further significant contributions to sustainability.[4] In line with stakeholder transparency, they have also outlined the criteria they will use to assess corporate performance. The *Financial Times*, reporting the findings of a survey of media, non-government organizations and leading CEOs, announced that BP was viewed by all these parties as the company that best manages environmental resources.

How did BP win such diverse and unanimous support? One survey respondent framed their selection of BP this way: 'They are huge – a damaging company . . . Their business causes a lot of damage to the environment. However over the years they have accepted their responsibilities and are constantly making efforts to reduce their impact on environmental resources. Although they have a long way to go, they deserve credit for their effort.'[5] Clearly, BP is in the early stages of the sustainability journey but already it is positioning the company as an industry leader.

Previous chapters have demonstrated that managers increasingly face consumer boycotts, public scrutiny, regulatory monitoring and fines over any failure to meet expectations around sustainability issues. The wish to avoid liability and reduce risk is a major driver for companies to review their strategies to include sustainability objectives. But sustainability can also be seen as presenting opportunities rather than potential problems. There is a better way of doing business that enables corporations to progress beyond pursuing efficiency measures to improve financial outcomes. The key to achieving this is to link corporate strategy to sustainability and progressively build relevant capabilities to support that strategy.

Corporations willing to adopt a strategic approach to sustainability can generate important ecological and community benefits.[6] However, these initiatives can also have other positive outcomes for the organization, such as:

- the generation of brand and reputational capital; for example, BP has been named in the UK as the leading corporation in managing environmental resources; in Australia, Visy Industries has been named the leading environmental firm in the good reputation index;[7]

- the development of innovative products and services for emerging markets;
- local community support for the organization's activities;
- difficult-to-imitate human and knowledge capabilities that are the basis for future competitive advantage; for example, Nucor Steel in the United States and Hewlett-Packard worldwide;
- industry leadership and in some cases the creation of a new industry.

Amory Lovins, Research Director of the Rocky Mountain Institute, emphasizes the business advantages of sustainability in relation to just one issue – climate change:

> I'd like to suggest that actually protecting the climate will be highly profitable rather than costly if we do the cheapest things first; and that pursuing profit motive will put industry in its rightful place as the largest part of the solution . . . The obstacles to achieving this profitable resolution are not technological or economic. Rather they are cultural and procedural.[8]

In other words, Lovins is arguing that our current corporate strategies, structures, cultures and norms prevent us from seeing solutions that can be both environmentally and economically beneficial. His message, in *Natural Capitalism*, is that the relationship between corporations and their environment is too complex to represent as either win–win or win–lose.[9] There are costs in incorporating sustainability objectives into corporate strategy but there are also very significant potential gains.

Making the changes needed to support sustainability does incur costs. However, for organizations acting strategically, protecting the environment and building human capital within the organization and society can provide significant new business opportunities. For example, AMB Property, a United States based property company, has found a lucrative competitive niche in transforming old brownfield industrial sites into thriving new industrial districts. Central to its approach is the integration of key community stakeholders as partners in the clean-up process. AMB also rewards its contractors for finding better solutions to the problems of environmental clean-up. The AMB case highlights that the challenge to renew the physical environment and make it fit for human habitation is a substantial strategic opportunity for business. This chapter builds the case for corporations to adopt a strategic approach to sustainability.

The importance of strategy

The last fifteen years of the twentieth century was a critical time for traditional organizations. In the preceding period of economic growth and relative stability, strategy was seen as developing and implementing top-down corporate plans and annual monitoring to see whether plan outcomes and objectives had been achieved. Like the five-year plans of the command economies of the former Soviet Union, corporate planning sometimes did not reflect the realities of corporate activity but nevertheless remained an important corporate ritual. Corporate strategic planning and its implementation is a very different process today and, to see why, we shall briefly review how the field developed.

The field of corporate strategy emerged in the 1960s from the work of several managerial thinkers, particularly Philip Selznick, Kenneth Andrews, Alfred Chandler and H. Igor Ansoff. They were actively involved as consultants to some of the leading US companies, including multinationals. These companies were confronting a series of problems emerging out of the growing pace of environmental change and the increasing size and complexity of their organizations. The executives were seeking more effective ways to control the activities of these growing organizations and to develop strategies to seize industry leadership and ensure the success of their international operations.[10]

Strategic management was subsequently popularized and developed further by the leading consulting companies, particularly the Boston Consulting Group and McKinsey's in the 1960s and 1970s. By the early 1970s, most large corporations were attempting to develop or had developed a corporate strategic approach with long-range plans to deal with environmental threats and opportunities. However, they were using what Lynda Gratton refers to as 'the top-down model of strategy'.[11] The top-down model is characterized by senior management formulating strategy and then pushing it down through the organization.

This approach to strategy suffered from several major limitations. First, it assumed that managers were rational decision makers who could make accurate forecasts and that organizations were passive tools to be directed to produce the desired outcomes. In fact, accurate forecasting is increasingly difficult in a turbulent world and organizations are often more political, chaotic and disorganized than a rational decision making model implies. In addition, the environment was generally taken to mean only the competitive market environment. Other major political and social factors (including the ecological environment) were generally left out of the analysis.[12] Finally, strategic planning often focused on the content of strategy and neglected the process of achieving it.[13] The assumption was that, if the strategy was formulated by the senior executive team, it would be automatically implemented throughout the organization.

The overly rational assumptions of the early strategic planners were widely questioned and led to a major debate in the field about the value of deliberate and emergent strategies.[14] As a result of this debate, researchers are now paying much more attention to three key issues that were formerly ignored:

1 the open-ended nature of strategy;
2 the impact of political groups in shaping the strategy process; and
3 the importance of an organization's resources and dynamic capabilities in shaping its ability to respond rapidly to turbulent and competitive environments.[15]

In particular, the debate on strategy has shifted beyond the traditional external elements of strategy such as industry structure, positioning and resources.[16] Current debates now emphasize that sustainable competitive advantages can be achieved by implementing value-adding strategies and by developing organizational innovation and agility. These strategies require the development of particular bundles and sets of capabilities that are not easily imitated and that can be used to transform and adapt the organization to changes over time. In other words, these capabilities are future-orientated and dynamic.[17] This approach to strategy can be characterized as a learning process which brings people together in an active engagement to design the future of the company.[18] In this chapter, we outline how strategic thinking will develop further as we move into the twenty-first century.

Hitt, Keats and de Marie argue that the following capabilities and competencies play an integral role in achieving strategic outcomes. We have linked some sustainability issues to these concepts:[19]

- *Strategic flexibility* The capability to adapt to fast-paced environmental change. The implication for sustainability is the ability to respond quickly to consumer and community demands and to create business opportunities.
- *Strategic leadership* The ability to develop a vision and mission and help build the values of the company that will achieve the stated intent of the mission. The challenge here is to incorporate sustainability objectives into the mission which can be acted upon.

- *Dynamic core competencies* The development and evolution of core skills and training and competency development. This requires investment in resources and people. Sustainability strategies require the development of core competencies to create value-adding opportunities.
- *Developing human capital* Focus on the development of organization learning, capturing and developing employee knowledge and identifying when to develop or rely on contingent workers. This amounts to a capability of higher-order learning – found in organizations such as Hewlett-Packard.[20] The focus is on long-term competency development.
- *Effective use of new technology* Extension of information systems into systems of procurement and supply management for value adding; design of environmentally responsive technologies and products/services. For instance, Interface has pursued a strategy based on the pursuit of long-life leasing deals for its products.
- *Engaging in valuable strategies* Taking advantage of global opportunities and developing strategic alliances and co-operative strategies. An extension of this to the ecological approach focuses on the development of partnerships with key stakeholders and local communities to review and monitor performance, to redesign products or services or to build local community capacity.
- *Developing new organizational structures and cultures* Valuing human capital and contributing to the sustainability outcomes and strategic goals of the organization. Such structures are designed to enhance and reward continuous innovation – this may be product or process orientated. The implication for sustainability is that the development of human and ecological competencies is reliant upon changes in structure and culture. Creating the conditions whereby these competencies become the basis upon which future competitive advantages are generated.

We think that Hitt *et al.*'s points are perceptive but we would add one further key characteristic of successful strategy: strategy is more than a set of business goals, financial objectives and means for pursuing competitive advantage in the market place. This is the traditional province of business strategy but it means nothing if the strategy is not known to all the members of the organization, strongly committed to by them and actionable in their terms. To be effective, strategy must be clearly articulated and embodied in specific action plans for every unit and individual in the organization.

We have explained how the current view of strategy differs from the traditional strategy model. But the current model of business strategy is only now beginning to take into account the importance of the ecological environment and human factors in achieving success. This is the issue we take up now. How can the strategy field incorporate the new demands of sustainability?

What is strategic sustainability?

What is meant by the term strategic sustainability? There is no clear-cut definition and several parallel interpretations exist. The first interpretation is the use of the word sustainability to mean corporate longevity and survival. If we were interested in how to achieve this kind of strategic sustainability then we would examine characteristics of those corporations that are long lived and strong performers.[21] For instance, as discussed in Chapter 4, de Geus has identified four characteristics of long-living companies. They show fiscal responsibility – these companies are not high-risk takers in the financial arena. They are aware of and in tune with their environment; they scan it constantly and respond quickly to emerging consumer demands. They have developed ways to experiment and to examine peripheral ideas and turn these into core activities or important side businesses. Finally, these companies have a sense of identity and community, and they work at maintaining good communal relationships.[22] De Geus's research highlights the fact that long-living companies, such as Shell, value human capital and seek to integrate the development of human capabilities into their long-term strategic approach.

There are limitations to adopting longevity as the measure of sustainability. Longevity is a poor indicator of whether an organization is pursuing goals that sustain the natural environment or society. However, the characteristics of long-living organizations do provide insights into how organizations adapt to changing environments. They are therefore useful in creating sustaining organizations.

The second use of the term sustainability focuses on an organization's engagement with its ecological environment. This is the approach adopted by Andrew Hoffman, Stuart Hart, John Elkington, Nigel Roome and others.[23] According to this approach, organizations which are seeking to realize strategic opportunities from the natural environment will develop a range of capabilities for understanding, processing and acting on ecological threats and opportunities.[24] This includes the generation of green products and services, refinement of supply chain procurement practices and the implementation of environmental management programmes, practices and techniques. Hoffman uses Volvo as an example of a company that was able to shift from environmental management to environmental strategy because it was able to adopt environmental values rapidly. In Volvo's case, the new environmental values were congruent with their existing values of safety and corporate responsibility. This enabled them to enlarge their existing values base to take in these other aspects of sustainability. Nevertheless, Hoffman claims that the adoption of a strategic sustainability perspective requires a cultural and behavioural shift within firms.[25] Such shifts do not occur easily or overnight but the resulting capabilities are hard to imitate and are a key source of competitive advantage.[26]

Interface

In 1994 Ray Anderson, Interface CEO and founder, instigated QUEST: a corporate programme designed to address the environmental consequences of manufacturing commercial carpets made primarily from petrochemicals. Anderson confronted the issue of huge quantities of their carpets ending up in landfill around the world.

QUEST was aimed at waste minimization through a variety of processes including the recycling of carpet. However, for QUEST to succeed as a programme, the organizational members needed to be strongly motivated to address the negative environmental impacts of key elements of the Interface 'value-adding' chain. This required a dramatic shift in the mindsets and motivation of everyone in the organization, from Ray Anderson to shopfloor workers.

While QUEST was a company-wide programme, decisions on how it was to be undertaken were delegated to each of the individual production facilities. Plants in individual countries were given the autonomy to pursue the QUEST programme according to local needs. Under these conditions, the Australian plant, for example, went from being number 27 – or worst in the organization – to number 1 by 1997.[27] In facilities across the world, small teams were established to address internal issues, such as waste reduction and minimization, and external issues, such as customer and supplier requirements. Company processes were then altered so that they aligned with the new focus on quality, waste reduction and recycling. For example, individuals and groups of employees were rewarded for attaining these goals. At Interface, the distinction between human and ecological issues has been increasingly integrated; new structures and processes have been established that reward progress in both areas and encourage the pursuit of excellence in each.

Source: Dunphy et al., 2000[28]

The third use of sustainability focuses on strategic sustainability as a suite of human resource practices and clusters of human capabilities that lead to high performance and enduring competitive advantages.[29] Such HR practices include the redesign of jobs to develop autonomy in decision making, the use of skills training to increase the organization's flexibility and the adoption of team-based organizational architectures to enhance work and increase innovation. High-performance workplaces require organizational systems which integrate HR practices such as particular approaches to recruitment and selection, the remuneration and the distribution of resources to value-adding activities, and knowledge management systems. Consequently, within this tradition, the focus of strategic development has been on creating value-based corporate cultures made up of committed individuals and supportive organizational systems. Gratton, for example, has shown that Hewlett-Packard built its success partly on the commitment, pride and trust of its employees – its competitive advantage has been based on the development and utilization of its human capital. According to Gratton, the development of human capital is a complex task that requires years of management commitment, action and skill. But the result is sustainable high performance.[30]

Human capital at Hewlett-Packard

A key factor in Hewlett-Packard's success has been the effective development of a workplace culture which attracts and retains skilled people committed to working in an entrepreneurial team-based environment which supports innovation. Hewlett-Packard has achieved a global reputation for building and utilizing human capital in the creation of new innovative products and processes. It is now utilizing this same human capital in its shift towards the development of sustainable strategies and eco design. At the core of the Hewlett-Packard approach to developing its human capital lie the following strategies:

- emphasis on creating careers, not jobs;
- promoting from within;
- developing and encouraging a culture of continuous learning and the expression of innovative ideas and practices;
- programmes designed to encourage diversity, profit sharing and the creation of a better work–life balance;
- programmes designed to build human capability in local communities.

These strategies rely on the development of enabling organizational structures such as the use of smaller division and cross-functional teams that enable employees to communicate freely, diffuse ideas and exchange knowledge. In turn, this has created an environment in which Hewlett-Packard is able to respond quickly and in an innovative fashion to customer and consumer expectations.[31]

For the purposes of this book, we identify strategic sustainability as being an organizational commitment to achieving competitive advantage through the strategic adoption and development of ecologically and socially supportive production processes, products and services and innovative human and knowledge resource management practices. What distinguishes our approach from the earlier strategic approaches we identified is the integration of the human and ecological sustainability traditions as a means of generating long-term competitive advantages. We have combined elements from all three traditions of strategic sustainability to define strategies to sustain the organization, society and the environment.

How strategic sustainability contributes to competitive advantage

What is the evidence that the strategic approach to sustainability can provide corporations with a basis for enduring competitive advantages? Recent research from the United States shows a positive relationship between a firm's performance on environmental indicators and its economic growth. When it comes to developing capabilities around sustainability, it pays to be green.[32] But the model of strategy we are advocating here goes beyond environmentalism: throughout this book we have viewed sustainability as including both human and ecological factors. Effective strategy in the future will draw competitive advantage from both areas. In this section we outline how this can be achieved and provide examples.

There is, however, an important point to make before we do this. Strategic sustainability represents more than the rhetorical commitment to human and ecological sustainability principles found in the glossy reports published by some corporations. These reports can be public relations exercises designed to conceal the corporation's lack of care for the community and the environment rather than an exercise in transparency. Strategic sustainability, by contrast, is a demonstrated commitment by the executive team and the board actively to pursue and develop corporate capabilities, products and processes that align sustainability initiatives with the corporation's overall strategic orientation. For instance, Australia Post, a government owned agency, was winner of the Good Reputation Index in Australia. It has developed a reputation for innovation and cutting edge ideas and has built its strategy on leveraging its reputation for trustworthiness and credibility.[33]

Strategic sustainability is also about the development and utilization of corporate competencies in both the human and the ecological areas. The two are loosely linked because developing ecological competencies within the organization necessarily relies on the development of proactive advanced-level human capabilities. Take the recent example of the Xerox Corporation where proactive designers and managers working in teams generated new products that were recyclable and reusable. This approach adopted by Xerox defied current trends that build in product redundancy and therefore waste. The team's zero-waste vision resulted in the establishment of a manufacturing plant that created virtually no waste.[34]

Strategic sustainability involves the organization in developing processes that institutionalize and systematize these capabilities so that they no longer depend on key individuals but are embodied in systems that act as an organizational memory. Based on a statistical analysis of change in over a hundred organizations, Turner and Crawford argue that high-performing organizations require both operational and transformational capabilities.[35] Operational capabilities contribute to the efficiency and effectiveness of day-to-day activities while transformational capabilities support change and strategic repositioning. This also holds true for organizations pursuing strategic sustainability. For instance, Boeing Australia is introducing New Business Development programmes designed to capture the skills of innovation and creativity of some key individuals in their organization. They are doing this to generate new business ventures and capture new market opportunities. This transformation has seen Boeing capitalize on its strength in winning defence contracts. It is using these capabilities to move into domestic aviation and to launch other new product and service areas. The focus of such corporate programmes is on the development and enhancement of the capabilities of their current staff. In other words, it is about building up the 'human capital' of the organization to enhance its reputation, to attract new business and capitalize on emerging opportunities for innovation. In the case of Boeing this involves reframing the business strategy and rebuilding the organization from its engineering-based orientation to a knowledge-based organization dedicated to the pursuit of entrepreneurship and intrapreneurship.[36]

Gratton argues that human capital contributes to the competitive advantage of organizations in three ways: first, when it is rare, that is, something other competitors lack; second, when it is valuable, that is, it has an impact on bottom line performance; finally, when it is difficult to imitate. Gratton goes on to argue that only human capacity can create these competitive advantages for corporations. She builds a strong case for managers to develop and integrate human capital into the core strategic directions of corporations in order to build long-term, sustainable competitive advantages.[37]

Volvo

At Volvo, a strategic approach to sustainability has meant concentrating on developing both ecological and human capabilities. This has led to the creation of internal cross-sectional project teams formed around the task of addressing key issues such as: changing structures and systems to capture the benefits of product recycling; restructuring organization systems for acquiring and diffusing environmental information; changing production processes for environmental efficiencies, and finally, meeting and extending European standards.[38] As Rowledge *et al.* state:

> Volvo's vision of environmental positioning has clearly moved beyond a compliance orientation in response to environmental regulation towards integrating consideration for sustainability into core business plans, products and operations. The most important thing about this evolution is that it is soundly based on prudent strategies and business planning. Rather than approaching environmental issues with an end of pipe mentality, Volvo instead addresses environmental considerations upstream in product and process design.[39]

The Volvo process of strategic sustainability is built on four key steps:[40]

1 Planning for sustainable development:
- leadership priority and organization alignment;
- diagnosis and analysis;
- a culture of openness and transparency;
- measurable environmental goals.

2 Organizing:
- comprehensive education and communication;
- establishment of infrastructure support for all operations.

3 Implementation:
- investment of resources in R&D, technology, product and people competence;
- formation of partnerships and alliances;
- practical change management strategies.

4 Review and monitoring.

This process is now being extended to the Volvo supply chain with the inclusion of the environment as a factor in the auditing of suppliers.

Sources: Maxwell *et al.*, 1997; Rowledge *et al.*, 1999[41]

Risks of the strategic approach

While the previous section outlined positive examples of corporations that were seeking to gain competitive advantages through the pursuit of strategic sustainability, this approach has some inherent risks. A focus on sustainability alone is clearly not enough to deliver competitive advantages. If the strategy is not viable in business terms, then a focus on sustainability will not save the organization. Consider the rapid rise and fall of many dot.com organizations. As Porter noted, many corporations and dot.coms assumed that the internet changed all the rules of competition. He argues that this led some organizations to make poor business decisions which undermined their own competitive advantage. For instance, many internet companies not only attempted to compete on speed, quality and innovation but also on being the lowest-cost provider of products and services. This led to many firms becoming unprofitable. As he states: 'The Internet per se will rarely be a competitive advantage. Many of the companies that succeed will be ones that use the Internet as a complement to traditional ways of competing, not those that set their Internet initiatives apart from established operations.'[42] In other words, many companies were swept up in the notions of the 'new economy', forgetting that conventional strategic rules about competing on value and cost still applied.

Similarly managers of organizations engaging in strategic sustainability need to understand that, as corporations, they must be profitable, add value and provide quality products and services. These are the conventional elements of any viable corporate strategy. For instance, while Interface and The Body Shop are held up as successful examples of companies pursuing strategic sustainability, both companies have recently experienced problems in maintaining the financial viability of their businesses. Elkington reports that The Body Shop lost ground to competitors because its product line was ageing and in need of revamping. He argues that this demonstrates the need for managers to maintain their focus on financial and strategic issues as well as social and ecological ones.[43] As a by-line on these issues, Anita and Gordon Roddick have now resigned from the board of The Body Shop.[44]

An analogy can be made between current efforts to institutionalize green strategies and earlier corporate experiences with the implementation of flexible manufacturing systems. At the height of competition between US and Japanese manufacturing firms, Jaikumar showed that Japanese firms outperformed US firms using the same or similar technologies.

Why? It appears that US firms used traditional organizational structures, systems and processes and did not modify their strategy to take account of the flexibility benefits associated with the new technologies. The Japanese, on the other hand, not only introduced the new technology, they also changed their structures and strategies to maximize the competitive advantages associated with its introduction. The story serves as a powerful reminder of the importance of linking the pursuit of sustainability with organization systems and strategic outcomes. It should also act as a warning: in the haste to develop corporate sustainability strategies, we should not overlook the need to make these strategies deliver competitive advantages.[45]

Beyond rhetoric and greenwash

What can we learn from our discussion of the risks of the strategic approach and from the successes of corporations such as Xerox, Hewlett-Packard and Volvo, which continually re-emerge as leaders in areas of strategic sustainability? One conclusion we could draw is that strategic sustainability can be fragile and difficult to maintain.

For instance, in the 1990s, Monsanto was hailed as a company that had achieved a remarkable turnaround. It adopted a strategy of moving from being a major polluter to pushing the boundaries of biotechnology and the new agriculturally based industries. In generating this transformation, the issues of strategic sustainability were key drivers. Monsanto's internal sustainability initiatives were promoted as being forerunners to creating the sustainable corporation.[46] They included the establishment of teams, a focus on waste and pollution reduction, and executive leaders who appeared to support key principles of strategic sustainability. Monsanto executives were keen to turn around the company's negative reputation concerning ecological and human resources. They set out to build a new image of an organization that valued community concerns, emphasized building human capabilities and was determined to move away from polluting industrial processes.[47] However, by the late 1990s and into 2000, Monsanto was once again attracting the ire of green and civil liberties groups and its commitment to sustainability was being questioned. What had gone wrong?

Monsanto had moved strategically to develop a range of genetically modified products. This was a product line which many outside Monsanto found ethically unacceptable. Environmentalists almost universally condemn Monsanto's ethics and its development and promotion of these products. In the case of Monsanto, first mover advantages were quickly lost due to external stakeholder criticism, which was very public and evoked broad consumer cynicism. Strategic proactivity in the new areas of biotechnology and genetic engineering requires the application of the precautionary principle. Monsanto provides an illustration of how easily a company can overlook this fundamental requirement of strategic sustainability. Had Monsanto maintained active and open links between strategic decision makers and third-party monitoring groups, it would have received an early warning that its developments in this area were unacceptable. These consumer concerns about genetic modification have now spread to food manufacturers, with many food manufacturers, particularly in the European Union, discarding genetically modified foods in order to avoid having to display GM food labels. As Robert Hadler, Corporate Affairs Director of Goodman Fielder, stated: 'The customer is always right and the customer is concerned about the effects of GM ingredients. The major retailers don't want products with GM in them.'[48]

Despite the strong commitment of its CEO and the introduction of sustainability teams, Monsanto found that strategic sustainability can be fraught with potential problems and hazards. There are some lessons to be learned from the Monsanto case. To achieve sustainability, companies need to remain nimble and continually reinvest in ecological and human sustainability capabilities. They need to maintain active and open links between strategic decision makers and third-party monitoring groups. In particular, strategic proactivity in the new areas of biotechnology and genetic engineering requires the application of the precautionary principle and transparency in operations.

The building of the human and ecological capabilities of an organization also contributes to its reputational capital. In their efforts to turn around poor or bad reputations, companies sometimes turn to 'spin doctors' and advertising, but this can expose the gap between what the organization says and what it does. Reputation must be realistic, monitored and constantly assessed, particularly in the global economy.[49] As Charles Handy puts it: 'Reputations matter and brands are fragile things.'[50] Furthermore, he argues that corporations have to redefine social responsibility – it is not enough to think of it as giving a little of your profits to the poor; it is about how you run your business and balance this with the demands of different stakeholders: 'Increasingly we want to know how they are making their money as well as how much they make.

They cannot turnover as much money as whole countries and not expect to be held accountable for the way they do it.'[51]

Table 6.1 outlines false postures that organizations sometimes adopt in dealing with sustainability issues. If your organization is adopting one of these postures, attempting to pass this off as strategic sustainability, then the deception will almost certainly be uncovered.

Table 6.1 *Strategic sustainability: false postures*

What strategic sustainability is not	*Risk to the organization*
Greenwash The use of corporate reports and misinformation to promote the public image of being sustainable	Damage to reputational capital as a cynical public votes with their dollars and shifts loyalties. For instance, Exxon lost US$3 billion in shareholder value after the *Exxon Valdez* incident. Similarly protests and consumer boycotts over its factories in developing countries hurt Nike's bottom line.
Green marketing Green product labels and the use of animals such as dolphins to create the image of green branding while obscuring the actual environmental impact of a company's processes, products and services	Consumer backlash against the organization and heightened cynicism about corporate and institutional pledges of self regulation.
EMS/TQEM These tools are useful in addressing complex sustainability issues but will not in themselves deliver strategic sustainability	A technological fixation: organizations can slip into the assumption that the implementation of such tools necessarily generates sustainability outcomes. A focus on tools alone can lead to missing strategic advantages which are eventually developed by competitors.
Fad surfing in the area of human resources Rhetoric about teams, virtual organizations, empowerment, culture change. Most employees have heard it all before. If translated into strategically relevant actions these concepts may help build sustainable capabilities and employee capital; but if rhetoric only, they create cynicism and resistance.	Alienation/cynicism and the flight of human capital as employees leave to find better employment prospects and to pursue their own values in a more honest corporate environment.

The winning formula

What is the winning formula to achieve strategic sustainability? What can we learn from our discussions of company cases and emerging research about how to integrate sustainability into strategy? First, corporations moving towards the attainment of strategic sustainability focus on building key capabilities for value adding and innovation. Second, they develop and utilize the corporate competencies needed to develop and enact these business strategies in the human and ecological spheres.[52] Third, the corporation develops processes that institutionalize and systematize these capabilities so that the organization is no longer reliant upon key individuals for best practice operations. The capabilities are embodied in the organization's systems and culture and are simply seen as 'the way we do business around here'. Finally, corporations must be embedded into local communities so that they are sensitive to community needs. The strategically sustainable organization will therefore give priority to cutting-edge human resource practices and look towards the creation of values-based cultures for sustainable outcomes. They will aim to become high-performance organizations (see Figure 6.1).

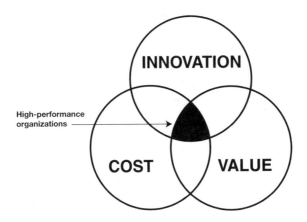

Figure 6.1 *The strategic target*

Achieving successful strategic sustainability also involves the following:

- *The move from efficiency to strategy* Building capabilities around achieving strategic goals involves moving beyond the compliance and efficiency phases to a strategic approach to sustainability. Strategic proactivity is much more externally focused and involves calculated risk taking. This is a significant value shift because the compliance phase reinforces risk avoidance and the efficiency phase reinforces cost minimization. By contrast, the development of new strategic options demands thoughtful risk taking and investment in R&D. Consequently, many organizations have to run an 'analyser' strategy, that is, they pursue a low-cost, low-risk strategy in traditional operational areas while accepting higher costs and significantly greater risks in areas involving new strategic developments.[53] To be successful this requires a more flexible managerial approach.

- *Introducing new tools and techniques* Various tools and techniques can be used to guide the development of strategic sustainability initiatives and in third-party monitoring and audits. One well known example is the use of the triple bottom line. John Elkington defines TBL as: 'sustainable development [that] involves the simultaneous pursuit of economic prosperity, environmental quality and social equity. Companies aiming for sustainability need to perform not against a single, financial bottom line but against the triple bottom line.'[54] Other companies, such as Hewlett-Packard and Du Pont, have experimented with the Balanced Environmental Scorecard, which links environmental performance to four key indicator areas: financial, customer, business processes and organizational learning.[55]

- *Linking operational processes to sustainable strategy* This involves the systematic and rapid translation of successful experimental ventures into standard operating procedures company-wide. For instance, Texas Industries operates a steel mill reliant on recycled scrap. A separate division, in the same town, then turns the slag from the mill into the raw material for its cement works. This has created synergies in product, resource usage and a reduction in energy waste, while increasing profits.[56]

- *Creating enabling structures and design* The development of sustainable business models and new organizational architectures can enhance an organization's responsiveness to environmental and social issues. Many traditional organizations have structures and designs that actually impede the development of sustainable business models. Networks and alliances in particular are appropriate to supply chain reorganization, recycling and stakeholder involvement.

- *Building employee knowledge and commitment* Firms adopting innovative and value-adding approaches to sustainability have emphasized the development of employee capital and corresponding competencies and have acknowledged their importance for long-term competitive advantages. They have set about creating commitment rather than control-based cultures and structures.

- *Executive leadership and stewardship* Innovative firms and corporations committed to the attainment of strategic sustainability have executive teams which support the development of sustainable products, services and processes for existing, emerging and future markets. Building an informed executive team takes time and may involve some change of membership. For instance, consider the comments by Bill Ford, Chairman of the Board at Ford Motor Company. He states: 'We see no conflict between business goals and social and environmental needs. I believe the distinction between a good company and a great one is this: A good company delivers excellent products and services; a great one delivers excellent products and services and strives to make the world a better place.'[57] The vision being outlined for Ford involves the shift from a traditional manufacturing company to a company that values its stakeholders: 'Our shared vision and my sincere hope is that Ford can become a company whose decisions and choices restore the environment and contribute to the creation of social and economic equity in communities around the world.'[58]

- *Developing differentiated stakeholder strategies* This involves designing and implementing various strategies that reflect the needs and interests of different stakeholders.[59] To achieve this, stakeholder representatives need to be actively involved. For instance BHP Carrington Silver Lead and Zinc Mine in Queensland has used third-party auditing by the North Queensland Conservation Council as a means of independently monitoring and reporting on the company's sustainable operation of this site. While the Council found that BHP performed better than their own targets and legislative requirements, they recommended that the mining operations look further into developing a product life cycle analysis and seek greater community involvement in risk assessment and revision of mining operations. Third-party scrutiny can be used to push organizations further towards the attainment of strategic sustainability and this can also prove to be of strategic advantage to the firm.[60]

We shall now expand on each of these points in the remainder of the chapter.

The move from efficiency to strategy

What does a review of the existing literature and case examples tell us about what the shift from the efficiency phase to the strategic phase involves? First, it is important to note that much of the literature in this area concentrates on environmental management rather than human sustainability. We shall deal with this literature first. Andrew Hoffman argues that the move from environmental management to environmental strategy requires organizations to shift their cultures, structures, reward systems and job responsibilities. In his view, the shift to strategic sustainability requires a radical overhaul of how corporations value their assets and how they define what is an asset.[61] The current strategic approaches are only starting to recognize the importance of culture and human capital in the attainment of strategic outcomes.

Furthermore, Hoffman argues that engagement with sustainability issues requires a holistic change. Piecemeal solutions such as retrofitting, fire fighting, end-of-pipe solutions and other technical programmes such as total quality environmental management (TQEM) and environmental management systems (EMS) are not enough. To be effective these programmes must be accompanied by a series of broader supporting organizational changes. Hoffman acknowledges that technical solutions can provide efficiency gains. However, he argues that they are easily imitated and will not provide long-term competitive advantages.[62] Increasingly companies will also require that their suppliers adopt a strategic approach to sustainability. For instance, the movement from efficiency to strategy has implications for a range of small and middle-sized companies. In their pursuit of new markets for green products and services, larger corporations will increasingly require their suppliers to obtain environmental accreditation and reach quality standards. The implication for those companies which supply the larger corporations is clear. They must act now to avoid the risk of having such systems imposed or, worse still, losing market share to others who have already implemented such systems. This has happened in some cases. IKEA, for example, now requires its furniture manufacturers, subcontractors, transport and logistics companies to implement and adhere to IKEA's high environmental standards. Customers are demanding high environmental standards and IKEA insists that those who participate in their supply chain deliver on IKEA's commitments to meet them.[63]

Key steps to strategic sustainability

This section outlines the five key steps required to shift an organization from an efficiency focus to strategic sustainability.

Step 1: Top team elaboration of corporate goals relating to sustainability
For corporations to shift to strategic sustainability, corporate goals need to measure and be redefined to include sustainability. This involves a thorough assessment of the strategic advantages that sustainability can provide. The executive team then needs to work with line managers to turn the revised goals into actionable strategies for individual business units. This is an iterative process as each individual business unit searches for new business opportunities in line with the corporation's overall sustainability agenda. Individual managers can also build on initiatives already undertaken through TQEM/EMS programmes or on skills development programmes, job redesign and pilot teaming initiatives. In the process, widespread involvement of staff at all levels leads to upward feedback about the goals and strategies which may result in some modification of them. For instance, at IKEA this required all senior managers to undertake training in The Natural Step and their mission and strategies to incorporate an environmental focus. Once this occurred, environmental training was then diffused throughout the organization.[64] It is important at this stage that the projects developed have clear strategic relevance and are not simply the ad hoc projects of individual enthusiasts.

IKEA's environmental goals

IKEA has adopted a systematic approach to environmental issues over the last ten years. They have followed a step-by-step approach to improving the environmental performance of their organization. This has typically involved the development of three-year plans – with clear objectives against which their performance can be managed. In their current three-year plan, 2000–2003, they have targeted the following areas for improvement:

- *products and materials*: reduce use of resources and increase use of recyclables and reusable materials;
- *forestry*: obtain forestry products from certified forests;
- *suppliers*: ensure that all suppliers adhere to the four-point supplier environmental accreditation scheme developed by IKEA;
- *transport*: measure and monitor the impact that the transporting of IKEA products has on the environment;
- *environment – retail*: concentrate on reducing waste and implementing energy efficiencies in retail outlets.[65]

Step 2: Development and systematic alignment of measurement systems with corporate goals This step involves the design and use of measurement systems to monitor ecological and human performance. Such systems are aligned with corporate objectives and linked to broader performance systems such as the triple bottom line. The aim is to use the resulting information to further drive the development of capabilities in product and process design to increase sustainability. At IKEA, for instance, cross-functional project teams were initially set up to identify environmental issues and to help integrate policies and practices across the organization.[66]

Step 3: Diagnosis of opportunities Opportunities for 'quick wins' are identified and resources channelled into those areas. In other areas of business activity, a constant scanning is taking place of internal opportunities to achieve strategic sustainability. Resources are shifted into research and development and future opportunity areas. Competitors and potential allies are identified. Resources are also shifted to the individual business unit level to support new developments there. Culture change programmes are designed, aimed at modifying corporate culture to support the drive to achieve sustainability goals. For example, the diffusion of The Natural Step programme at IKEA followed a cascading model. Managers undertook the programme, followed by employees so that everyone in the organization had a shared understanding of the emerging strategies. Opportunities had been identified for improvements in key areas. The focus of attention shifted to product design, then to purchasing, then to wholesale activities and, finally, to retail.

Step 4: Implementation and diffusion of successful practices both internally and externally Successful product and service practices, measurement systems and human resource approaches are then diffused internally. Slow-moving business units are linked to 'star' or good performers to improve the performance of these areas. At the senior management level, more time is devoted to engaging suppliers and other external parties to take part in the initiatives. At the grass-roots level, business unit performance is supported by the development of key performance indicators (KPI) for all relevant staff.

Step 5: Review, monitoring and alignment Results of initiatives on both the ecological and human sustainability fronts are made available internally and externally. Third-party auditors are invited to review the strategic directions, challenge strongly held corporate assumptions and generate ideas for future opportunities for competitive advantage.

Employees and managers alike are rewarded for strong performance on triple bottom line measures. Feedback mechanisms are used to further develop and enhance human and ecological capabilities and develop the next range of sustainable products, processes and services.

Introducing new tools and techniques

The movement towards strategic sustainability has raised new issues over the tools, techniques and methods that corporations use to monitor their performance (for example, the triple bottom line) and inspire corporate transformation (such as The Natural Step). Earlier chapters referred to programmes and systems such as total quality environmental management (TQEM) and environmental management systems (EMS). In this section we outline the benefits of such programmes – particularly the measurement systems that enable organizations to collect information on their performance and that enable them to set targets and goals. This monitoring of human and ecological performance, established in the compliance phase, is an essential element in the attainment of strategic sustainability. We shall examine first the operational benefits of such systems, then move on to explore how they can be used to inform the strategic directions of corporations and, finally, outline some risks involved with the use of measurement systems.

As we saw in Chapters 4 and 5, moving through the compliance and efficiency phases requires that organizations develop systems for collecting and evaluating information on performance. Generally, in these early stages, monitoring and data collection systems focus on operational activities. For example, environmental reporting systems may focus on monitoring pollution or waste levels, with the goal being to use TQEM programmes to move towards zero waste or zero emissions at particular business unit locations. In pursuing human sustainability in the compliance and efficiency modes, organizations will often monitor their performance in terms of operational factors, such as health and safety incidents and absenteeism. Such monitoring systems allow individual managers and business units to comply with legislative requirements and track costs. These systems form the base from which broader strategic sustainability initiatives can be launched.

As corporations develop strategic sustainability initiatives, they systematize and expand such information systems. The Fuji Xerox Eco Manufacturing plant in Sydney, Australia, exemplifies this approach.

When they began to retrieve components of their damaged office equipment, instead of allowing them to be thrown into landfill, they found that they could analyse where faults had occurred and why. This product information was then used to redesign components to extend their life. For instance, the redesign of a small roller spring, worth only 5 cents, saved millions of dollars by significantly extending the working life of each roller. Or in the case of their new team-based organization, teams become responsible for collecting information on their own performance in terms of product, processes and customers. They use this information to leverage further performance improvements, identify gaps in their skills and knowledge base and develop proactive programmes to address these limitations.

Corporations that have moved into the strategic phase increasingly align their internal tools and systems with other reporting initiatives of environmental and social performance. Such ambitious initiatives are being undertaken by Shell, BP, ABB, Daimler-Benz, BT and Nortel.

Clarke notes the following trends in the movement towards broader measurement systems:[67]

- an increased willingness to use such systems to engage with a broader range of stakeholders interested in different elements of the company performance;
- a shift towards complementing the measurement of tangibles with those of intangibles – that is, the social capital of the firm;
- the broadening of social and environmental reporting both within the organization and in public forums and the development of more systematic ways of reporting;
- the creation of a sense of legitimacy in the process by increasing involvement of external parties in the auditing and verification process.

Finally, however, as with any reporting system, there exist some inherent challenges. We know of one corporation in the process of implementing triple bottom line reporting systems which has faced difficulties in several areas. These include: the problem of aligning current internal systems with the more macro variables associated with triple bottom line reporting; uncertainty over what to measure – particularly when it comes to external factors such as community engagement and satisfaction, and working out how to integrate different measures to create broad indices of performance particularly on environmental and social reporting. New forms of auditing such as triple bottom line are important mechanisms for leveraging the corporation to achieve strategic sustainability. However, they need adapting and customizing to the needs of specific organizations.

Linking operational processes to sustainable strategy

We mentioned earlier in this chapter that in the efficiency phase the prime focus of sustainability initiatives was on creating operational systems. As the organization moves into the strategic phase, these systems have to be linked to the emerging sustainability strategies so that they can support them.

However, to be effective, the linking of operational systems to sustainability strategy requires a shift in values and culture. Several writers have identified the need to change traditional values, the way managers typically view organizations and technical problems.[68] Value shifts by employees, engineers and other key stakeholders are important prerequisites in identifying innovative solutions to existing problems and potential new opportunities.

For instance, Amory Lovins provides examples of how strategic knowledge can be linked with operational processes and emphasizes the importance of changing values to identify such opportunities: for instance, realizing that 'changes in the size of pipes' could modify the flow of processes in a plant and result in efficiencies for business units. This case provides a clear example of the linking of operational knowledge, embedded in the minds of scientists, engineers and employees of the organization, with the strategic approach of gaining long-term sustainability outcomes, embedded in the minds of executives.

In other words, organizations need to create cultures which provide opportunities for employees to undertake 'out of the box' thinking and play 'maverick roles' in identifying strategic sustainability opportunities. The human sustainability tradition already has developed processes which can be utilized to solve problems – such as total quality management (TQM) practices. However, TQM systems are tightly controlled and managed problem solving approaches and must be modified to provide for creative thinking if organizations are to integrate operational and strategic practices. Operational thinking cannot be allowed to dominate: managers also need creative thinking for strategic initiatives. Contradictions need to be managed so that the two mindsets can co-exist.

At a more macro level, the new field of industrial ecology also provides insight into the benefits of linking operational and strategic processes. The operational processes revolve around finding industrial synergies in the industrial eco system in order to create closed-loop industrial systems. This involves the creation and management of strategic alliances between different firms within the industrial eco system. It requires the development of competencies in the management of strategic alliances, in the exploration of industrial interconnections and in the management of trust. Cohen-Rosenthal believes that central to the success of effective industrial ecology applications are skills in human decision making, imagination and learning.[69] He reports a comment made by Tachi Kiuchi, managing director of Mitsubishi Electric and chairman of the Future 500, a high-level group exploring industrial ecology:

> When I visited the rainforest, I realized that it was a model of a perfect learning organization. A place that excels by learning to adapt to what it doesn't have. A rainforest has almost no resources. The soil is thin. There are few nutrients. It consumes almost nothing. Wastes are food. Design is capital. Yet rainforests are incredibly productive. They are home to millions of types of plants and animal, more than two thirds of all biodiversity, so perfectly mixed that the system is more efficient, and more creative than any business in the world. Imagine how creative, how productive, how ecologically benign we could be if we could run our companies like rainforests.[70]

Creating enabling structures and designs

Organizations will fail to address ecological and social issues unless systems, designs and structures are changed to support sustainability initiatives. Organizations can impede the attainment of sustainability in three ways: first, rigid corporate structures can insulate organization systems and processes from a broad range of relevant information: systems that rely on inspired leaders rather than establishing structural or systemic solutions are particularly vulnerable; second, the established routines and systems of many corporations promote and protect the status quo: sustainability initiatives, particularly in the strategic sustainability phase, can be a threat to command and control style management systems, managers who have risen to power in the command and control systems frequently resist the transition to alternative enabling organizational structures; finally, many current organization designs limit or deny access to a range of stakeholders whose participation is vital for the pursuit of sustainable initiatives. Traditional organizations tend to be focused on a limited set of stakeholders, in particular boards of directors and shareholders. Other stakeholders, such as unions, green groups and community groups, are often seen as hostile forces that may harm current organizational performance. Redefining these groups as resource and information opportunities rather than problems demands a significant shift of perspective.

However, organizational design can play an important contributing role in the development of human and ecological capabilities. Hierarchies are killers of creativity and initiative and impede the use of employee knowledge. Companies such as Xerox and Monsanto have found that team-based structures are more conducive to the generation of employee knowledge and empower employees to use such knowledge. Team-based structures enable employees to have input, discretion over decision making and provision of information. Team-based organization architectures, which include project teams and virtual teams based on new information technologies, provide the basis for capturing and utilizing employee knowledge and competence in real-time situations.

Ericsson Australia

Ericsson Australia has set about developing an organizational precinct for fostering innovation. 'Precinct 42', located in its Melbourne office, has been set up with the purpose of delivering more integrated and faster technological solutions. An entire floor has been set aside for teams of employees to work across a mix of technologies to encourage the cross-fertilization of ideas. At any one time, eight teams work in the location – sharing ideas and creating new products. Teams leave the Precinct once they have reached the product development stage. New teams are then sent into the Precinct to start the process over again.[71]

Building employee knowledge and commitment

Strategic sustainability requires employee input and commitment. The successful implementation of various operational programmes such as total quality environmental management is reliant on human capital and workforce skill. The experience of firms such as Interface and Placer Dome demonstrates the need to develop and utilize employee capital and knowledge to achieve innovation, agility and high performance.

Organizations that have shifted to the strategic approach value human resource practices around new workplace cultures, enhanced adaptability, team-based work and project work and are keen to experiment with new ventures, such as virtual teams, that characterize 'silo busting' approaches to sustainability. The focus in these organizations is on developing and promoting talent, increasing autonomy and being responsive and flexible. Similarly these firms typically create reward structures that allow managers to foster these conditions and that encourage employees to look beyond their organization by rewarding their efforts in community assistance and community building.

In a recent empirical study, de Sac-Perez and Garcia-Falcon examined the ability of an HR system to facilitate or inhibit the development of organizational capabilities. They found that an HR system has a positive influence on the development of organizational capabilities and that those organizations that combine their HR practices to create and develop strategic capital actually demonstrate higher organizational performance.[72]

The innovative performance of Nucor Steel, a US-based firm, is reliant in part upon the development and utilization of its human capital. At the heart of this strategy lies a social ecology that enables Nucor to: create knowledge internally through the encouragement of experimentation; acquire external knowledge as a consequence of good reward structures and a reputation for being an 'ideal employer'; and finally, retain and use the knowledge it has developed. By social ecology, we mean the culture, structure, information systems, processes, people and leadership that enable the company to pursue its knowledge management approach. The concrete actions that Nucor have taken include: the use of group incentive schemes; the encouragement of experimentation and 'play'; risk-taking; rewards for knowledge sharing; and transfers within the company to diffuse knowledge. These have helped create Nucor's innovative approach to knowledge management and human capital development.[73]

Building executive leadership and stewardship

Strategic proactivity is a demonstrated commitment by the senior executive team and the board to actively pursue and develop corporate capabilities, products, processes and designs that align sustainability with the corporation's overall strategic orientations. Strategic proactivity encourages the use of distributed leadership approaches – rewarding innovation and initiatives that drive the company further towards its sustainability goals. Strategic proactivity opens the corporation to third-party scrutiny, as a way of improving or embedding sustainability practices within the organization. In particular, one of the key drivers of sustainability performance for an organization is the commitment by the executives to the large-scale changes and reforms required for sustainability to take place. They outline and live a compelling vision for the organization. For example, Greg Bourne, General Manager of BP Asia Pacific, states that:

> We must demonstrate our commitment, not just talk about it. As individual corporations and as individuals within corporations, we must show by our actions and their results, that we are serious about the Triple Bottom Line. We must also be leaders beyond just our corporations and actively engage with the community and government to help Australia's progress down the path towards sustainable development. At a time when the community is sceptical of big business, there is a unique opportunity within the sustainable development agenda for us to show that our interests are broader than just our financial bottom lines, our share price and our options package.[74]

While executive leadership is crucial for sustainability, such leadership needs to be reinforced by the corporate values, the funding of corporate change programmes and willingness to transform organizations towards these ends. Robert Eckert, CEO of Mattel, the toy manufacturer, highlights the importance of social strategies in building and developing the human capital of the organization. He believes that it is important for CEOs and other senior managers to address people's needs and expectations and in turn reward their efforts by taking time to communicate openly and honestly. These values then become sources of human capital within the organization.[75]

The success of senior managers is determined by their ability to draw together different programmes and operations and to embed sustainability initiatives within the overall strategy of the organization. Therefore the senior executive role is not only about formulating commitment but about integrating the transformation into the business strategies of the organization.[76] Reinhardt argues that, 'Managers need to go beyond the question: "Does it pay to be green?" and ask instead, "Under what conditions do particular lines of environmental investment deliver benefits to shareholders?"'[77]

Developing differentiated stakeholder strategies

Business alone cannot achieve sustainability. To achieve sustainability, corporations also require inputs from both governments and communities. Some organizations have already built capabilities associated with forming internal communities of practice that are fluid structures formed around areas of interest and expertise in organizations. An example of a community of practice may be a community of professionals who gather and share information around particular technical problems or solutions. Such communities generate the diffusion and acceptance of tacit knowledge that can be transferred into innovative solutions and actions within organizations. Their contribution to the attainment of sustainability outcomes for organizations lies in their ability to collect, process and diffuse knowledge of a technical and specialized nature to find rapid and innovative solutions. This is a vital component of strategic success.

One method to use in developing a stakeholder strategy is values-based environmental management. It is an approach that aims to develop a strong relationship between corporate strategy and how stakeholders view the organization. The questions proposed by values-based environmental management include: Do stakeholders value your performance? Do products and services contribute to solving environmental issues? Does the stakeholder see you as a problem or part of the solution?[78] Attracta Lagan, Foundation Director of the St James Ethics Centre, states that: 'We're finding that values-based companies are outperforming others on the stock exchange when performance is measured over the long term.'[79]

Analysing stakeholders

Polonsky suggests a four-step process to analyse stakeholder approaches and identify strategic actions:

Step 1: Identify the stakeholders   That is identify those who have a vested interest in the outcomes of environmentalism.

Step 2: Determine the stakes   What is each group's stake in the issue? Is it large or small? What specific issues do they revolve around?

Step 3: Determine how expectations are met   Use this to assess the gap between expectations and performance.

Step 4: Adjust the strategy   Strategy is adjusted to minimize/deal constructively with the stakeholder expectations and the gap in performance.[80]

Moving beyond strategic sustainability

Hart and Milstein state:

> To capture sustainable opportunities managers must fundamentally rethink their prevailing views about strategy, technology and markets . . . Managers who treat sustainable development as an opportunity will drive the creative destruction process and build the foundation to compete in the twenty-first century.[81]

We agree with Hart and Milstein. To attain strategic sustainability managers must develop ecological and human capabilities within the organization. These capabilities enable the organization not only to keep abreast of sustainability issues but to obtain sustainable competitive advantages.

This chapter has outlined some organizational pathways to strategic sustainability. The challenge now, for those who aspire to move beyond strategic sustainability, is to generate the new business models of corporations that move beyond the pursuit of competitive business advantage in order to contribute to a fully sustainable society. This emerging model of business we discussed in Chapter 3. The critical issue of how to move organizations towards this model is the issue we take up in the next two chapters.

 ## Phase 5: Strategic proactivity

Human sustainability (HS5)

The workforce skills mix and diversity are seen as integral and vitally important aspects of corporate and business strategies. Intellectual and social capital are used to develop strategic advantage through innovation in products/services. Programmes are instituted to recruit the best talent to the organization and to develop high levels of competence in individuals and groups. In addition, skills are systematized to form the basis of corporate competencies so that the

Ecological sustainability (ES5)

Proactive environmental strategies supporting ecological sustainability are seen as a source of strategic business opportunities to provide competitive advantage. Product redesign is used to reduce material throughput and to use materials that can be recycled. New products and processes are developed that substitute for or displace existing environmentally damaging products and processes or satisfy emerging community needs around sustainable organization is less vulnerable to the loss of key individuals. Emphasis is placed on product and service innovation and speed of response to emerging market demands. Flexible workplace practices are strong features of workplace culture and contribute to the workforce leading more balanced lives. Communities affected by the organization's operations are taken into account and initiatives to address adverse impacts on communities are integrated into corporate strategy. Furthermore, the corporation views itself as a member of the community and as a result contributes to community betterment by offering sponsorship or employee time to participate in projects aimed at promoting community cohesion and well-being.

issues (reforestation; treatment of toxic waste). The organization seeks competitive leadership through spearheading environmentally friendly products and processes.

Notes

1 M. Porter and C. van der Linde, 'Green and competitive: ending the stalemate', *Harvard Business Review*, 1995, September–October, 130.
2 Anon., 'Action agenda for the private sector', *Business Week*, 1999, 3 May.
3 P. May, V.Vinha and N. Zaidenweber, 'Royal Dutch/ Shell', in M. Hastings (ed.) *Corporate Incentives and Environmental Decision-making*, Centre for Global Studies, Houston Advanced Research Centre, Texas, 1999, p. 88.
4 BP, *Environmental and Social Review*, 2000, http://www.BPamoco.com/alive (accessed 4 December 2001).
5 Michael Skapinker, 'Best environmental companies', *Financial Times*, 1 February 2002.
6 N. Roome, 'Developing environmental management strategies', *Business, Strategy and Environment*, 1992, 1(1), 11–23.
7 Visy aims to be a leading provider of packaging and recycling services in the paper and paper products industry.
8 A. Hoffman, *Competitive Environmental Strategy*, Washington, D.C.: Island Press, 2000, p. 162.

9 P. Hawkin, A. Lovins and L. Lovins, *Natural Capitalism*, Boston, Mass.: Little Brown, 1999.

10 D. Dunphy and A. Griffiths, 'Corporate strategic change', in M. Warner (ed.) *International Encyclopaedia of Business and Management*, London: Thomson Learning, 2002.

11 L. Gratton, *Living Strategy: Putting People at the Heart of Corporate Purpose*, London: Financial Times/Prentice-Hall, 2000.

12 A. Schaefer and B. Harvey, 'Stage models of corporate greening: a critical evaluation', *Business Strategy and the Environment*, 1998, 7, 109–23.

13 A. Pettigrew, *The Awakening Giant*, Oxford: Basil Blackwell, 1985.

14 H. Mintzberg and J. Waters, 'Of strategies deliberate and emergent', *Strategic Management Journal*, 1985, 6, 257–72; H. Mintzberg, *The Rise and Fall of Strategic Planning*, New York: Free Press, 1995; Gratton, *Living Strategy*.

15 Dunphy and Griffiths, 'Corporate strategic change'.

16 M. Porter, *The Competitive Advantage of Nations*, New York: Free Press, 1990.

17 K. Eisenhardt and J. Martin, 'Dynamic capabilities: what are they?', *Strategic Management Journal*, 2000, 21, 1105–21; C. Prahalad and G. Hamel, 'The core competence of the corporation', *Harvard Business Review*, 1990, 68(3), 79–91.

18 Gratton, *Living Strategy*.

19 The basic competencies outlined are based on: M. Hitt, B. Keats and S. de Marie, 'Navigating in the new competitive landscape: building strategic flexibility and competitive advantage in the 21st century', *Academy of Management Executive*, Nov 1998, 22–47; M. Hastings, 'Oil companies in sensitive environments', *Business Strategy and Environment*, 1999, 8, 267–80; S. Sharma and H. Vrendenburg, 'Proactive environmental strategy and the development of competitively valuable organizational capabilities', *Strategic Management Journal*, 1998, 19, 729–53.

20 Gratton, *Living Strategy*.

21 A. de Geus, *The Living Company*, Boston, Mass.: Harvard Business School Press, 1997; J. Collins and J. Porras, *Built to Last*, London: Century, 1994.

22 De Geus, *Living Company*.

23 J. Aragon-Correa, 'Strategic proactivity and firm approach to the natural environment', *Academy of Management Journal*, 1998, 14(5), 556–67; M. Starik, *Management and the Natural Environment*, Fort Worth, Tx.: Dryden Press, 1997.

24 B. Piasecki, K. Fletcher and F. Mendelson, *Environmental Management and Business Strategy*, New York: John Wiley, 1999.

25 Hoffman, *Competitive Environmental Strategy*, pp. 160, 181.

26 S. Hart, 'A natural resource based view of the firm', *Academy of Management Review*, 1995, 20(4), 986–1014.

27 A. Griffiths, 'New organisational architectures: creating and retrofitting for sustainability', in D. Dunphy, J. Benveniste, A. Griffiths and P. Sutton (eds)

Sustainability: The Corporate Challenge of the 21st Century, Sydney: Allen and Unwin, 2001, pp. 219–35.

28 For further information on the Interface case see: L. Rowledge, R. Barton and K. Brady, *Mapping the Journey: Case Studies in Strategy and Action Towards Sustainable Development*, Sheffield: Greenleaf Publishing, 1999.

29 J. Pfeffer, *Competitive Advantage Through People*, Boston, Mass.: Harvard Business School Press, 1994; D. Dunphy and A. Griffiths, *The Sustainable Corporation*, Sydney: Allen and Unwin, 1998.

30 Gratton, *Living Strategy*.

31 P. Crittenden and D. Dunphy, *Hewlett-Packard: A Corporate Sustainability Case Study*, UTS, Faculty of Business Working Paper no. 19, 2000.

32 M. Russo and P. Fouts, 'A resource based perspective on corporate environmental performance and profitability', *Academy of Management Journal*, 1997, 40(3), 534–59.

33 L. Getter, 'Australia Post delivers the goods', *Sydney Morning Herald*, 2001, 22 October, 3.

34 P. Senge and S. Carstedt, 'Innovating our way to the next industrial revolution'. *MIT Sloan Management Review*, 2001, Winter, 24–38.

35 D. Turner and M. Crawford, *Change Power: Capabilities that Drive Corporate Renewal*, Sydney: Business and Professional Publishing, 1998.

36 D. Hine and A. Griffiths, interview at Boeing Australia, March 2001.

37 Gratton, *Living Strategy*, p. 11.

38 J. Maxwell, S. Rothenberg, F. Briscoe and I. Marcus, 'Green schemes: corporate environmental strategies and their implementation', *California Management Review*, 1997, 39(3), 118–34.

39 Rowledge *et al.*, *Mapping the Journey*, p. 49.

40 Ibid.

41 J. Elkington, *Cannibals with Forks*, Gabriola Island: New Society Publishers, 1998, p. 119.

42 M. Porter, 'Strategy and the Internet', *Harvard Business Review*, March 2001, 63–78.

43 J. Elkington, *Cannibals with Forks*, p. 333.

44 Anon., 'Anita Roddick off Body Shop board', *Sydney Morning Herald*, 2002, 15 February, 7.

45 R. Jaikumar, 'Post industrial manufacturing', *Harvard Business Review*, 1986, November, 69–76; A. Griffiths, 'New organizational architectures', in D. Dunphy, J. Beneviste, A. Griffiths and P. Sutton (eds) *Sustainability*, Sydney: Allen and Unwin, 2000.

46 S. Hart, 'Beyond greening', *Harvard Business Review*, 1997, January–February, 66–76; J. Magretta, 'Growth through global sustainability', *Harvard Business Review*, 1997, January–February, 79–88.

47 J. Elkington, *The Chrysalis Economy*, Oxford: Capstone, 2001, p. 96.

48 M. Metherell, 'Gene labels scare off food makers', *Sydney Morning Herald*, 2001, 15 November, 1.

49 L. Gettler, 'Reputation: it's priceless', *Management Today*, 2002, Jan/Feb, 5.
50 C. Handy, *The Elephant and the Flea: Looking Back to the Future*, London: Hutchinson, 2001, p. 82
51 Ibid., p. 83.
52 R. Orsatto, 'The ecological competence of the organization: competing for sustainability', paper presented to the 16th EGOS Colloquium, Helsinki, Finland, July 2000.
53 R. Miles and C. Snow, *Fit, Failure and the Hall of Fame*, New York: Free Press, 1994.
54 Elkington, *Cannibals with Forks*, p. 3.
55 G. Wilson, and D. Sasseville, *Sustaining Environmental Management Success*, New York: John Wiley, 1999, p. 208.
56 Anon., 'Case studies: visionary leadership', *Business Week*, May 3 1999.
57 Ford Motor Company, *Connecting with Society*, Detroit: Ford Motor Co. 2000, p. 3; http://www.fordmotorco.com (accessed 4 December 2001).
58 Ibid., p. 6.
59 B. Hirsh and P. Sheldrake, *Inclusive Leadership*, Melbourne: Information Australia, 2000, p. 20.
60 Business Council of Australia, *Towards Sustainable Development: How Leading Australian and Global Corporations are Contributing to Sustainable Development*, Melbourne: Business Council of Australia, 2001.
61 Hoffman, *Competitive Environmental Strategy*.
62 Ibid.
63 B. Natrass and M. Altomare, *The Natural Step for Business*, Gabriola Island: New Society Publishers, 1999, pp. 47–74.
64 Ibid.
65 http://www.ikea-usa.com.
66 Nattrass and Altomare, *Natural Step for Business*.
67 T. Clarke, 'Balancing the triple bottom line: financial, social and environmental performance', *Journal of General Management*, 2001, 26(4), 1–11.
68 Hoffman, *Competitive Environmental Strategy*.
69 E. Cohen-Rosenthal, 'A walk on the human side of industrial ecology', *American Behavioral Scientist*, 2000, 44(2), 245–64.
70 Cited in ibid., p. 259.
71 D. Stace and D. Dunphy, *Beyond the Boundaries*, Sydney: McGraw-Hill, 2001, p. 132.
72 P. de Sac-Perez and J. Garcia-Falcon, 'A resource based view of human resource management and organizational capability development', *International Journal of Human Resource Management*, 2002, 13(1), 123–40.
73 A. Gupta and V. Govindarajan, 'Knowledge management's social dimension: lessons from Nucor Steel', *Sloan Management Review*, 2000, 42(1), 71–80.

74 G. Bourne, 'Business leadership for sustainable development: an Australian perspective', paper prepared for World Business Council for Sustainable Development, *The Road to Rio + 10, and Beyond*, Melbourne, 17 September 2001.

75 R. Eckert, 'Where leadership starts', *Harvard Business Review*, November 2001, 53–62.

76 S. Banerjee, 'Managerial perceptions of corporate environmentalism: interpretations from industry and strategic implications for organizations', *Journal of Management Studies*, 2001, 38(4), 479–513.

77 F. Reinhardt, 'Bringing the environment down to earth', *Harvard Business Review*, 1999, July–August, 149–56, esp. p. 150.

78 J. Blumber, A. Korsuold and G. Blum, 'Value based environmental management and sustainability', in G. Wilson and D. Sasseville (eds) *Sustaining Environmental Management Success*, New York: John Wiley, 1999, p. 220.

79 A. Lagan, 'Lively conversations with the future', *Future News*, 1998, 3(5), 2.

80 M. Polonsky, 'Incorporating the natural environment in corporate strategy: a stakeholder approach', *Journal of Business Strategy*, 1995, 12(2), 152–5.

81 S. Hart and M. Milstein, 'Global sustainability and the creative destruction of industries', *Sloan Management Review*, 1999, 41(1), 22.

Part IV
Pathways to sustainability

7 The incremental path

Setting the scene

For a significant part of the twentieth century most managers used incremental change programmes to modify their organizations. Transformative change programmes were only employed in times of crisis, which were the exception rather than the rule. So the history of the development of systematic approaches to incremental change extends throughout the twentieth century. As a result, we now have a comprehensive set of tools available to make incremental change and we know some of the key ingredients for successful change programmes of this kind.

Early in the twentieth century scientific management theories led to an emphasis on technically and operationally focused change. Later human relations theories dominated and the focus switched to an emphasis on changing the social systems of the organization through interventions such as supervisory training and motivational programmes. All of these approaches advocated making relatively slow-paced change. They also tended to ignore technological issues. However, in the 1970s, incremental change theories began to address both social needs and technical efficiencies in a more balanced way. The dominant approaches became organization development (OD) and socio-technical systems (STS) theory. The STS approach developed in the UK and Scandinavia under the intellectual leadership of Trist and Emery, while they were working from the Tavistock Institute of Human Relations in London. The approach was widely adopted after the Second World War, particularly in Scandinavia and Australia where it became strongly linked to the industrial democracy movement.[1]

The STS approach derived from general systems theory in the natural sciences and used open organic systems as its metaphor for organizations. The diagnostic model was socio-technical systems analysis, that is a detailed approach to analysing both the technical and social systems. The ideal organization was a representative democratic community composed of work teams, learning through participative action research. STS theory strongly influenced the empowerment movement in the USA, particularly through the work of Davis, Cherns, James Taylor and others at the University of California, Los Angeles, and of Lawler and others at the University of Southern California. It also continues to influence action research in a range of countries, particularly in the Netherlands. STS theory consistently advocated incremental change as a necessary condition for workforce involvement.[2]

While STS and OD theories of change were developing in Europe, North America and Australia, in Japan quality management techniques were adopted with enthusiasm. The Japanese combined the TQM emphasis on statistical controls, stemming from the work of Deming and others, with the participatory shop floor practices of the earlier human relations movement. The human relations movement advocated employee participation in decision making and strongly emphasized social factors. By including employees in the quality improvement process, Japanese managers harnessed employee knowledge and competencies to overcome variances from ideal quality standards. The human relations/OD, STS and TQM approaches to change have all strongly supported incremental rather than transformative changes. Incremental change appeared ideally suited to the operating environments of many organizations in the late 1960s, 1970s and into the early 1980s, particularly when it achieved a balanced emphasis on both technical and human factors.

This emerging movement for incremental change was led by self-proclaimed management heretics (like Emery and Trist) who saw their mission as overturning the prevailing management orthodoxies of the time. The paradigm espoused by the Organizational Renewal Movement heretics contrasted significantly with the dominant managerial ethos of the 1960s and 1970s. Their criticisms were directed at inefficiencies in bureaucratic organizations, but even more at the dehumanizing and exploitative effects of bureaucratic managerialism on the morale and satisfaction of the workforce.[3] They advocated incremental change to shift organizations to be more effective in terms of the core business and more responsive to employee needs.

However, in the period from 1985 to 1999, under pressure from economic reforms, increasing globalization and international competition, many companies found that they were significantly out of alignment with their operating environment. For example, they found that their core technology was suddenly obsolete or that their major customer segment had shifted its preference to another type of product or service. In these circumstances, incremental changes were often insufficient to strategically reposition organizations. So in the late 1980s and the 1990s many organizations abandoned incremental change for radical, transformational change. Change of this kind is covered in detail in Chapter 8. Many organizations have recently moved into a period of mid-range change: that is, many managers are recognizing that their organizations need the flexibility to move between the two approaches in order to stay in alignment with market conditions. Some commentators have suggested that contemporary organizations need to be 'ambidextrous', that is, with the ability to manage both incremental and revolutionary approaches to change.[4]

Incremental versus transformational change

In this chapter, we discuss those incremental change approaches that are characterized by participative management and collaborative forms of work, and that require basic operational change and work redesign. However, our overall approach is not that we should go back to these past approaches, but rather that they represent a part of our armoury of change that needs to be utilized under the appropriate conditions. In other words, the approach to change that we advocate is not about pursuing the 'one best way' but rather of identifying the appropriate strategy for the appropriate situation. However, when it comes to the study of the environment and organizations, Orsatto points out:

> The majority of literature on corporate environmental management assumes reformism as the guiding principle for organizational change. Incrementalism is the basic principle of the standards of environmental management systems such as the ISO 14000 series . . . These programs assume that through incremental improvements organizations would achieve eco-efficiency and, eventually, ecological sustainability.[5]

However, some advocates for sustainability question whether it can be achieved by changing corporations incrementally. In their view, incremental change is not enough: transformational changes are required to achieve sustainability.[6] Most recently, Hart and Milstein, in their prophetically titled article 'Global sustainability and the creative destruction of industries', argue that: 'the emerging challenge of global sustainability is a catalyst for a new round of creative destruction that offers unprecedented opportunities. Today's corporations can seize the opportunity for sustainable development, but they must look beyond continuous, incremental improvements.'[7] Building on the work of Joseph Schumpeter, these authors view incremental change as simply maintaining the status quo. Furthermore, they argue that at some point in the future, those organizations that have only changed incrementally will fail because they did not 'change the fundamental manner, in which they provide products, processes and services'.[8] In their view, the operations of current businesses are so inimical to sustainability that only radical change will create a sustainable world.

Another strong advocate of revolutionary, transformational change is Michael Hammer, the champion of business process re-engineering. The title of his path-breaking article, 'Re-engineering work: don't automate, obliterate', exhorts managers to take radical, not incremental action to achieve human and technological efficiencies. His argument is that organizations are competing in new times and that traditional 'silo' structures and organizational forms are no longer appropriate to achieve competitive advantages. If corporations want to be more productive, they need to engage in 'silo busting' activities and reorganize core activities along business process flows.[9] So what really works best, incremental or transformational change?

We want to make it clear that making change of any kind is difficult. As Beer and Nohria state:

> Despite some individual success, change remains difficult to pull off, and few companies manage the process as well as they like. Most of their initiatives – installing new technology, downsizing, restructuring or trying to change corporate cultures – have had low success rates. The brutal fact is that about 70 per cent of all change initiatives fail.[10]

However, there are circumstances where incremental change can effectively create new values, structures and processes which support the building of sustainable corporations. Our collective experience of consulting and research in organizations indicates that incremental change is often a viable means to achieve sustainability outcomes. The approach that we take in this and the next chapter is situational. We argue that managers should adopt the kind of change programme that suits the organization's specific situation. Significant gaps between corporate strategy and performance, for instance, do require larger, more robust transformational changes. Smaller gaps, new strategic opportunities, capability development or changes in the workforce skills mix, however, may be achieved through incremental or continuous change initiatives. As Abrahamson states:

> To change successfully, companies should stop changing all the time. Instead they should intersperse major change initiatives among carefully paced periods of smaller, organic change using processes I call tinkering and kludging. By doing so companies can manage overall change with an approach called dynamic stability.[11]

So arguments for transformational change are compelling in some circumstances, but unconvincing in identifying it as the sole means to achieving sustainability outcomes. Incremental change has an important role to play in the development of the corporate capabilities, cultures and practices that lead to the creation of sustainable organizations but, as we shall discuss further in the next chapter, transformational change is sometimes needed.

To extend this notion further, the change strategy employed must not only be situational, it must be connected to and driven by an organization's strategy. Without this, it becomes 'change for change sake'.[12] Incremental changes are best suited to organizations that require minimal strategic realignment. Where organizations are already meeting many of the demands of key stakeholders for sustainable practices, incremental strategies are effective in keeping the organization aligned to incremental changes in stakeholder expectations.

What is incremental change?

Sometimes it helps to explain a concept by first defining what it is not. For our purposes, incremental change is not large-scale transformational or revolutionary change of the kind often associated with business process re-engineering, downsizing, corporate spin-offs, mergers/acquisitions or strategic unbundling. Incremental change does not include radical changes in strategy, structure, capability or organizational realignment. Rather incremental change is planned and emergent, continuous and ongoing and for the most part impacts on the organization's day-to-day operational processes.[13] Incremental change includes changes to the way people work (job redesign; teamwork); changes to an organization's business unit processes (quality management; STS redesign); and changes to reward systems, information systems and technologies. As Stace and Dunphy note: 'corporate wide total quality management, service quality and team building programs are often a feature of this type of organization change. Leadership is primarily consultative in style.'[14] Furthermore incremental change can be used to generate new capabilities, for example, through multi-skilling or forming project teams or creating new values and modifying corporate culture (customer service, empowerment and leadership development programmes).

Macquarie Bank is a highly successful Australia-based global organization that has used incremental change strategies to maintain its strategic alignment, even in a highly competitive and turbulent environment: 'The Bank has maintained a constant incremental adjustment process for about two decades . . . one executive described it this way: "We never stay still, but we don't change in quantum leaps – our corporate culture would preclude that; running a business on partnership concepts means that policy decisions are not dramatic, they evolve."'[15] The Bank's success at managing and maintaining an incremental change strategy can be attributed to a variety of factors:

- the development and incorporation of a values and goals statement that also elaborates on how the process of change should be managed;
- the creation of a culture of constant innovation;
- the development of an organization structure that is flexible, modular and reliant upon a collegial workforce, creating adaptive responses to rapidly changing market conditions.[16]

We focus here on planned approaches to change of the kind described by Porras and Silvers:

> Organizational change is typically triggered by a relevant environmental shift, that once sensed by the organization, leads to an intentionally generated response. This intentional response is planned organizational change and consists of four identifiable, interrelated components (a) a change intervention that alters (b) key organizational target variables and that then impacts on (c) individual organizational members and then . . . [results] in (d) organizational outcomes.[17]

In designing incremental change programmes, managers are faced by a variety of choices and options. They could attempt to pursue sustainability initiatives by developing corporate-wide programmes – based for instance on empowerment or The Natural Step[18] – or they could buy off-the-shelf programmes of the kind provided by consulting companies or tailor them in-house, or they could seek to encourage more organic, bottom-up initiatives where changes are initiated and trialled in pilot programmes in different parts of the organization.

These choices reflect the complexity of issues that managers face in implementing change programmes. One of these issues relates to the scope of the programme. The implementation of corporate-wide programmes can have a significant impact in raising awareness throughout the organization and lead to a variety of consistent initiatives. However the broad scope of such programmes can also dilute valuable energies and disperse scarce resources. The result can be a loss of momentum. By contrast, pilot programmes can work spectacularly because resources are focused and the scope is limited. But they may not be subsequently diffused through the organization. Packaged change programmes offer organizations quick access to tools and methods for implementing change. After all, why reinvent the wheel? But they may not meet the needs of a particular organization and those in the organization can lose the opportunity to develop skills in change design.

There is no one recipe for successful change: the approach must be carefully chosen on the basis of an analysis of the situation and the availability of resources; so we suggest here some principles in designing incremental change programmes. First, where possible, organizations should look internally for change agents. The knowledge and capabilities need to be internalized so that organizational learning takes place and skills are retained in house so that they can be used for future change programmes. If external experts are required, the organization should leverage their knowledge and capabilities and transfer these to internal change agents. Second, as much of the change programme as possible should be designed internally. If 'packaged programmes' are used, they need to be modified to suit the organization's unique culture and operating conditions. Change agents need a deep understanding and awareness of the culture of the organization before imposing a set of solutions on those who work there. Finally, significant outcomes can be achieved through small interventions. Donella Meadows states:

> Folks who do systems analysis have a great belief in 'leverage points'. These are places within a complex system (a corporation, an economy, a living body, a city, an eco system) where a small shift in one thing can produce big changes in everything.[19]

Identification of key leverage points is crucial in generating change outcomes. We return to this below.

Benefits of incremental change

There are positive benefits for organizations that implement incremental changes. This section outlines a number of them.

The development of small wins

Whether planned or emergent, incremental change strategies allow organizations to achieve what Weick describes as small wins:

> A small win is a concrete, complete, implemented outcome of moderate importance. By itself, one small win may seem unimportant. A series of wins at small but significant tasks, however, reveals a pattern that may attract allies, deter opponents and lower resistance to subsequent proposals. Small wins are controllable opportunities that produce visible results.[20]

This strategy allows support to be built for the changes being implemented.

Take, for example, the case of Panasonic Matsushita. Its incremental change approach was built on the 'small wins' model of establishing the change programme's credibility. Initially, their approach to sustainability started out as a series of informal meetings between a group of managers who believed that the organization could achieve savings by reducing waste and energy use. Within five years this informal approach had developed into a planned and structured approach to pollution prevention through recycling, energy efficiency and supplier choice. In the process they made significant cost savings as well as process and quality improvements. Having successfully achieved their first goal, they have now implemented an EMS to assess, manage and minimize the impact of their business operations on the environment.[21]

Many of the efficiency gains achieved by firms such as Scandic, Ikea and Sony relied initially upon achieving straightforward cost efficiencies:

'picking the low-hanging fruit'. These easily gained benefits contributed to building momentum and became the basis upon which later successes were built. The concept of small wins as a strategy can be applied to ecological efficiencies, process improvements and the development of broader cultural changes. The key to the success of a small-wins strategy lies in the ability of the change agent to draw isolated and scattered innovations into a coherent, integrated programme. Otherwise, small wins can easily be picked off by forces opposed to change or may simply wither away.

Capability development

Another benefit of many incremental change strategies is their ability to extend and develop new technical, operational and human capabilities within an organization. Technical capabilities are developed primarily through the introduction of new technologies and multi-skilling. Operational capabilities are developed by giving employees the technical skills and authority to make product and process improvements. Human capabilities are developed through up-skilling, knowledge development and empowerment.

We return to the case of Volvo, discussed in Chapter 6. Volvo's shift beyond compliance involved the development and integration of both ecological and human capabilities. This was achieved by the establishment of cross-functional project teams to work on corporate-wide key issues relating to sustainability; the implementation of broad communication and training programmes to educate employees and managers alike; and investment in R&D and technology. The performance of these programmes against sustainability goals was constantly reviewed, monitored and adjusted accordingly.[22]

Volvo executives were able to build on the existing corporate culture, which valued safety and social responsibility, by linking sustainability to their mission and values statements. Subsequently the programme focused on developing technical capabilities in product design, remanufacturing and recycling. These technical capabilities were embodied in the organization's standard operating and manufacturing procedures and policies. People capabilities were developed through team-working initiatives and the training of employees in sustainability awareness workshops, and were built on existing projects which had encouraged widespread employee participation.

Positive culture changes

Incremental change programmes are often focused on culture-building activities. In its steel operations, BHP Biliton implemented a pilot culture change programme to assist with the spin-off of its steel making operations into a new business. It centred around story-telling and developing positive future images of where the steel-making business was heading. This was designed as a powerful yet incremental means to build on the existing corporate culture. Shanahan and Maria state that 'we know that story-telling – particularly when used in industries heavily entrenched in rigid mental models – can succeed in removing obstacles to strategy development and process improvement when other methods fail'.[23] Story-telling and other culture change programmes can open up lines of communication, create integration opportunities, commitment to new values and personal empowerment.[24]

Particular organizational cultures influence the uptake of innovative practices in different ways. A recent study by Jones *et al.* found that corporate cultures with a 'human relations orientation' demonstrated higher readiness for change when it came to the implementation of a new information technology system. This was in direct contrast to those organizations that reported hierarchical, command and control style cultures. Furthermore, those organizations that had developed reshaping capabilities – that is, change competencies – also showed greater readiness for change and higher usage of the IT systems once they had been implemented.[25] Incremental changes that build positive culture and values can enhance an organization's readiness for change and acceptance of new practices. This was also the case at Scandic corporation, highlighted in Chapter 5. The successful redefinition of corporate values to 'profound caring' and the subsequent expression of this in greater stakeholder involvement and support depended on prior customer-orientated values.

Efficiency improvements

Incremental changes when implemented successfully can lead to improvements in operational performance. The drive towards eco-efficiency at Sony, for instance, has brought about improvements such as a 50 per cent improvement in the ratio of recycled parts and materials, 50 per cent reduction in dismantling time and 50 per cent reduction in the use of styrene foam.[26] These results came from implementing EMS in manufacturing operations and the design of products. Operational efficiencies are not limited to changes in technical production systems. For instance, in a study of automobile manufacturing assembly plants, MacDuffie found that bundles of innovative HR policies – from selection, through multi-skilling, to job redesign and the introduction of teams – improved overall organizational performance. Furthermore, companies in which these bundles of HR practices were linked to the creation of flexible production systems outperformed traditional organizations where this link was missing.[27] Similarly, a study of steel finishing lines in the United States found that those organizations that used innovative work practices, including incentive pay, teams, flexible work arrangements, training and offering employment security, demonstrated higher levels of productivity than those organizations based on more traditional approaches.[28] These large empirical studies add weight to the thirty years of case studies, anecdotal evidence and broad industry surveys which have shown the benefits of such practices in creating high-performance organizations.[29]

New organizational structures

Incremental change strategies can be used to generate new organizational structures, systems and reporting relationships while maintaining the on-line operational capacity of the organization. For instance, STS redesigns which result in what are now known as 'high-performance work organizations' have generated a sophisticated methodology for the implementation and evaluation of team-based organizations. These new organizations have flatter reporting structures; are reliant upon the devolution of responsibility and autonomy; have shifted from control to commitment-based systems and changed the way that production is organized. Creating high-performance work organizations can take years, but many organizations in Europe, the USA and Australia have benefited from the use of such team-based approaches to change. They represent powerful successful models which can be emulated. Citing the work of Ostroff and Smith, Stace and Dunphy note that the concepts of team based organizations can be used to enhance new organizational structures such as networks. These organizations demonstrate the following characteristics:[30]

- they organize around processes by linking workflows and relying on teams;

- they keep hierarchies flat and remove the temptation to build control-orientated management systems;
- they assign ownership of processes and performance to teams;
- they link performance to customer satisfaction;
- they combine managerial and non-managerial activities to encourage self-management;
- they link customers and suppliers to teams;
- they focus on developing trust and competencies.

Development of change competencies

Incremental change programmes are an excellent vehicle to develop change agent skills and the change competencies of managers and employees. For example, incremental change provides environmental managers not only with the technical and process skills required for further change but also the opportunity to develop important skills needed for building and maintaining coalitions, designing educational programmes, extending leadership skills for culture change and negotiating with community representatives.[31] Daily and Huang argue that successful EMS implementation requires cultural changes.[32] Change agents can use opportunities around incremental change to create cultures which empower employees as well as implementing team-working initiatives which support sustainability.

For example, Australia Post used the opportunity of a major technology change in its mail sorting operations to develop the consultative, participative and change agent skills of its line managers. Prior to the development of this participative technology implementation process, Australia Post had experienced and engaged in decades of industrial war with unions and employees over the introduction of new technologies. As a result of developing the change agent skills of line managers, developing a participative approach with employees and a consultative approach with unions, they were able to reverse this disastrous situation to capture many productivity and efficiency benefits.

Benefits of incremental change

- Development of small wins – small successes can be used to overcome areas of resistance and develop a powerful force for change

- Capability development – incremental changes can be used to develop human and technical competencies
- Positive culture change – incremental change can modify values and build commitment through employee involvement and participation
- Efficiency improvements can be generated as a consequence of making process improvements, changes to product or work design
- Creation of new organizational structures based on teams, virtual teams and improvements in reporting systems and feedback loops
- Development of change competencies

Potential pitfalls of incremental change

The first major pitfall to threaten organizations that are changing incrementally is misfit: moving out of alignment with the firm's dynamic market environment. To avoid this, organizations need constantly to monitor and evaluate their current environments and develop competencies to anticipate future trends. Without such capabilities, they can become vulnerable to what Strebel refers to as 'breakpoints': significant events that face organizations with a major environmental discontinuity such as loss of a major market or a new technology that makes the existing technology obsolete.[33] Confronted with a crisis of this kind, the advocacy of incremental changes is usually a form of organizational complacency and dysfunctionality. When organizations experience turbulent and transformed conditions, incremental changes will fail to realign them with the new environments. Under these conditions, we advocate the use of transformational change strategies instead.

The case of Qantas highlights this point. In 1993 Qantas was merged with Australian Airlines to form the global and domestic carrier, Qantas. The CEO, James Strong, adopted a transformational leadership style. He pursued cost cutting and undertook other significant changes required for the airline to compete during a period of intense global competition. This was major transformational change. However, when the cost cutting was over, the senior team moved towards more incremental change that encouraged employee participation and used a more collaborative style of leadership. Radical change may be necessary to bring an organization back into alignment with its environment but, as radical changes are slowed and absorbed, incremental change can be used to continue to modify the culture and build key capabilities.[34]

The gradualism of incremental changes means that they are susceptible to regression and abandonment particularly if there is no clear link between the change programme and performance. Where success is not clearly defined, senior managers may withdraw their support from incremental changes and shift priorities for resources to other areas of organizational activity. Incremental changes do not usually occur in all parts of the organization at the same time or at the same pace. However, to attract continued managerial support, they must show significant performance improvements and clearly contribute to business results. Most of the cases that we have presented in this book demonstrate positive examples of successful change. However, not all cases have happy endings. In one energy company that we are familiar with, the change agent responsible for implementing sustainability programmes within the organization found that her time was spread too thinly across a range of projects in the organization. Innovations that she had started foundered as she switched her attention to other projects. The lack of resources meant that she was unable to establish clear performance improvements beyond some compliance activities. As a result, momentum was lost and the change programme petered out.

Employee cynicism over the 'latest management fad' can be fatal for incremental change programmes. Employees and managers alike 'batten the hatches' when senior executives launch the organization into the next alphabetically listed change programme. Abrahamson refers to 'perma-frost' organizations[35] where change-fatigued middle managers block and actively resist initiatives from both below and above. Under these conditions, incremental change stands a significant chance of failure, disappearing like water into sand. A manufacturing organization that one of us researched, Bendix Mintex, had been through the 'alphabet soup' of change programmes. After many false starts they finally settled on a team-based approach to change. However, before this could succeed they needed to overcome employee cynicism about seeing this as just 'the latest fad'. They succeeded in overcoming the cynicism by including key opinion makers in the change process from redesign to implementation. Furthermore they actively sought and encouraged employee suggestions on how the redesigned organization should work. By the time they began to implement the new redesign they had achieved a groundswell of support from the workforce, who wanted to see their own ideas put into practice. They became a successful team-based organization.[36] Table 7.1 outlines major threats to the success of incremental change programmes and how these can be overcome.

Table 7.1 *Overcoming limitations of incremental change*

Major issues	Action strategies
Lack of fit with external environment	Constant monitoring of the external environment of the firm and a preparedness to engage in transformational change if necessary.
Deceasing managerial support for change programme	Demonstrate and promote performance improvements. Develop small wins approach, market success in order to win management support.
Change fadism	Maintain programme consistency and link the programme to overall corporate strategies and values statements.

Major issues in the movement between phases

Moving from non-responsiveness to compliance

The organizations in most need of change are those in the rejection and non-responsiveness phases. In our view, the movement from rejection (Phase1) to compliance (Phase 2) is a transformational change of the kind we deal with in Chapter 8. So in this section we concentrate on the movement from non-responsiveness to compliance (Phase 2 to Phase 3). Non-responsive organizations tend to disregard the impact of their actions on the natural environment, the communities in which they are located and the value of their human capital. These corporations are economically, socially and ecologically blind or blinkered. In some cases, traditional values and a focus on operational and cost issues act as blinkers, resulting in a narrow view of what constitutes the firm's environment. Generally, business activities in these firms are concerned primarily with short-term profits to the detriment of broader societal and environmental responsibilities. This may be across all the organization's activities or in particular areas. For example, some corporations don't apply the same 'home base' standards to their activities in other parts of the world, particularly third world regions and countries. Esmeralda Explorations Ltd were owners of the Baia Mare Aurul gold mine. When a tailings dam burst, spilling 95 tonnes of cyanide into the environment, they denied responsibility, claiming that there was no connection between the spill and the poisoning of the Lapus and Somes rivers in Romania and the Tisza in Hungary.[37] One doubts whether they would have made the same arguments in their home country.

Non-responsive corporations are characterized by a blatant disregard for legislative and social standards. They may be willing to dump waste, clear fell old growth forests, engage in poor OH&S standards and hide facts from the public about the damaging nature of their activities and/or products. However, there are many examples of organizations, which once acted in this way, abandoning these approaches and supporting significant sustainability initiatives. Given the willingness of the board, CEO, senior managers and major financial investors, these organizations can make the shift from non-responsiveness to compliance using incremental change strategies. How is this to be achieved?

- Where there is organizational reluctance to initiate change, external pressure can be brought to bear on the organization through public protests and/or court action.
- By ensuring that someone with authority in the organization takes charge of the change process. Non-compliance can have major effects on the profitability, risk liability and the reputation of the corporation. Consequently, the change agent responsible for the shift needs to be a senior manager who reports directly to the CEO and has the power and authority to implement the changes. This should be someone with credibility and integrity who is respected throughout the organization.
- By making a comprehensive evaluation of legislative obligations. The survey should cover legislative requirement areas such as pollution, waste and licensing, mining and logging, and OH&S and other workplace codes. Similarly the organization needs to develop an understanding of its insurance risks, potential liabilities and obligations to bodies such as securities commissions.
- By undertaking a review of existing operations to see whether and where they fail to comply with the legislative requirements. Areas requiring immediate action are then targeted and resources allocated. It may be necessary to design and run training programmes and management awareness sessions, to institute searches for new technologies and to establish measurement and reporting systems. In some cases decisions may be made to disengage the company from activities that involve future risks or are not cost-effective to operate.
- By using the human resources system to link management performance to these new goals in order to ensure that programmatic changes, such as OH&S initiatives, are accurately monitored and measured. Timelines and specified performance goals are set for the changes to be implemented. This phase requires standard project management skills.

- By putting feedback loops in place in critical compliance areas to ensure that compliance is monitored and managers are rewarded according to their performance against these standards.
- By using auditing bodies to review and monitor corporate progress against plans. This may also involve the use of international agencies, such as the International Standards Organization and its ISO 14000 series as a basis for environmental management systems. A summary of moving from non-responsiveness to compliance is provided in the box.

Pathways from non-responsiveness to compliance

- Appoint a senior manager with authority and reputation to implement the change process
- Undertake an evaluation of the key legislative requirements
- Review existing operations and identify areas for immediate attention
- Align programmatic changes to goals
- Create feedback loops in critical compliance areas
- Use auditing bodies to assess compliance

This approach to incremental change is unusual because it is directive in character. Transformational strategies are more often associated with a directive approach to change initiated by senior executives. However, in ensuring compliance, significant responsibility for shifting the organization and its operations lies with senior management, who must institute and support clearly defined standards and rules. While there is a directive element in this change process, this does not exclude employee participation in making compliance-related procedures succeed.

Compliance to sustainable efficiency

For many corporations the incremental shift from compliance to efficiency is a natural extension of the capabilities, knowledge and practices developed in the earlier phase. For instance, compliance monitoring systems – particularly attempts to reduce emissions – often result in organizations also implementing process improvements and installing new technologies that enable the organization to move beyond compliance. Similarly, we find that organizations investing in compliance activities also start to invest in resources, specialist knowledge and skills (developing environmental managers, shifting from a narrow personnel focus to a broader HRM focus); and new technologies (monitoring systems; human resource information systems). For instance, at this stage there is usually a movement from personnel management to human resource management. Such a transition involves a shift in focus away from issues such as pay scales and legislative compliance activities towards the development of a more strategically orientated human resources function which contributes to gaining competitive advantage.

What are the incremental steps involved in shifting organizations from compliance to efficiency?

- Efficiency programmes often start on the periphery of an organization as innovative line managers use their business units to experiment with such practices as job redesign, teamwork or reorganization of the supply chain. This often occurs in problem plants – the poor performers – and is part of a push to improve performance. Sometimes, however, efficiency programmes may be initiated by a senior manager or CEO, who develops a particular commitment to sustainability, inspired by programmes such as The Natural Step. For instance, Interface's Australian operations went from being the 'worst performer' to being their number one performing plant out of twenty-seven plants scattered around the world, largely because of the CEO's personal enthusiasm for sustainability.
- Learning from the pilot experiments is normally brought together and evaluated. Successes and failures are talked about and initiatives extended. Managers who lead the changes in these business units walk-the-talk. Their actions and commitment are matched by their willingness to utilize the knowledge of employees, question current organizational orthodoxies and push responsibility down the line. Robert Eckert, CEO of Mattel, attributes their turnaround, in part, to a 'walk-the-talk' approach that encouraged employee empowerment and contributed to human capital development.[38]
- In both HR and ecological areas, incremental change results in an increased emphasis on capability development. Typical initiatives include education programmes, cross sectional problem-solving teams, reviews of barriers and enablers, and a willingness to try new ideas and suggestions. Meanwhile successes are monitored in both a tangible form (costs; waste; quality) and in an intangible form (stories; shifts in culture and values). These shifts often become part of the organization's folklore and help employees develop a 'can do' attitude.

- We often notice that there is a point where the confidence building activities, the devolution of authority, the education programmes and capability development all begin to crystallize. This becomes a critical leverage point. At this time there is the opportunity to shift the programme from a series of isolated small wins and grow more independent support for organization-wide change. It is important to seize the opportunity and provide the resources needed to significantly expand the programme.

When this critical mass for change is harnessed, the programme develops its own momentum: for instance, efficiency gains are diffused to other parts of the organization. Problem areas outside the boundary of the business unit, such as product design and supply chains, now become open to influence and change. After the economic and other benefits of the efficiency changes have been demonstrated, the programme is championed by senior management and extended throughout the organization. As this happens, it is useful to dramatize and celebrate successes and reward key contributors to the change program. These steps are summarized in the box.

Steps in moving from compliance to sustainable efficiency

- Look for efficiency opportunities at the periphery of the organization or in poorly performing plants
- Collate pilot projects' experiences and evaluate
- Increase capability development
- Monitor success and incorporate success stories into organizational folklore
- Identify leverage points and generate critical mass support
- Look for opportunities to create programme momentum
- Identify and work on problem areas
- Extend the programme with management support

Efficiency to strategic proactivity

With each additional incremental step, organizations can build increasing depth of technical and human capabilities. We also see changes in the organization's culture, such as increasing employee commitment, and more indicators of its movement towards high-performance activities. There is often also a corresponding shift from products to services and increasing diffusion of sustainability practices to suppliers and customers. For instance, in the HR area there is usually active recruitment and more retention of highly skilled people with strong sustainability values; challenging executive development programmes are developed and delivered and new opportunities created for exciting and meaningful careers. In the ecological area, we see the emergence of strategic alliances with suppliers and customers and active engagement with community groups in the establishment of new products and services.

Our case study analysis indicates that the following characteristics assist in shifting a firm from efficiency to strategy by incremental processes:

- senior level recognition that the efficiency gains achieved through value adding, and the capabilities developed along the way, are sufficiently valuable to be further integrated into the core strategic activities of the organization. For instance at BP, Sir John Browne has played an integral role in setting targets and values for sustainability and linking them to BP's core business strategies;
- the diffusion of strategic goals for sustainability to all key business units and managers within the organization. Along with that, responsibility for the attainment of sustainability goals is integrated into management reward and performance systems. Hedstrom *et al.* give the example of Shell: 'Shell is developing a new management system to address its financial, environmental and social performance in an integrated manner, applying business rigour to each. The system will strengthen and integrate nine business processes across all three dimensions of sustainable development, including performance management (comprising standards, metrics and verification) and internal and external engagement. It will be built largely on existing processes . . .';[39]
- allocation of significant corporate resources into key areas such as research and development, knowledge management, alliance formation, industry networking and social partnerships;
- systematic exploration of opportunities for strategic alliances. However, by this time, suppliers are accountable for the impact of their products and processes on sustainability outcomes. Training and resources are provided to those willing to change;
- accreditation systems such as EMS, TQEM, design for environment, team work, communities of practice and networking become common features of organizational life. Operational and efficiency gains are constantly improved upon and linked to strategic objectives;
- finally, corporate strategies are constantly revisited in light of the

performance of products and services; new directions are initiated; there is openness to third-party auditing and systematic assessment of the impact of the organization on communities.

These steps are summarized in the box.

Steps in moving from efficiency to strategic proactivity

- Senior level support built on the gains made in the efficiency stage
- Diffusion of strategic goals relating to sustainability to all parts of the organization
- Allocation of corporate resources to key areas
- Identification of strategic alliances and other emerging opportunities
- Use of accreditation programmes
- Strategies revised in light of performance

Strategic proactivity to the sustaining corporation

Incremental change can also facilitate the shift from strategic sustainability to the sustaining corporation phase. We view these changes as cumulative. In becoming sustaining corporations, organizations do not abandon the strategic approach or the capabilities that they have acquired and built as they moved through prior phases. Rather, the shift from strategic sustainability to the sustaining corporation requires an expansion and modification of the value base of the organization. In particular we identify three key changes:

- change programmes that focus on shifting the behaviours and values of organizational members. These are designed to produce extensive culture change. For instance, employees may be rewarded for undertaking community projects or taking an organizational sabbatical working on ecological issues. For example, since 1984, Patagonia, a successful manufacturer of outdoor equipment, has committed 10 per cent of its annual profits to grass-roots environmental groups and has adopted the following mission statement: 'Patagonia exists as a business to improve and implement solutions to environmental issues.' As an expression of its values-based culture, Patagonia runs an internship programme for employees whereby they can work, fully paid, for up to two months in a non-profit environmental group of their choosing. Patagonia executives see these types of programmes as falling under the banner of their strategy – 'It's the right thing to do';[40]

- the use of external parties to monitor, evaluate and encourage future performance: while not essential, this helps create momentum for further change. Third parties can also be used to challenge prevailing assumptions and organizational complacency. More importantly, the sustaining organization will start to challenge others within their industry or supply chain to implement a broad sustainability agenda;
- a focus on design for environment, product and service innovation and the education of consumers and supply chain members on the role that they can play in creating viable alternative business models for sustainability and a sustainable society. These steps are summarized in the box.

Steps in moving from strategic proactivity to the sustaining corporation

- Build on previous capabilities from efficiency and strategic stages
- Focus on shifting behaviours and values to create large-scale cultural change
- Use external parties to drive and challenge performance
- Invest in innovation in product and process redesign and consumer education
- Diffuse sustaining practices to others in the supply chain and other organizations interested in benchmarking

---

Steps involved in incremental change

Up to this point, we have discussed how generic incremental change can help shift organizations from one phase to another. These suggestions outline 'critical paths' organizations can take in the pursuit of sustainability objectives. In Chapter 1 we outlined a model of the phases of corporate sustainability. This model identified six phases in corporate progression towards full sustainability. These are:

- rejection;
- non-responsiveness;
- compliance and beyond;
- efficiency;
- strategic proactivity;
- the sustaining corporation.

These phases emphasize that there is an enormous difference in the readiness of organizations to move to sustainable practices. Some firms are highly advanced in terms of having sustainable human resource practices; others have scarcely given them a thought. The same is true in the area of ecological sustainability: some firms are actively working towards practices that sustain and renew the environment while others continue to exploit the environment. Because traditionally the two kinds of sustainability have rarely been seen as connected, there can also be a lack of conjunction between an organization's current position on one dimension and on the other. The ideal of a fully sustaining corporation is outlined in Figure 7.1: The sustainability change matrix. The figure combines the scales of the two dimensions in the phases of corporate sustainability in a matrix. In the upper left-hand quadrant we have those organizations with relatively few human and ecological sustainable practices, being actively rejecting, indifferent or simply minimally compliant to both human and ecological sustainability standards. The goal is to move corporations to the lower right-hand quadrant, which represents varying degrees of active involvement on the base of efficiency, strategic advantage or fully sustaining practices.

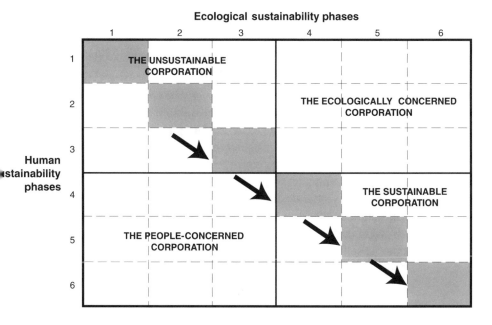

Figure 7.1 *The sustainability change matrix: incremental paths*
Source: Adapted from D. Dunphy, J. Benveniste, A. Griffiths and P. Sutton, *Sustainability: The Corporate Challenge for the 21st Century*, Sydney: Allen and Unwin, 2000, p. 256

Figure 7.1 outlines the incremental changes that organizations could take in shifting from an unsustainable to a sustainable corporation position. These represent 'ideal type' incremental changes. We have not documented here all other possible incremental change scenarios; for instance, those organizations that have already made substantial progress on either ecological or human sustainability (quadrant 2 and 3) may also be able to take more evolutionary and incremental paths to sustainability.

Here we identify eight generic steps involved in creating sustainable organizations through the use of incremental change strategies:

Step 1: Begin with future workshops/search conferences The incremental changes discussed in this chapter focus primarily on operational issues (such as product, process and people changes) and take place in strategic business units. However, starting change programmes at this level does not preclude having a vision or strategic direction. The cases of Scandic, Ikea and Patagonia all point to the importance of having a clear vision and strategic goals to move the organization or specific units forward. Future workshops and search conferences are tools that can be used to generate discussion, participation and commitment to the developing vision for sustainability and developing a plan for realizing the vision. They are also useful for identifying problem areas and potential strategic opportunities. Such events also act as leverage points to motivate and harness employee energy to the change.

Step 2: Assess the organization's current position in relation to sustainability This step addresses the questions: Where is the business unit currently in relation to sustainability practices? What are the barriers and enablers for making sustainability work? What influence will the existing corporate or unit culture have in facilitating or blocking sustainability initiatives? What are the activities that will need to be undertaken in order to shift the business unit from its present position to that outlined in the search conference? In some cases, such as Shell, assessing the current position also involves opening up the organization to external stakeholder evaluation and criticism.

Step 3: Evaluate the type of change programme needed This stage addresses the issue of the approach to be taken. Will the changes introduced be programmatic? That is, will the change programme seek coverage rather than depth – using change tools such as education programmes, The Natural Step workshops or competency training, or will the change approach encourage the emergence of organic innovations within identified business units? The choices made here will impact on the types of change strategies used, on resource needs and expectations for performance. On the whole, we advocate progressing through organic innovations which are piloted and then diffused through a more programmatic approach, although the type of change programme needed may differ for different countries. The multinational bank, the ING Group, controls every aspect of its operations in the Netherlands through an EMS. This is more difficult in some countries; policies on investment concerning life sciences, coal energy and fur, for instance, are each considered separately.

Step 4: Identify change agents   We shall comment in more detail on change agents in Chapter 9. However, change agents should be enthusiastic, knowledgeable about business processes and engender confidence and optimism. Furthermore, a team of change agents playing different facilitative, technical and coalition-building roles can have more impact than one change agent acting alone. For instance, at one manufacturing organization, the implementation of world-class manufacturing involved the formation of a change unit in which a variety of roles were played. The role of the senior executive leading the team was that of the strategist/political operator. It was his role to garner senior support and protect the change programme in its infancy. The operations manager played a task-focused role: he designed and implemented the change programme. His activities were directive and he was responsible for maintaining the momentum of change. His directive style of leadership was complemented by the change facilitator who concentrated on the social relations side of the change. The change facilitator was assisted by a shopfloor employee who was a key opinion maker. The change unit was coached by an external consultant who also played an important role in gathering information and providing a template for action and training. These roles were co-ordinated and influential in creating a successful multi-skilled unit that turned around a brownfield manufacturing site into one that was competitive and world class.

Step 5: Pilot new practices and innovations   In incremental change programmes there is usually time to pilot test proposed changes. This allows competency deficiencies and operational problems to be identified and then addressed, rather like debugging a software program before its widespread adoption. Once the effectiveness of pilot programmes has been established, they can be used to build broader support throughout the organization. Pilot programmes are also an ideal way to test the appropriateness of the tools, and redesign techniques and forms of participation that will be used in the subsequent full-scale incremental change programme.

Step 6: Harness further resources When pilot programmes have been shown to be effective, diffusion of the changes requires access to further resources: time, money, people and management support. Areas of resistance within the organization need to be progressively incorporated into the programme. These areas may require a more intensive use of resources, particularly skilled change agents with high levels of interpersonal skills. If middle managers and supervisors are resistant to change, senior management support will be necessary to ensure that the programme is not sabotaged.

Step 7: Communicate and extend the program The success of the pilot needs to be communicated throughout the organization and some of those involved in making the changes in the pilot situation used as change agents to initiate the changes elsewhere, working with line managers.

Step 8: Align organizational systems For the successful initiatives to turn into truly programmatic changes, operating systems, reward systems, information systems and reporting structures will need to be modified. These modifications should be designed to enhance the robustness of the change and to prevent regression in the pilot site and diffusion areas.[41] Without these broader changes, pilot sites can end up becoming 'islands of innovation in a sea of mediocrity'. As Shelton argues, they run the risk of 'hitting the green wall'.[42] The steps of incremental change are summarized in the box.

Eight steps of incremental change

- Begin with future workshops/search conferences
- Assess the organization's position
- Evaluate the type of change programme needed
- Identify change agents
- Pilot new practices and innovations
- Harness further resources
- Communicate and extend the programme
- Align organizational systems

These eight generic steps by themselves do not guarantee the success of an incremental change programme. A great deal depends on the support given to the changes by senior management, readiness for change on the part of the workforce and the skill of change agents. However, omitting one of these steps can seriously affect the potential success of the change programme. A fully fledged incremental change programme normally moves through all eight steps.

Conclusion

In this chapter we have outlined some of the key characteristics of successful incremental change programmes. We have noted that incremental change strategies are useful for organizations seeking to move between one phase of sustainability and the next. However, as we discussed earlier in this chapter, not all organizations will be able to move forward fast enough on the path to sustainability by using incremental change strategies. The next chapter outlines transformational change strategies – that is, strategies which change the mindsets, cultures, structures and products of organizations in radical ways to obtain sustainability outcomes.

Notes

1 D. Dunphy and A. Griffiths, *The Sustainable Corporation*, Sydney: Allen and Unwin, 1998, p. 56.
2 D. Dunphy and A. Griffiths, 'Corporate strategic change', in *International Encyclopedia of Business and Management*, London: Thomson Learning, 2002, pp. 1169–75.
3 A. Griffiths and D. Dunphy, 'Heresies to orthodoxies: organizational renewal in Australia 1966–1996', *Management Decision*, 2002, 40(1), 74–81.
4 M. Tushman and C. O'Reilly, 'Ambidextrous organizations: managing evolutionary and revolutionary change', *California Management Review*, 1996, 38(4), 8–30.
5 R. Orsatto, 'The ecological modernisation of industry: a study of the European automobile field', doctoral thesis, University of Technology, Sydney, 2001, p. 35.
6 See, for instance, the work of D. Korten, *When Corporations Rule the World*, San Francisco: Berrett-Koehler, 1995; D. Korten, *The Post Corporate World*, San Francisco: Berrett-Koehler, 1999.
7 S. Hart and M. Milstein, 'Global sustainability and the creative destruction of industries', *Sloan Management Review*, 1999, 41(1), 23–33, esp. 24.
8 Ibid., p. 24.
9 M. Hammer, 'Re-engineering work: don't automate, obliterate', *Harvard Business Review*, 1990, 104–12.

10 M. Beer and N. Nohria, 'Cracking the code of change', *Harvard Business Review*, 2000, May–June, 133–41, esp. 133.

11 E. Abrahamson, 'Change without pain', *Harvard Business Review*, 2000, July–August, 75–9, esp. 75.

12 D. Stace and D. Dunphy, *Beyond the Boundaries*, Sydney: McGraw-Hill, 2001, p. 64.

13 For further detail on the debates over planned versus emergent change, refer to B. Burnes, *Managing Change*, London: Pitman Publishing, 1996; K. Weick, 'Emergent change as a universal in organizations', in M. Beer, and N. Nohria, (eds) *Breaking the Code of Change*, Boston, Mass.: Harvard Business School Press, 2000; K. Weick and R. Quinn, 'Organizational change and development', *Annual Review of Psychology*, 1999, 50, 361–86.

14 Stace and Dunphy, *Beyond the Boundaries*, p. 110.

15 Ibid.

16 Ibid., p. 111.

17 J. Porras and R. Silvers, 'Organization development and transformation', *Annual Review of Psychology*, 1991, 42, 51–78, esp. 82.

18 See the work of R. Henrik, H. Daly, P. Hawkin and J. Holmbery, 'A compass for sustainable development', *International Journal of Sustainable Development and World Ecology*, 1991, 4, 79–92.

19 D. Meadows, 'Places to intervene in a system in increasing order of effectiveness', *Whole Earth*, 1997, Winter, 78–84, esp. 78.

20 K. Weick, 'Small wins: redefining the scale of social problems', *American Psychology*, 1984, 39(1), 40–9, esp. 43.

21 S. Benn, interview with D. Lett, Manager, Personnel and Administration, and A. Holmes, Supervisor – Local Purchasing, Panasonic Matsushita Pty Ltd, Penrith, Sydney, 29 August 2000.

22 J. Maxwell, S. Rothenberg, F. Briscoe and I. Marcus, 'Green schemes: corporate environmental strategies and their implementation', *California Management Review*, 1997, 39(3), 118–34.; L. Rowledge, R. Barton and K. Brady, *Mapping the Journey*, Sheffield: Greenleaf Publishing, 1999.

23 M. Shanahan and A. Maria, 'Creating change through strategic storytelling', *PRISM*, 1998, Q4, 99–108, esp. 100–1.

24 Ibid., 101.

25 R. Jones, N. Jimmieson, N. and A. Griffiths, 'The role of organizational culture and reshaping capabilities in creating readiness for change: implications for change implementation success, unpublished manuscript, School of Management, Queensland University of Technology, 2001.

26 Rowledge *et al.*, *Mapping the Journey*, p. 136.

27 J. MacDuffie, 'Human resource bundles and manufacturing performance: organizational logic and flexible production systems in the world auto industry', *Industrial and Labor Relations Review*, 1995, 48(2), 197–221.

28 C. Ichniowski, K. Shaw and G. Prennushi, 'The effects of human resource management practices on productivity: a study of steel finishing lines', *American Economic Review*, 1997, June, 291–313.

29 For a review, see J. Pfeffer, *Competitive Advantage Through People*, Boston, Mass.: Harvard Business School Press, 1995.

30 Stace and Dunphy, *Beyond the Boundaries*, pp. 97–8, citing the work of Ostroff and Smith.

31 N. Roome, 'Developing environmental management strategies', *Business Strategy and the Environment*, 1992, 1(1), 11–23.

32 B. Daily and S. Huang, 'Achieving sustainability through attention to human resource factors in environmental management', *International Journal of Operations and Production Management*, 2001, 12, 1539–52.

33 P. Strebel, *Breakpoints: How Managers Exploit Radical Change*, Boston, Mass.: Harvard Business School Press, 1992.

34 Stace and Dunphy, *Beyond the Boundaries*, p. 104.

35 Abrahamson, 'Change without pain', 76.

36 J. Mathews, A. Griffiths and N. Watson, *Socio-technical Redesign: The Case of Cellular Manufacturing at Bendix Mintex*, Industrial Relations Research Centre, UNSW Studies in Organizational Analysis and Innovation, University of New South Wales, 1993.

37 'Greenpeace warns of further water contamination in Romania and Hungary', press release 14 March 2000; 'Cyanide spill mine takes first step towards bankruptcy', Environment News Service, 16 March 2000.

38 R. Eckert, 'Where leadership starts', *Harvard Business Review*, 2001, November, 53–62.

39 G. Hedstrom, S. Poltorzycki, and P. Stroh, 'Sustainable development: the next generation of business opportunity', *PRISM*, 1998, 4th Quarter, 5–20, 17.

40 Rowledge *et al.*, *Mapping the Journey*, p. 97.

41 R. Walton, 'The diffusion of new work structures: explaining why success didn't take', in P. Mirvis and D. Berg (eds) *Failures in Organization Development and Change*, New York: John Wiley, 1977, pp. 243–61.

42 R. Shelton, 'Hitting the green wall: why corporate programs get stalled', *Corporate Environmental Strategy*, 1994, 2(2), 5–12.

8 The transformational path

- Why transformational change?
- Step 1: Know where you are now
- Step 2: Develop the vision – the dream organization
- Step 3: Identify the gap
- Step 4: Assess the readiness for change
- Step 5: Set the scene for action
- Step 6: Secure basic compliance first
- Step 7: Move beyond compliance
- Step 8: Establish the performance criteria for 'compliance plus'
- Step 9: Launch and manage the transformational change programme
- Step 10: Maintain the rage

Why transformational change?

For some organizations, the move to sustainability can be incremental. As outlined in the last chapter, there are many organizations, particularly in the service sector, which touch the earth lightly and already contribute substantially to the health and welfare of their workforce and the community. For these organizations, progress towards full sustainability can be a process of unspectacular but systematic and sustained development of awareness, policies and practices. These are the fortunate organizations.

There are many other organizations, however, that have been, or will soon be, subjected to unprecedented and unanticipated public pressures to make radical change. Why? Because some of their current policies or practices are revealed as plundering and polluting the planet, destroying the human capital assets of the organization or fracturing community relationships. We have given many examples throughout this book of organizations that have found themselves in such a situation and have had to respond by initiating radical, transformative change. In fact, some of today's leading corporate advocates of sustainability, whose managers have blazed a trail to sustainable practices, have been companies whose reputations suffered at some point because of unacceptable and unsustainable practices. For example, in the mid-1990s Shell faced a barrage of international criticism over its proposal to sink the redundant Brent Spar oil platform in the North Sea; this crisis was followed by more international criticism over its apparent support for a cruel dictatorship in Nigeria. Shell responded with a series of roundtable meetings in fourteen locations throughout the world where it faced up to its severest critics for a frank exchange of views. As a result, it made a fundamental re-evaluation of its ethical position and business strategies, giving social and environmental sustainability issues a significant place in its core business strategies.

We are moving into a period of history when organizations engaging in unsustainable operations will have their 'licence to operate' questioned by activist community groups or government watchdogs.[1] If organizations persist in these behaviours, they will be forced into crisis mode to extricate themselves, salvage their public image and retain market share. The community is increasingly suspicious of 'greenwash' so the change has to be more than simply a cosmetic makeover. What is required sometimes is large-scale, transformative change: that is, a leap into a fundamental redefinition of the company or some significant aspect of it. This may involve developing a new definition of the business the company is in, a new strategic orientation or realignment, a new structure, a significant change in the workforce skill mix or profile and/or a substantive change in corporate culture.

Other companies may choose to change transformationally even though they are not subjected to external pressures to do so. Some of these will be companies whose managers see the significant business opportunities that are emerging in sustainable development and who wish to lead in taking up these opportunities. To do so they may have to reinvent the organization, for example by moving from manufacturing petroleum-based products to manufacturing and recycling products based on natural fibres while building a wholly new business operation that services and recycles – this is the story of Interface, the international commercial carpet company. Other companies will be led by managers who are personally committed to contributing to a more sustainable world and who see their companies as instruments for accomplishing this. The move from a single-minded focus on creating short-term profits to embodying an ideological commitment to social justice and ecological diversity may also involve transformative change. The story of how Interface transformed its operations includes change of this kind as well.

We are addressing here what Robert Quinn refers to as 'deep change'. Quinn writes:

> Deep change differs from incremental change in that it requires new ways of thinking and behaving. It is change that is major in scope, discontinuous with the past and generally irreversible. The deep change effort distorts existing patterns of action and involves taking risks. Deep change means surrendering control.[2]

Corporate transformations are not to be initiated lightly for they are difficult to accomplish, often risky for the careers of the change agents involved and can have significant impacts on the lives of others, not all of which may be positive in the short term. In fact some have questioned whether it is possible to manage such change at all.[3] In our view, it is often possible to bring about transformational change, and we have documented many successful cases.[4] However, the magnitude of the task is often underestimated by managers, who consequently under-resource the process and fail to assemble the skills required to accomplish large-scale, fundamental change. On the other hand, while transformative change involves risk, there are times when failure to initiate transformative change results in the business being out of business. Not doing anything can be a greater risk than initiating transformational change.

Given the magnitude and urgency of the changes needed to bring about sustainability in society, we are confident that over the next few years many organizations will have to undergo corporate transformation. The good news is that many already have done so over the last quarter century due to the globalization of business, increasing competition and world economic recessions. Tough as these times have been, we have learned a great deal about how to reinvent organizations (and how not to). We can therefore draw on this experience and use what has been learned from it to manage the kind of transformational change needed to achieve full sustainability. In addition, we now know that 'long-living companies', that is companies that survive for many years, undergo at least one significant period of transformational change and sometimes several. As mentioned earlier, de Geus has documented the histories of twenty-seven companies that lasted from 100 to 700 years – companies such as DuPont, Kodak, Mitsui, Sumitomo and Siemens.[5] Their ability to initiate and manage transformational change has been a major contributor to their longevity.

In addition, there are an increasing number of organizations whose basic corporate strategy is continually to transform or 'reinvent' themselves to maintain a competitive edge. Brown and Eisenhardt capture this well:

> For firms such as Intel, Wal-Mart, 3M, Hewlett-Packard and Gillette, the ability to change rapidly and continuously, especially in developing new products, is not only a core competence, it is also at the heart of their cultures. For these firms, change is not the rare, episodic phenomenon described by the punctuated equilibrium model but, rather, it is endemic to the way these organizations compete.[6]

Those organizations which see the development of new sustainable technologies, processes and products as central to their strategic success may choose to use continuous transformational change as a way of continuously dominating their emerging markets.

This chapter outlines the practical process by which change agents can reinvent and reconstruct organizations into responsible instruments for creating products and services that contribute to a fulfilling life on a healthy planet. In the process, this makes a significant contribution to their own financial success and sustainability as viable organizations.

So how is transformative change initiated and effectively implemented? We outline the steps involved in the process and give concrete examples of successes and failures.

Step 1: Know where you are now

Transformative change involves reinventing the organization – creating a compelling image of a desirable future organization dramatically different from the current one. But before charging off into the future, it is important to know the starting point: the organization as it is now. This is not a minor task, particularly in a large, complex company. It is easy to assume that the organization's current strategic identity is known and understood – after all, many people in the organization may have been around for years. Yet everyone in an organization has a different experience of it – organizations are not primarily buildings, equipment, finance and organization charts. Rather they are constructs in the minds of those who work in and with them, who buy from them and supply to them. They are primarily subjective realities, images that have been forged from individual and collective experience over time, and these subjective realities are usually partial and fragmentary and differ widely from one person to another. It is not enough to create a vision of the future and build an informed commitment to it. It is necessary first to build a shared understanding of the organization's current reality and of the need to radically shift that reality.

As Lynda Gratton notes:

> Working at the level of meaning in an organization requires a new way of thinking. To understand meaning it is not sufficient to simply consider what the organization is doing with regard to its tasks, the reporting structure or policy statements. We have to understand how the organization is perceived by its individual members. Working at the level of the 'unwritten rules of the game' provides us with such an opportunity. This level of analysis begins to answer questions about what is important around the organization, what people have to do to get on, what really motivates and excites individuals, and which factors send the most positive messages.[7]

So up front of any transformative change programme we must assess the current reality. How?

There are two basic sources for constructing a shared view of the organization's current situation. The first source is carefully chosen members of the organization including preferably some who have left. What can be gained from this source is a précis of the history of the organization, an outline of its defining formative moments. How did it come to be what it is? Who played key roles? To what extent were issues of sustainability taken into account along the way? The other source consists of representatives of key stakeholders – customers and suppliers, for example – who have dealt with the organization throughout its history. What is their experience of the organization? Have their expectations, particularly around sustainability (for example, pesticide-free food products), been met in the past? Are they being met now? To what extent are they currently expecting sustainable practices? Even if they are not, how would they respond to the development of such products and services?

There are various ways in which this information can be elicited; for example, through surveys, interviews, focus groups, and analysis of organizational and community records. Sometimes valuable information about the expectations of external stakeholders can be gleaned from members of the organization who have roles that require regular contact with a key stakeholder group. For example, we were working with a port authority to identify key stakeholders and their expectations. The CEO mentioned the fishermen and their reaction when the authority closed off access to the authority's wharves where tugs were moored. The move was made because of persistent vandalism to the tugs while they lay beside the wharves. After protests from the fishermen at the closure of the wharves to the public, the authority built a new wharf, at considerable expense, from which boat owners could operate. This, the CEO thought, had resolved the issue. 'For the boat owners,' remarked the head of security, 'but not for all the fishermen whose equipment was only rods and hand lines. They're still mad as hell about being excluded from their favourite fishing sites.' Most organizations have a wealth of information about external stakeholder attitudes which is not accessed, integrated and assessed by the senior executive team, let alone made known throughout the organization as part of creating the consensual reality needed to launch a change programme.

An important part of assessing current reality is to identify the core cultural values of the organization and the entrenched behavioural mores that control much of day-to-day behaviour in the organization. Here a trained outsider can often make the most useful contribution by focusing a fresh independent eye on the customary ways members of the organization undertake everyday business. The best observer is someone who is sensitive to the differences that often exist between espoused and enacted values – what people say they support versus what they actually do. Managers, for example, often express the view that 'people are our major asset' but their actual human resource practices may not reflect this stated belief. What are the prevailing views on sustainability issues held by the dominant coalition and other key groups such as trade union members, salespeople, maintenance workers, research and development staff? What is the result, in practical terms, for the welfare of the workforce, for the community, for the environment?

'Telling it the way it is' can be confronting for many members of the organization. Some organizational members will have a strong personal stake in preserving fictional views of the organization's current reality, for their own identities are bound up in maintaining the fiction. For example, they may not welcome a realistic assessment of the organization's impact on the environment. They may seek to 'shoot the messenger' who brings the disconfirming views. Remember the strenuous action of cigarette manufacturers who sought to disconfirm scientific evidence of the link between smoking and cancer. We emphasize strongly here that the basis for effective transformational change is widespread consensual agreement on the current organizational reality. It is necessary to be honest, sometimes brutally honest, to bring this about. This is easier to achieve when members of the dominant elite(s) are open to acknowledge different viewpoints and willing to absorb new information even when it challenges their traditional views. In fostering this openness, the credibility of the source of such information can also make a critical difference: respected external change agents with authority and expertise are more likely to be heard than insiders or outsiders without these attributes. A combination of confrontation by concerned community groups and, in parallel, a significant challenge from one or more sources whom executives respect and trust can provide the jolt needed to create the initial momentum for change.

In this regard, Byong-Wook Lee outlines some of the prevailing assumptions about waste in a Korean steel producing operation. These assumptions had to be confronted before waste and the associated pollution could be significantly reduced. The commonly held views were that 'change of waste management is expected to have very limited effect upon the company's financial performance' and that 'there is little room to reduce wastes through changes in the steel making process'.[8] Neither view was accurate, but the beliefs were deeply entrenched in the traditional culture of the organization.

If we are travelling through the countryside and are unsure of the terrain, it is useful to have a map. But even a map is useless unless we know where we are now. Travelling to the future is similar; we need to be sure of our current situation so that we can begin to change it. Like travelling by car or boat, in organizations we are not stationary and, in order to change direction, we must take into account the organization's current direction and momentum. This is particularly important when we propose to accelerate dramatically the pace of change for, in turning and accelerating at the same time, it is easy for managers to lose control of the process. Nevertheless, with foresight, wisdom and skill, transformational change can be exciting, challenging and effective.

Step 2: Develop the vision – the dream organization

Transformative change is an opportunity to rethink the raison d'être of the organization. Organizations are organic entities, social systems, which take on a life of their own often independent of those who brought them into being. They are shaped initially by the purposes of their founders but modified by external social pressures, by momentous and sometimes unanticipated events. Organizations sometimes actively shape the economic, physical and social environments in which they operate; they both shape and are shaped by these forces. They sometimes lead changes in their environments; more often they lag behind.

Organizations are, however, human creations, held in place by the values and actions of those in and around them. What has been created by human thought and action can also be recreated. However, to use an analogy, remanufacturing is a different process from manufacturing. In remanufacturing, the physical basis of metals, for example, may have been changed by heat, vibration and wear. In remanufacturing, therefore, different processes have to be invented to produce the same or similar outcomes that result from manufacturing from raw materials. The same is true of transformative change: changing an organization that has already developed a history and a culture requires a different approach from creating a new organization. We are intervening in a system that has already developed powerful properties and processes of its own and these processes are usually deeply embedded in the minds, emotions and lives of the members of the organization and its external stakeholders. Changing the organization involves changing those in it, often including ourselves; it often also involves changing the expectations of those outside.

The first step in transforming an organization is to creatively imagine one or more future realities (scenarios) that the organization will face. The future is usually three to ten years out – the time chosen depends fundamentally on an estimate of how long it will take investments made now, in capital, human and technical capabilities, to be realized. This scenario planning begins with an identification of: (a) the major current trends that are likely to affect the future viability, success and sustainable contribution of the organization; and (b) who the critical stakeholders are likely to be in the future, for they may be different from those the organization relates to now. Scenario planning of this type first emerged in the Royal Dutch Shell Group in the 1970s and has since been elaborated and widely used under the general heading of 'strategic scenarios analysis'.[9] It is widely used: for example, the US Marines are creating scenarios that apply network technology to urban warfare and, as a consequence, are reshaping their traditional military organization.[10]

In constructing future scenarios, it is neither necessary nor wise to eliminate alternative scenarios for one 'most likely' scenario. Rather, a vision may be elaborated for the most likely scenario but parallel visions roughed out for 'best case' and 'worst case' scenarios. The purpose of the exercise is not simply to create a strategy for the future but also to create a purposeful process of engaging people inside and outside the organization in scoping out possible new paths ahead – to engage them in a critical debate about possible alternative futures. The aim is to build the commitment of all critical stakeholders to a challenging new future role for the organization.[11] At the same time, it is important to avoid locking the organization into an irrevocable path to a future that may never eventuate. The organization needs to be proactive, to create direction and momentum but also to retain the flexibility to adapt to unanticipated developments.

A critical part of this process of strategic realignment is to move from an identification of key future stakeholders to an imaginative construction of how their expectations may affect the organization in the future. This is an opportunity to engage these stakeholders in a dialogue about how they view their future – to give them voice. It is important also that as many members of the organization as possible are in a position to hear for themselves these voices from the stakeholders or their representatives. For example, Qantas, the Australia-based airline, made forums with groups of its frequent flyers and employees, from managers to baggage handlers, an important part of its transformational change programme. Qantas employees were trained to ask questions of customers, listen and take notes. This not only resulted in vital competitive information on how the airline could improve its services but it also transformed the understanding and attitudes of Qantas staff to customers. The airline still uses forums of this kind on a regular basis so that the change is ongoing and updated and so that staff are fully engaged with issues of customer satisfaction.

This exercise leads into a definition of the most critical issues facing the organization. The natural next step is to ask: What will these anticipated changes mean for our organization? What problems will we face? What opportunities will be available to us? What values will we stand for?

These questions centre on defining a new identity for the organization and developing an innovative strategic intent to guide the organization in its future decision making. An important facet of this process is defining a set of core values in which human and ecological sustainability have a central place. For example, the Co-operative Bank in the UK has a history of pioneering ethical business practices and instituting community-minded policies. In their 1998 *Partnership Report*, the bank extended its list of key stakeholders beyond shareholders, suppliers, customers, staff and their families to include local communities, national and international society and future generations. The bank aims to deliver 'value' to each of these stakeholders – value as defined by the group itself and not by the bank. As a result, for example, the bank does not invest in firms which violate human rights. It also operates a credit card scheme where a proportion of profit made from money spent by customers on their cards is donated to organizations such as Amnesty International and Greenpeace.[12]

These core values also define how the organization will measure performance in the future. Stace and Dunphy express the change occurring in this area as follows:

> As the era of industrial capitalism recedes, it is evident that the strategic benchmarks of organizations are changing. In the classical era of industrial capitalism, strategic benchmarks were nearly all expressed in financial or market terms: the typical measures were net profit, return on investment, return on earnings and market share. Organizations compared themselves and were driven by these or similar ratios. It was as if the unwritten law of each organization was to become the biggest and most profitable, quite often by immolating competitors. Today we are witnessing a sea change. Why? Because shareholders are not the only organizational constituents of the firm: stakeholders, customers, network and alliance partners are just as important.[13]

As noted elsewhere in the book, numerous organizations are now adopting triple bottom line performance criteria or comparable approaches that reflect a significant broadening of values and acceptance of a multiple stakeholder approach. Involving forward-thinking stakeholders in the process of renewing the corporate vision and strategic intent is an important part of building 'relationship capital'. Creating an engaging dialogue with key stakeholders ensures that their interests are taken into account and that they know this. It also enlists their active support for the emerging changes in the organization's operations.

The central challenge of transformative change is to unleash the imagination of organizational members and stakeholders so that they collaborate in creating a vision that breaks out of existing cultural assumptions to create a prototype for a truly sustainable and sustaining organization. Whereas incremental change can often be successfully generated and led entirely by people internal to the organization, transformative change almost always needs input from outsiders. The outsiders need to be informed, radical, lateral thinkers who can and will challenge existing assumptions about the current organizational platen and accepted best practice. For example, Placer Dome, an international mining company, invited major critics of its current environmental and community relations practices (for example, Greenpeace) to examine, critique and propose new policies and procedures acceptable to them.[14]

The vision must be spelled out as clearly as possible and personally endorsed by senior management. However, at this stage it represents a new identity, a change of direction, an idea in process to be explored, tested and progressively given shape through future action. It must also be formulated in a way that speaks to the hearts and minds of the key players in the organization and to stakeholders whose support will be needed for it to be realized. It has to have a clear relationship to the core business strategies of the organization. Ideally the essence of the new identity can be expressed simply and directly, for example, BP = Beyond Petroleum, signifying that the company is repositioning itself to phase out its dependence on petroleum and to become a significant player in the development of alternative energy sources.

Nigel Roome has documented the development in 1996 of an environmental vision at Abitibi-Price, a Canadian manufacturer of newsprint and added value papers:

> Under the guidance of the vice-president for Environmental Affairs, Brian Young, a process was set up to clarify the company's environmental vision and to make it part of the company's business process. The critical issue was that the company's overall vision 'to be the finest' needed to be supported by a clear understanding of what this meant for the company's environmental performance and environmental management practices of the whole company rather than what it meant in terms of investments and technology. The aim of the overall process was to:
>
> • clarify the vision;
> • develop a detailed outline of the 'finest' environmental management system operating within the normal business cycle;
> • achieve a vision during the 1996 planning cycle that would ensure that environmental action became a part of the business process, rather than a compliance afterthought.[15]

Roome provides a detailed account of how the vision was generated and how commitment to it was built throughout the company.

Step 3: Identify the gap

Having reached this point, now is the time to pull back from the dream and to create a realistic assessment of the gap between the organization's current situation and where the new vision seeks to position itself in the future. The Corporate Sustainability Matrix around which this book is constructed provides a way of estimating and describing the gap as well as indicating how to move forward. To do this, you need to work independently through the human sustainability column and the ecological column – an organization may be at a different stage in each of these areas (see p. 246). It is possible for the same organization to have a highly strategic approach to human sustainability (Phase 5) but to be lagging in terms of compliance in the ecological area (Phase 2) – for example, a mining company which has first-rate human resource policies but which has environmentally destructive operations.

The outputs of Steps 2 and 3 above supply the information needed to position, in the matrix, where the organization is now and where it aspires to be, and over what time span. The differences between current and envisioned future positions in the matrix define the gap to be bridged. Let's take the case of a bank, for example, which has systematically built its HR strategies over a ten-year period, using them to attract and retain some of the best talent in the industry. The bank has also been concerned about its contribution to the community and also used its community relations to support its progressive, 'concerned and caring' image. This places it in Phase 5, strategic sustainability (HS5), in the area of human sustainability. However, it has given little thought to its environmental impact. It uses huge amounts of paper, most of which is not separated for recycling. It constantly updates its computers, printers and so on, but commits them by truckloads to landfill. It is discussing developments in the ethical investment fund area but has not yet launched such a fund or developed an alliance with another financial institution that has. This places it, for ecological sustainability, in Phase 2, non-responsiveness (ES2). So its overall position on the Sustainability Change Matrix, Figure 8.1, is at point A. Now it aspires to be a leader in the introduction of both human and ecological sustainability practices by moving towards HS6 and ES6. Clearly it needs, at the most, incremental change in the human sustainability area. But its transformational change programme needs to centre on ecological sustainability, where it has a lot of ground to make up before it reaches its ideal position at or near point B. The gap between the current phase and the desired future phase defines the bridge the organization must cross in order to emerge transformed.

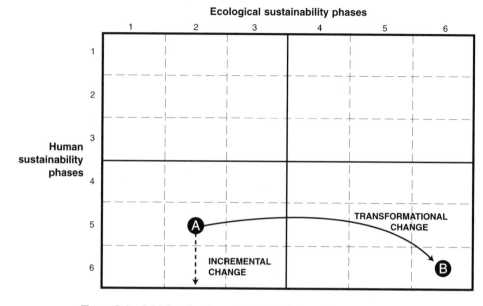

Figure 8.1 *Bridging the gap: what kind of change?*
Source: Adapted from D. Dunphy, J. Benveniste, A. Griffiths and P. Sutton, *Sustainability: The Corporate Challenge for the 21st Century*, Sydney: Allen and Unwin, 2000, p. 256

If the organization is complex, having divisions and units with differentiated operations, market environments and cultures, the process of positioning on the matrix may need to be analysed for each differentiated unit. This implies that the organization may have to pursue a complex change strategy that is a mix of both incremental and transformative change, depending on the current character of the subunits. The more differentiated the change strategy in this regard, the higher will be the cost of coordinating across ongoing strands of the change programme. Resources, human and financial, need to be allocated to ensure that the various change initiatives move the organization as a whole on its chosen trajectory rather than spinning off on their own orbits.

The most obvious output of this stage of the design process is a realistic assessment of the nature of the gap to be bridged – the gap between the organization's current commitment to and performance on key sustainability indicators and the new vision for the future. This gap may be substantially different for human and ecological sustainability and may also differ from one part of the organization's operations to another.

If the process has been well managed to this point, an important secondary output is that commitment to change is already building among key opinion leaders within the organization and significant external stakeholders. Transformative change is always a political process and a central task of change agents is to build active support among constituent groups, or at least receive tacit acceptance of the desired changes. This is not always possible: there are usually individuals and groups who have a significant stake in the existing order, the status quo, and whose interests are threatened by change. It would be naive not to expect active and passive resistance from them. What is often harder for change agents to accept, however, is the resistance that often comes from some of those who are disaffected from the status quo and who stand to *benefit* from the proposed changes. Some people cannot project themselves into a future world, cannot assess realistically how their interests will be served by change, or actually prefer to remain locked in, complaining, to the security of a known if debilitating role rather than break the chain and be free. We cannot make people change; we can only provide opportunities for them to change themselves.

Step 4: Assess the readiness for change

For those who have been intensely involved in the diagnostic process described in steps 2 and 3, it is easy to assume that the organization as a whole is poised and ready for change, or that, if there are points of resistance, these will simply fade away as the change proceeds. This is usually far from the truth. Planning change is the easy part; intervening in an ongoing system that is alive, has its own compelling logic and of which we are only a small part is a huge challenge. Even formal authority has limited validity in a transformative change process. Ordering people to change is seldom effective; change by memorandum and edict usually fails. Leadership, not management, is the critical element in transformative change. Leadership at all levels is vital in creating the bursts of energy that must spark responses in opinion leaders and build momentum for change. This is an issue we will deal with in more detail in our final chapter.

Transformative change may involve authoritative action, even coercion, but its success depends ultimately on emotional contagion across the living networks of human relationships that make up an organization. There must be a compelling intellectual agenda for change, but that is not enough to transform deeply entrenched behavioural patterns built up over years of repetitive action. People are more than minds; they have hearts and spirits as well and the agenda for change must also appeal to people at emotional and spiritual levels. The sustainability agenda has the potential to do this. For example, most parents care about the world that their children and grandchildren will inherit. Most people want to work for organizations that are seen to be making a contribution to community life. We seek meaning and purpose in our lives: the great opportunity that faces managers and change agents in the move to sustainability is to actualize the opportunity this represents to enhance the sense of meaning people derive from coming to work each day. A transformative change programme can catalyse meaning and provide opportunities for the development of wholeness through purposive and fulfilling work.

As Debashis Chatterjee points out: 'Organizations are not merely structures of units and departments but living fields of creative intelligence of the people who constitute the organization.'[16]

Step 4 involves identifying the important internal and external organizational stakeholders whose attitudes and actions could affect the success of the proposed change programme, and working out how their interests may be affected by the changes. It may be appropriate to consult with them beforehand if this has not already happened. Again, where possible, the change programme should be modified to ensure that the interests of as many key players as possible are served by the unfolding programme of change. However, in transformative change, there are usually some groups whose entrenched interests will be threatened. If this is the case, positive alternatives can sometimes be developed to reduce the win–lose nature of the situation. If not, then conflict can be expected and strategies developed to minimize the threat their opposition will represent for the repositioning of the organization. We stress that transformative change is a political process characterized by conflict and power plays. Those initiating the change need to develop a clear understanding of the sources of their authority and power to initiate and carry through the desired changes, build political alliances to support their initiatives, and anticipate potential sources of opposition and indifference. Sustainability is a relatively new ideology and support for it cannot be assumed but needs to be won progressively.

Step 5: Set the scene for action

There are three additional issues that need to be addressed in creating a base for effective action: awareness of the need for change; identifying change leaders; and assembling the resources needed for the change programme.

Before change can happen, those in the organization must be aware of the need to change. In creating an awareness of the need to change, it makes sense to start where there is the most potential energy for change, that is, with those who are already aware of and committed to the changes. In today's organizations there are usually articulate advocates of sustainability who understand at least some of the key issues and who are impatient for change. There are also others who are aware but tend to be 'covert' believers, less articulate but waiting for encouragement and clear opportunities before becoming involved. The awareness-building process can start by bringing these people together and identifying the potential contributions they can make to the change process both individually and collectively. One of their most important resources will be the informal networks of others in the organization whom they can influence, so creating a process by which the 'ripples' of awareness can spread out through the natural links between people in the organization. In the early 1990s, for example, Scandic Hotels, the hotel chain in Scandinavia we discussed earlier, embarked on a change programme to improve the environmental and economic performance of all its hotels. In the first year alone, employees identified more than 1,500 potential innovations which resulted in significant savings and reduced the hotels' environmental impact. In 1997 it was rated in the top 100 most desirable companies to work for in Sweden and successfully attracted large numbers of environmentally conscious guests.[17]

Another important step in building awareness is to open windows on the world and on the future for those in the organization. The more that those in the organization can be given access to leading thinkers and organizational practices in corporate sustainability, the more compelling the case for sustainability becomes and the more engaged they will be. Lectures, seminars, site visits, articles, videos and books can all help build a compelling case for change. They are an important part of creating an intellectual agenda for the change programme.

But effective change programmes require leadership and resources as well as ideas. The next task therefore is to identify change leaders at all levels of the organization, to bring them together around creating a practical agenda for change and to win their commitment to make the change happen. This team (or partnership of several teams) will become the guiding coalition driving the change programme. To be effective, this group needs to have representatives of all key power groups, formal or informal, in the organization who have the capability to make the programme succeed or fail. It needs to include at least one member of the top team so that its work is linked to the core business strategies of the organization. The change leaders include those who have the requisite technical knowledge in areas such as human resource management, corporate social responsibility and the natural environment. They also need to have the EQ (emotional intelligence) skills required to work effectively with people and the SQ (spiritual intelligence) skills needed to provide the wisdom to make sound choices in the face of complex problems.[18] We shall discuss the role and relevance of these factors in more detail in Chapter 9.

However, even the best leaders cannot accomplish effective large-scale change without the necessary resources of time, personnel support and finance. Some of the best-planned change programmes fail because senior executives believe that key personnel can simply act as change agents in their 'spare time' and that change programmes do not need the kinds of resources that would be considered essential to a well-run operational task of similar magnitude. Managing a large-scale organizational change programme is equivalent to an engineering project such as creating a new mine, building a skyscraper or installing an organization-wide IT system. Because there may be no visible end product, justifying the time involved and the provision of the necessary resources often demands building a convincing case for equivalent support.

If enthusiasm has been engendered for change, those who assume leadership can readily underestimate the time needed for deep change. Lynda Gratton, through UK-based The Leading Edge Research Consortium, has had the opportunity to monitor several transformational change processes in leading companies. One of the companies studied was Glaxo Wellcome, the world's largest drug company by sales. Their position was challenged because of cost cutting in drug purchases and the introduction of 'managed care'. In 1988 Glaxo chairman Richard Sykes and his senior team reviewed their business strategy, deciding to move away from a single product focus to the concept of disease management, closer partnerships with their customers and speedier delivery of drugs. Gratton details how it took two years of intensive targeted activity to transform the company's functional, hierarchical structure to a process-driven, customer-focused culture with effective multi-disciplinary teams. Only then, two years later, did the company begin to pick up the performance benefits it had aspired to; over this period it also created a stable of new drugs to fuel its continuing success in the future. But it was really the late 1990s before the new culture they had envisaged ten years earlier was hard and soft wired into the organization and the benefits fully realized.[19] Stace and Dunphy provide comparable case studies of transformational change in two companies, Qantas and ICI's Botany Plant in Sydney. The Qantas change programme went through several phases over the six years from 1993 to 1999, moving backward and forward from transformative to more incremental change; the ICI change programme went through three distinct phases, transformative, incremental and transformative again, over the ten years from 1987 to 1997.[20] Deep change takes real time.

While incremental change can often be effectively undertaken with resources internal to the organization, transformative change usually requires the use of competent, qualified and experienced external consultants. Cultural shifts require a rethinking of cherished assumptions, the challenging of existing patterns of behaviour and the generation of novel alternatives. In this process, it is valuable to have the assistance of parties who have not been socialized into the current corporate culture and who have moved across a variety of organizations in different industries. Organizations undergoing cultural change have characteristics of both chaos and order and this is becoming a normal pattern of corporate change in a much more dynamic and unpredictable world.[21]

Step 6: Secure basic compliance first

We want to stress here that securing compliance with legal requirements and the legitimate expectations of stakeholders is the necessary base from which transformational change to more advanced stages must be made. No matter how urgent the need to move the organization forward to other stages of sustainability, it is dangerous to skip this stage – dangerous because failure to comply with legal requirements for health and safety, for example, could lead to costly lawsuits and a damaged corporate reputation. In the USA, Honda had to pay US$267 to settle claims that it disconnected pollution monitoring equipment on 1.6 million cars. They contravened America's Clean Air Act and the fine was their reminder that the US government is now taking air pollution seriously.[22]

It is not only dangerous to skip this stage but also irresponsible because the health and safety of employees, of the community and the environment is the first responsibility of any organization in the twenty-first century. In addition, transformational change inevitably creates disorder that can increase the risk of non-compliance. Consequently it is important to create clear guidelines for compliance first and to build a tight control system that is actively maintained at a grassroots level. This needs to be backed up by clear managerial accountability to hold compliance in place when everything else is changing. It is vital to ensure that compliance norms are internalized and to create a working set of operational procedures to reduce corporate risk to a minimum. Contingency plans for damage control also need to be in place in case the compliance procedures fail (for example, in a mining operation, a tailings dam collapses in an unprecedented downpour despite well thought out measures to prevent this).

It is not only compliance to legislation that is important: as we pointed out in Chapter 4, companies must also meet the strong expectations of stakeholders even if these do not have legal standing. For example, Monsanto set out to model sustainable development but experienced global outrage when it developed genetically modified seeds that would not reproduce themselves; this meant that farmers would have to buy new seeds from Monsanto every year.[23]

Compliance is the base platform on which sustainability can be built. We outline here the necessary tasks to be performed in achieving compliance:

- Identify potential risks through undertaking a risk analysis.
- Establish the priorities for risk reduction.
- Decide who will take charge of the compliance generating process, keeping in mind that this is an opportunity to begin to identify and develop change leaders for later stages in the path to sustainability. Create a task force to plan and guide the process.
- Estimate the resources needed to achieve compliance and assemble these resources.
- Develop a co-ordination and communication plan that links line and staff responsibilities.
- Set criteria for success and construct an ambitious schedule for completion.
- Establish a monitoring and review process that is understood, transparent and widely reported.

In a transformational change process, the priority is to achieve compliance effectively and rapidly. This can be accomplished by creating a number of task forces in important areas of sustainability such as OHS, EEO, water and energy conservation, and then having these task forces operate in parallel. (In an incremental change programme, these key compliance areas might be tackled sequentially.) The cost of organizing in parallel lies in the need for greater co-ordination across the teams to ensure that the end result is a well-integrated and mutually consistent set of policies and procedures. Therefore there is a need for an effective liaison role in linking the teams together as they work on their focal issues.

Step 7: Move beyond compliance

With an effective compliance base in place, it is now time to put the organization into fast forward mode. At this point it is useful to return to the sustainability matrix and to confirm the decision, made in step 1 above, to move towards either the phase of 'strategic sustainability' or to 'the sustaining corporation' (see Figure 8.1). In addition, the gap between where the organization is now and where it aspires to be needs to be reviewed. Now is the time also to outline the major steps through which the change programme should move and the time frame for this. The resulting change programme must be challenging but achievable. For example, if significant cultural change is needed, then the schedule would normally cover three to five years.

There are two possible transformational change paths to take at this point: either to attempt to take the organization in a leap forward to Phase 5: strategic proactivity, or to Phase 6: the sustaining corporation. Obviously the latter is the goal involving the biggest stretch but both involve moving rapidly through Phase 4: efficiency. This has significant implications; for instance, it may be possible to pick up some of the key achievements of the efficiency phase along the way but there is a real risk that transformational change of this order will actually work against making efficiency gains, at least in the short term. The speed and extent of large-scale transformational change often brings significant inefficiencies because of the level of disorganization involved. Similarly the larger leap from the compliance phase to the sustaining corporation runs the additional risk of losing some of the advantages to be gained in the strategic proactivity phase. It is possible to lose strategic focus and direction and so place the sustainability of the organization itself at risk. It seems that something like this happened at Interface, the international carpet firm.[24]

We wish to stress that transformational change, unlike most incremental change, involves significant risks. These risks should not be taken lightly as they can endanger the viability of the firm itself and can damage the careers of many involved. There are situations, however, when these risks are warranted: for example, when the core business of the organization is clearly no longer ethical (cigarette companies); when the firm's production processes need to be completely replaced because they are dangerous to the workforce and society (organochlorines); or when there is a significant strategic opportunity that demands major reorganization (alternative energy generation).

The critical questions to be answered in this step are: Where are we going in terms of sustainability? How fast must we make the changes? Can we assemble the resources needed to make this schedule realistic? Where are the critical gaps in our expertise that we must fill? Where is the most resistance likely to occur? How will we know we are succeeding? The answers to these questions form the outline of the emergent change programme. Other useful questions are: Can we identify positive models for the changes we need to make – either within our own organization or in other organizations? What other organizations have attempted to travel this path? Can we access them and assess their level of success? Were their attempts successful or unsuccessful? Where they were successful, what can we learn from their achievements? Where they were unsuccessful, what can we learn from their mistakes? Site visits are often useful in making these assessments and maximizing learning from the experience of others.

In drawing up the programme for change, it is vital to ensure that the sustainability goals adopted are integral to the overall business plan for the organization. Sustainability must be a business imperative, not simply an add-on or option. In transformational change, sustainability initiatives can contribute significantly to business performance, particularly to future corporate repositioning. Von Weizacker *et al.* give a multitude of examples of companies that have dramatically reduced their use of resources and at the same time significantly increased their profitability.[25] In addition, sustainability initiatives can be important in securing the support of key stakeholder groups for the organization's strategy of repositioning itself in new markets. However, other stakeholders may perceive some sustainability initiatives as a threat to their interests. For example, suppliers who find their materials or products bypassed for others with more sustainable characteristics may be alarmed to see their business being diminished. As stated before, transformational change is always a political process. It is important therefore to understand which stakeholders will be important for success and to attempt to secure their support or, if necessary, neutralize their opposition.

One way of securing stakeholder support is to define the value proposition for key stakeholder groups. In 2001 the winner of Australia's 'Good Reputation Index', initiated by two leading Australian newspapers, was Australia Post. Back in the early 1990s it seemed to many that new technologies of communication would take an increasing share of business away from the government instrumentality. Since its corporatization in 1987 the opposite has happened. In a major transformation of its business operations, Australia Post increased its pre-tax profits sixfold to $392 million in 1999–2000 and the proportion of wages to revenue dropped from 67 per cent to 44 per cent. The corporation built on its reputation of trustworthiness and credibility to establish a retailing and delivery culture. It now also operates Australia's largest financial network which processes 48 per cent of the nation's financial transactions. Its value proposition to its customers is to be a one-stop shop for a whole range of commercial services from the traditional postal services to office supplies and the payment of bills.

The questions to answer at this stage are: Where will this change programme or its outcomes add value for this particular group of stakeholders? How could it diminish value, as the stakeholder perceives it? How can the positive value proposition be most effectively communicated to each stakeholder group? How can any negative perceptions be managed to ensure that the programme of change is not undermined by any resulting opposition?

Step 8: Establish the performance criteria for 'compliance plus'

If the change programme is to be seen to contribute significantly to the core business of the organization and to the well-being of the community and the environment, then we need to define the criteria for performance. How shall we judge whether the programme is successful? What performance criteria shall we use for this?

There are two kinds of performance criteria to use; the first is 'output criteria'. What are the outputs we are seeking in terms of such factors as decreased waste or community contribution? The second kind of performance criteria is 'process criteria'. What characteristics of the process of change are we seeking to create (for example, the progressive engagement of key interest groups in the change programme or a more collaborative set of relationships between different organizational units)?

Many change programmes fail to define performance criteria at all and, as a result, they falter or fail. If we don't know what we are trying to achieve or fail to reach agreement on the goals of change, confusion and chaos will reign. Most successful change programmes define output criteria and this helps keep them on track. But in our experience few change programmes define process criteria. However, the quality of the developing change process can be critical in achieving sustainable performance. There is a tendency in transformative change programmes to sacrifice the quality of the change process in the interests of achieving the desired performance outputs quickly. The result can be resentment, cynicism and a failure of key groups to engage and commit to longer-term performance.

Output criteria relate to the following kinds of performance for existing products and services:

- reduced costs, increased profitability;
- added quality;
- innovation, flexibility and speed of initiation and response to market shifts;
- increased market share.

In addition, other criteria may relate to the process of strategically repositioning the organization:

- entry to new markets;
- development of new products and services;
- industry leadership;
- enhanced public profile and reputation;
- creation of a new industry.

Beyond these traditional measures of effective business performance, other criteria might be:

- elimination of waste and sources of pollution;

- building workforce capability to contribute to the development of sustainable operations;
- building workforce commitment to continue to build the company's future sustainability performance;
- development of new environmentally beneficial production processes;
- contributing to strengthening community relationships;
- increasing stakeholder support, including licence to operate and increased trust;
- significantly reducing the organization's ecological footprint.

These outputs may significantly increase the real wealth of the organization. An important issue to be decided early in the change programme is, therefore, how these benefits are to be distributed among the organization's stakeholders. The traditional answer for a listed company is that the increased wealth would be divided between the shareholders and reinvestment in the company's future growth, usually in the form of capital assets. In the new world of business that we have been describing, capital assets are becoming less important than intellectual capital and stakeholder relationships assume greater significance. Therefore the increased wealth represents an opportunity to invest in the further development of the capabilities of employees and in strengthening key stakeholder relationships, rather than increased investment in buildings and hardware.

Process criteria are ways of assessing whether the change process itself is generating the quality of relationships and capabilities needed to sustain future change. Criteria that may be used here include:

- progressive engagement of key individuals and groups, both internally and externally;
- development of concrete, actionable plans for delivery of the outputs above;
- progressive development of skilled and committed change leaders at all levels;
- a climate of trust and more collaborative relationships between organizational subunits;
- a culture of non-defensive learning.

An important issue to be addressed in regard to process quality is the style of change leadership that will be adopted to bring about the desired transformation. Research on change programmes shows that as the scale and speed of change increase, there is a shift to more directive styles of leadership.[26] In addition, the research also shows that the majority of organizational members understand the necessity for this and support it. So in large-scale transformational change, it is not necessary or appropriate that all decisions be made participatively. The executive team needs to decide early in the change programme what issues will be dealt with by executive decision and are therefore non-negotiable. Safety, for example, is generally regarded as a non-negotiable value. Similarly, the team should decide what kinds of decisions will be made participatively, that is, where individuals, groups, stakeholders or their representatives will be encouraged to participate, influence or determine outcomes. The rationale for this decision making approach needs to be clearly understood throughout the organization.

However, if management is to take a decisive lead, their actions must consistently model their rhetoric. As Alan Pears has pointed out, it is important for senior managers to set visible examples: 'Where senior managers drive fuel-guzzlers and insist that reports be submitted on non-recycled paper printed single-sided, it is difficult for staff to believe the organization is serious about larger environmental issues.'[27]

Step 9: Launch and manage the transformational change programme

The reader may be wondering whether we would ever get to this point, that is, of doing what we set out to do. Is all this taxing groundwork necessary? Why not simply get on with it and launch the change programme in the first place? We can only reiterate that launching transformative change programmes is a risky endeavour and that a great deal of the success comes from careful preparation in advance. While this preparation consumes time, it can be carried out efficiently and significantly raises the chances of a successful outcome. Managing a change programme has some similarity to painting a house: a large part of the business of doing a first-rate job lies in the careful preparation of surfaces and selection of the appropriate paints. The painting is the easier part.

There is an extensive literature on how to conduct successful change programmes. We do not intend to cover this in any detail but refer the reader who is unfamiliar with the literature to read selectively from the list we provide (see Further reading, pp. 305–6). Here we shall simply outline some of the key steps in a programme designed to move the organization rapidly along the path to sustainability:

- Create and communicate the main focus of the programme so that all in the organization understand the direction and rationale for change (for example, BP = Beyond Petroleum; Woolworths = the Fresh Food People).
- Map the main subprojects in sufficient detail to clarify for change agents how the change is expected to happen, ensuring that the link to business strategies is clear.
- Build a network of change agents (line and staff personnel, internal and external consultants); break the overall change programme down into projects that can be handled by multi-disciplinary task forces led by these change agents.
- Establish a change co-ordination team consisting of executives and other strategically located change agents; clarify authority for decision making and accountabilities against goals and time lines; pay particular attention to the roles of frontline supervisors and ensure that they have a clear role to play.
- Monitor the emerging trajectory of change and remediate where necessary; the monitoring should be of both output and process performance criteria; seek and respond to grassroots feedback.
- Create and celebrate early wins and publicly reward those responsible for them.
- Progressively enlarge the sphere of engagement – go with the energy; remember that opposition is a natural part of the engagement process (apathy and cynicism are more serious threats).
- Create momentum, feeding in resources where necessary.
- Communicate and dramatize success; foster transparency and truth.
- Ensure that, as the capabilities for organizational reshaping develop, they are reinforced and progressively translated into intellectual capital.
- As change goals are reached, consolidate them in new operational systems under the control of committed and competent operational managers (not change agents) and operational teams.
- Ensure that the operational managers achieve efficiencies as the new systems are debugged and routinized.
- Check that key stakeholders perceive that the promised value propositions are being delivered; consolidate their support.
- Build reward systems that reinforce and renew the core values of the new culture and reinforce the behaviours that support the emerging system. These behaviours then become the cultural norms supporting the next stage of sustainability development. It is vital that achievement of sustainability outcomes is a major criterion in staff assessment for career advancement.

Step 10: Maintain the rage

In a dynamic world, change is an ongoing process. When the goals have been achieved, the change process may become incremental rather than transformative, but change continues. Organizations ossify unless they continue to change with their environments. Therefore it is essential to continue the process of environmental monitoring and identification of emerging stakeholder interests around issues of sustainability. The organizational members need to ensure that the organization maintains its leading edge position; it is easy to fall behind the leading edge through becoming complacent.

Those organizations that move to the stage of becoming sustaining corporations can improve their performance even further by contributing to a growing industrial ecology. As discussed earlier, an industrial ecology is an active network of organizations for exchanging ideas, products and services in sustainable ways. The best-known example of this is an eco-industrial park in the town of Kalundborg in Denmark, discussed in Chapter 5. Several companies in the town created a system of exchange whereby the byproducts ('wastes') from one company's operation became a resource or raw material for another.[28] Networks and alliances of organizations like this, working actively to promote and model sustainable practices, are epicentres for the development of the new sustainable economy. As their success becomes apparent, they contribute to a developing climate of political and community support for the enhancement of human capability and environmental regeneration. Any optimistic scenario for the future depends on widespread transformational change designed to bring about a different form of economy to that existing today. Networks of transformed organizations are a major dynamic for transforming the economy as a whole.

In the box below we have outlined ten steps to creating a successful transformational change programme. These steps are distilled from the experience of many change agents working on a range of transformational change programmes and adapted to the task of moving organizations rapidly towards sustainability. They are a useful guide but in reality, as we have noted, the change process will be more chaotic than this indicates. Nevertheless the steps can help us assess our progress in managing change and they set a direction to work towards. Leadership is the decisive factor that determines whether we succeed, and we turn to that next in Chapter 9.

Ten steps to creating a successful transformational change programme

1 Know where you are now.
2 Develop the vision – the dream organization.
3 Identify the gap.
4 Assess the readiness for change.
5 Set the scene for action.
6 Secure basic compliance first.
7 Move beyond compliance.
8 Establish the performance criteria for 'compliance plus'.
9 Launch and manage the transformational change programme.
10 Maintain the rage.

Notes

1 J. Elkington, *Cannibals with Forks: The Triple Bottom Line of the 21st Century Business*, Oxford: Capstone, 1999.
2 R. Quinn, *Deep Change: Discovering the Leader Within*, San Francisco: Jossey-Bass, 1996, p. 3.
3 I. Palmer and R. Dunford, 'Who says change can be managed? Positions, perspectives and problematics', unpublished paper presented at the International Research Workshop 'New Ways of Thinking about Organizational Change: Discourses, Strategies, Processes, Forms', University of Sydney, 26–27 Nov. 2001.
4 D. Dunphy and D. Stace, *Under New Management: Australian Organizations in Transition*, Sydney: McGraw-Hill, 1990; D. Stace and D. Dunphy, *Beyond the Boundaries: Leading and Re-creating the Successful Enterprise*, 2nd edn, Sydney: McGraw-Hill, 2001.
5 A. de Geus, 'The living company', *Harvard Business Review*, 1997, March–April, 51–9.
6 S.L. Brown and K.M. Eisenhardt, 'The art of continuous change: linking complexity theory and time-paced evolution in relentlessly shifting organizations', *Administrative Science Quarterly*, 1997, 42, March, 1–34, esp. p. 1.
7 L. Gratton, *Living Strategy: Putting People at the Heart of Corporate Purpose*, London: Financial Times/Prentice-Hall, 2000, p. 18.
8 Byong-Wook Lee, 'Waste costing for a Korean steel producer', in K. Green, P. Groenewegen and P.S. Hoffman (eds) *Ahead of the Curve: Cases of Innovation in Environmental Management*, Dordrecht, Netherlands: Kluwer Academic Publishers, 2001, esp. pp. 63–7, 71.
9 Stace and Dunphy, *Beyond the Boundaries*, pp. 71–3.

10 J. Garreau, 'Point men for a revolution: can the marines survive a shift from hierarchies to networks?', *Washington Post*, 6 March 1999, A01.

11 L. Gratton, *Living Strategy*.

12 J. Benveniste, 'Quality of work, home and family life', in D. Dunphy, J. Benveniste, A. Griffiths and P. Sutton (eds) *Sustainability: The Corporate Challenge of the 21st Century*, Sydney: Allen and Unwin, 2000, pp. 102–23, esp. p. 117.

13 Stace and Dunphy, *Beyond the Boundaries*, p. 83.

14 J. Benveniste and D. Dunphy, *The Path Towards Sustainability: A Case Study of Placer Dome Asia Pacific*, Centre for Corporate Change, Australian Graduate School of Management, University of New South Wales, 1999.

15 N. Roome, 'The role of visioning in environmental management and organizational change: the case of Abitibi-Price', in K. Green, P. Groenewegen and P. S. Hofman (eds) *Ahead of the Curve: Cases of Innovation in Environmental Management*, Dordrecht, Netherlands: Kluwer Academic Publishers, 2001, pp. 19–40, esp. p. 29.

16 D. Chatterjee, *Leading Consciously: A Pilgrimage Towards Self Mastery*, Oxford:Viva Books and Butterworth-Heinemann, 1999, p. 39.

17 B. Smith and J. Yanowitz, 'Sustainable innovation and change: the learning-based path to growth', *Prism*, 1998, 4th quarter, 35–45.

18 D. Goleman, *Emotional Intelligence*, New York: Bantam Books, 1996; D. Zohar and I. Marshall, *Spiritual Intelligence: The Ultimate Intelligence*, London: Bloomsbury, 2000.

19 Gratton, *Living Strategy*, pp. 4–6, 32–6.

20 Stace and Dunphy, *Beyond the Boundaries*, pp. 138–53.

21 See D. Hock, *Birth of the Chaordic Age*, San Francisco: Barrett-Koehler, 1999.

22 C. Handy, *The Elephant and the Flea: Looking Backwards to the Future*, London: Random House, 2000, p. 82.

23 Ibid.

24 For an account of this, see J. Elkington, *The Chrysalis Economy: How Citizen CEOs and Corporations Can Fuse Values and Value Creation*, Oxford: Capstone, 2001, pp. 220–3.

25 E. von Weizacker, A.B. Lovins and L.H. Lovins, *Factor 4: Doubling Wealth – Halving Resource Use*, Sydney: Allen and Unwin, 1997.

26 Stace and Dunphy, *Beyond the Boundaries*, pp. 106–18.

27 A. Pears, 'Towards ecological sustainability: technologies and processes', in D. Dunphy, J. Benveniste, A. Griffiths and P. Sutton (eds) *Sustainability: The Corporate Challenge of the 21st Century*, Sydney: Allen and Unwin, 2000, pp. 167–90, esp. p. 183.

28 H. Tibbs, 'Industrial ecology: an environmental agenda for industry', *Whole Earth Review*, 1995, September–October, 120–34.

9 Leading towards sustainability

- Facing up to the future
- Key factors in change agent competency
- Achieving mastery
- Starting with self-leadership
- Seeking cosmocentric consciousness
- Building or assembling the skills needed for diagnosis and action
- Creating dialogue and shared scenarios
- Identifying and dealing with resistance to change
- Learning as we go
- Making it happen
- Contributing to living networks
- Who are the leaders/change agents?
- Building alliances of change agents
- Constructing the sustainability agenda
- Owning your power and changing corporate culture
- Putting the jigsaw puzzle together

Facing up to the future

Leadership is the creation of new realities. In this final chapter we discuss the leadership of change and the roles that different kinds of change agents can play in constructing the new reality of the sustainable corporation. Transforming the way we do business is no minor task and will require the inspiration, energies and skills of more people than are currently engaged in the task. If we are to create a sustainable world, we need many more effective leaders. Despite powerful forces moving global society towards sustainable practices, the difficulties of making the shift are formidable. There are many people who see their interests threatened by these developments and who have a strong investment in maintaining current practices. This is particularly true of those who have deeply entrenched positions of power in the traditional system. In the face of the principalities and powers of this world, of presidents and politicians, terrorists, drug lords and arms merchants, multinational magnates and media barons, star war scenarios, germ warfare and genetic manipulation, we may well ask: What is the value, if any, of *my* puny actions?

In raising the issue of change leadership, we cannot ignore how much easier it is to accept the status quo, to respond to our fear of change and our desire for certainty, to opt out rather than to engage actively in attempting to change the organizational world. Most of us, if we are honest, would rather let someone else lead in this kind of endeavour. Change of the order we are advocating here threatens us with uncertainty and chaos. It is much easier to hold on to traditional ways of doing things and to accept the leadership of others who don't question the status quo. The past, because of its familiarity, seems to offer us security – more security, at least, than a divergent and uncharted future. However, as we have argued throughout this book, many past practices are unsustainable. If we want the world we know and love to survive, we must change it. If we are to survive and thrive ourselves, we too must change. To change, however, requires the rawest kind of courage.

Paradoxically, only by relinquishing the security of the known, letting go, and choosing to risk the unknown can we realize the full potential of our past. The acrobat, flying through the heights of the circus tent, must let go of the trapeze bar before turning in space to grasp the bar she hopes her partner has launched towards her with perfect timing. The excitement, beauty and meaning of the act come from the completion of the full trajectory.

Choosing to lead change similarly involves courage, risk taking and the development of high levels of skill. These are the focus of our discussion in this chapter. The chapter is also designed to help you answer some basic questions about your own potential role as a leader of sustainable change:

- How do I equip myself to be an effective leader?
- Where shall I start?
- Who can I work with to have the most impact?

> We are entering an era, I believe, when world class enterprises will build . . . sophistication in understanding and tapping the intelligence and spirit of human beings.
>
> *Source*: P. Senge[1]

Key factors in change agent competency

What do we need to be effective change leaders? We need clarity of vision, knowledge of what we wish to change and the skills to implement the changes. But none of these can be fully effective without maturity and wisdom. In the end it is who we are, not what we know or can do that makes the crucial difference in effecting organizational change. Ideally change agents need the following characteristics – but note the provisos that follow.

Goal clarity

'I know what outcomes I want to produce.' Yes, we do need to know what we want to achieve, but our understanding of the goal doesn't have to be precise when we begin. What we need is a 'strategic intent', a direction, a deep, intuitive response to the organizational situation in which we find ourselves, an aspiration to nudge our organizational world a little closer to the ideal of sustainability. Jaworski tells of a meeting he had with physicist David Bohm in 1989 – a meeting that proved to be a life-changing experience. Bohm spoke about how 'thought creates the world . . . we participate in how reality unfolds'.[2] Jaworski went on to read Bohm's work and was particularly struck by his concept of 'implicate order' – the notion that 'the totality of existence is enfolded within each "fragment" of space and time – whether it be a single object, thought or event'.[3] As change agents, our role is to be part of the process by which the implicate order unfolds. We don't control this process; we are co-creators; midwives aiding the birth of a new order.

Role clarity

'I know what to do to produce change.' Of course, when we start, we often do not know what to do. We may not have a clue about what to do to make change happen. This is a paradox we face as change agents – we need to find a viable and effective role to play in midwifing the future but everything seems to conspire to block us. Reflecting on my own experience as a change agent, I realize that I floundered about for years, often getting in my own way and others'. My estimate is that it took about eight years to learn the most important lesson of 'not doing', that is, understanding that most of the time I cannot significantly affect the course of change and am better not doing anything at all for a while but wait, listen, watch and reflect on the process.[4] Out of that reflective process, an understanding emerges of the role I can play, and where and how I can be effective. Timing and skill then become all important. Disciplined inaction is an opportunity to cultivate the inner stillness through which we appreciate the unfolding of the implicate order and our role in it. And then we must act decisively.

Relevant knowledge

'I have or can access the knowledge required to produce the outcomes I want.' Corporate change processes demand depth of knowledge and in the area of sustainability that knowledge is often not gained easily. Sustainability cuts right across traditional disciplinary boundaries. In a particular project, for example, we may need knowledge of the political processes of the organization, technical knowledge about energy conservation, water purification and chemical pollutants, knowledge about the attitudes of key external stakeholders. It would be an unusual person who had this knowledge at the beginning of a change programme. But we don't need all the knowledge before we start; we can acquire it as we go along, in partnership with others more knowledgeable than ourselves in some of these areas, and learn as we go.

Relevant competencies and resources

'I have or can assemble the skills and resources to make it happen.' Again, we may not have the skills we need when we first take up a role as organizational change agent. Acquiring skills is a lifetime endeavour. So, we need to be realistic about the skills we have and start the change process in a way that builds on our current skill level. However, the only effective way to learn skills is through experimentation and practice. To acquire them, we take faltering steps at first but, with practice, our steps become firm and purposeful. Mentors and models help so, if we are relatively unskilled, another criterion of where to start the change process is to find others who do have the necessary skills and work with them. To begin, we need only a subset of the skills demanded by the full change programme and, if we work with others, we do not need the full repertoire of skills ourselves.

Self-esteem

'I believe I can do it.' Sometimes this one is the toughest call of all, but a passionate belief in the profound importance of the change we are initiating is a great help. Being a change agent is not for the faint hearted. Emotional resilience is a fundamental requirement. We are often called on to persist in the face of adversity, derision, contempt, anger. Changing entrenched power structures can be a career-threatening experience. But then, abandoning the cause of sustainability is a planet-threatening experience. If we choose to undergo some adversity, at least in the end we have the satisfaction of knowing that we stand for life, for hope, for a viable future for us all.

If we believed we need the five characteristics so starkly listed above without the added provisos, we would never start to try to change corporations. These are ideals to be worked towards; they set a direction for our learning – they are not the starting line we must cross to begin. They define mastery in this field and we discuss below the path to mastery – it is a long path and we learn primarily by doing. If we choose well, we also learn by apprenticeship to others more experienced and skilled than ourselves and by finding models and mentors. But definitely by doing.

We need to learn to live with ambiguity and a degree of chaos. Managing corporate change is rather like white-water rafting or surfing. The first lesson is not to try to control the environment but to move with it. Like rafting or surfing, success in change leadership comes from being willing to change our internal psychological world.

Achieving mastery

But that's only Change Leadership 101. As in any field of serious endeavour, learning of this kind is a lifetime commitment. We start as novices and may achieve mastery but that takes effort, time and commitment. Table 9.1 outlines the stages in achieving mastery as a change agent.

Mastery involves bringing all our awareness, knowledge, skills and energy to bear on the task before us; but it implies a history of disciplined learning, experimentation and practice over a significant period of time. Master potters, tennis players and ballet dancers, for example, are not

Table 9.1 *Stages in achieving change agent mastery*

1. Novice: learning 'the rules'	We seek clear guidelines for how to act in different situations; for example, many novices are drawn to The Natural Step programs which offer simple rules for instituting sustainable practices. We seek the codified knowledge of others who have done it.
2. Advanced beginner: beyond rules to strategies	We realize that in many situations, the rules don't work. Making change is more complex than we thought. Rules become more blurred and evolve into thoughtful strategies.
3. Competence: disciplined effectiveness	We develop a 'feel' for the complexity of change, select cues and respond to them on the basis of our accumulating experience. Our knowledge now is more tacit; our strategies are now evolving to include deeper levels of awareness.
4. Proficiency: fluid, effortless performance	We have internalized the strategies and they are backed up with high levels of skill. Intuition now dominates and reason is secondary.
5. Mastery: acting from our deepest intuition with confidence and flow	We become one with the changes we are making and are changing ourselves and our organizational world at the same time. Our inner and outer worlds are one. What we do often seems effortless and spontaneous.

created overnight or by two-day training courses. There are no short cuts, no quick fixes. But as we achieve mastery, we often have the ability to create the reality we want because we respect and work with the change process. We are not frustrated by it but accept that what happens is what we get to work with. The path before us opens to a series of opportunities rather than problems.

Chatterjee writes eloquently of the need for change agents to develop personal mastery:

> Personal mastery is a journey towards a destination we may call an *integral being*. Integral beings experience a life of oneness with themselves and their universe. They act from the wholeness of this experience. There is harmony and a unique synchronicity between their beliefs and their actions. Their bodies, minds, and senses orchestrate themselves to the effortless rhythms of the universe.[5]

Similarly Handy talks of change agents as 'alchemists' who don't react to events but shape them. He characterizes them as passionate about what they are doing because they have a conviction of its importance. He also sees them as being able to leap beyond the rational and logical and stick with their dream, if necessary against the 'evidence'.[6] In fact, they are changing the world as they go, building excitement and momentum. Like water finding its way down a hillside, they simply go around obstacles and dissolve resistance.

Starting with self-leadership

Being a change agent means living in and between two worlds. One is the world of inner experience, of personal meaning, of selfhood. The other is the outer world of action. The inner world is the real challenge for change agents. Paradoxically the secret to changing the world about us is only discovered within ourselves. Mahatma Gandhi had a very clear idea about where his leadership began. He said: 'I must first be the change I want to bring about in my world.'[7] Our ability to model in our own lives – in our attitudes, words and actions – the changes we wish to bring about: this is the most powerful intervention we ever make. Our integrity is the test of the worth of what we advocate. After all, if we cannot bring about the changes within ourselves, do we have the right to ask others to make these changes? And if we cannot make the changes ourselves, what chance do we have of success in changing others?

Quinn writes of how important it is for organizational change agents to make deep change at the personal level: 'To make deep personal change is to develop a new paradigm, a new self, one that is more effectively aligned with today's realities.'[8] He sees a vital link in our ability to make deep change within ourselves and the effective leadership of organizational change. Leaders who are prepared to make deep change within themselves, in Quinn's view, make transformative organizational change possible.

Recent research on leadership effectiveness reinforces the notion that change leadership requires particular kinds of psychological strengths. In particular, Luthans draws on developments in positive psychology – a field which emphasizes building on people's personal strengths rather than focusing on their weaknesses. He reviews research into the contribution of personal strengths to performance improvement in the workplace. He finds that these characteristics include 'realistic hope, optimism, subjective wellbeing/happiness and emotional intelligence'.[9] These are, of course, the characteristics of mature, emotionally healthy human beings as well as effective change agents.

Through reviewing the change agent literature and discussions with change practitioners, Dunphy has identified the following as important personal characteristics for change agents:

- personal resilience and persistence;
- realistic self-esteem, self-direction and initiative;
- tolerance of ambiguity;
- flexibility and adaptability;
- clear focus;
- enthusiasm and motivation;
- ability to inspire others;
- political awareness and sensitivity;
- empathy;
- sense of humour;
- a helicopter view;
- commitment to continuous learning.[10]

We all fall short of this ideal, of course, but attempting change leadership is one way to acquire these characteristics.

Seeking cosmocentric consciousness

In bringing about deep change leading to sustainability, the old Newtonian worldview of a mechanistic, atomized universe doesn't help; nor does the 'objectivist' stance, so deeply inculcated by a traditional scientific worldview, based on the myth that knowledge is created by scientists who stand outside the universe they are studying.

Chatterjee draws on Indian spiritual tradition in describing the importance of meditation in helping us relinquish both our belief that the world is made up of discrete objects and the egocentricity associated with this belief. In his view, we can progress from being egocentric personalities attached to material objects to cosmocentric individuals in a harmonious relationship with nature. The egocentric person feels empowered by the objects he or she can possess. By contrast, cosmocentric consciousness frees us from the clutter of objects and possessions so that the universal consciousness that flows through the entire universe also flows through us.[11]

Albert Einstein wrote eloquently in the same vein:

> A human being is part of the whole, called by us the Universe, a part limited in time and space. He experiences himself, his thoughts and

feelings, as something separated from the rest – a kind of optical delusion of his consciousness. This delusion is a kind of prison, restricting us to our personal desires and to affection for a few persons nearest to us. Our task must be to free from this prison by widening our circle of compassion to embrace all living creatures and the whole of nature in its beauty.[12]

This mystical view is also supported by many other leading physicists who have been involved in redefining scientific views of the universe.[13] Jaworski calls this type of awareness 'unity consciousness'. Unity consciousness releases us from the cultural boundaries we have internalized and allows us to experience the interrelatedness of the universe and to become part of its unfolding future.[14]

Jaworski speaks of an experience in Chartres cathedral that led him to think about two different notions of freedom. The first is 'freedom from', that is the freedom to escape oppressive circumstances. He then turns to the other kind of freedom:

> But another notion of freedom was beginning to make its way into my consciousness at this time, far below the surface – the freedom to follow my life's purpose with all the commitment I could muster, while at the same time, allowing life's creative forces to move through me without my control, without 'making it happen'. As I was to learn over time, this is by far a much more powerful way of operating.[15]

Organizations too have their collective consciousness. Quinn writes of the change agent listening to the inner voice of the organization which calls for the realignment of internal values and external realities. He regards the inner voice of the organization as 'the most potent source of power in the organization':[16] 'Preparation, reflection, and courage are needed to hear the inner voice. The inner voice will provide direction if people have the courage to listen and the commitment to change.'[17] In our view, responding to the inner voice includes voicing the unspeakable – speaking for the interpersonal underworld that exists in most organizations but fails to gain official recognition. This is the world of collective fear and despair, of latent rebellion, of long-remembered anger, of irreverent humour and cynicism. Giving voice to these aspects of the organization's life is often like pointing out that the emperor has no clothes. This is also the world of high dreams and ideals: people's hopes and yearnings for more fulfilling and meaningful work. These aspirations have often been submerged by disappointment and discouraging experiences but can rise to the surface again with compelling power.

To develop cosmocentric consciousness is to care, and caring is an important part of effective leadership. Effective change leaders are passionate about the changes they support; their actions are value driven. They care about the environment, they care about the community, they care about the individuals with whom they work.

Empathy, caring and love are not popular terms in the current managerial vocabulary. They are, however, words we can dare to speak and to live. Professor Leo Buscaglia, an outstanding academic educator, recounts how deans from other schools would call to invite him to give a visiting lecture. They would eventually ask him for the title of his lecture and, when he said 'Love', there would be an embarrassed silence on the other end of the phone, followed by a remark like: 'Could you make that Love comma As A Behavior Modifier?'.[18]

True knowledge of the world and of others comes from empathetic understanding, not cold objectivity. Love is the matrix from which community is born; love creates the 'we' from the 'I'. From conception to old age, maturity and health are products of supportive social relationships. Without empathy, caring, compassion, respect, tolerance and love, organizations cease to be communities, trust dissolves and all relationships become calculative. As we have discussed earlier in this book, the nature of modern organizations means that they don't operate effectively without trust. But trust does not grow automatically; in organizational life, it is built consciously, purposefully over time by those who care.

Cosmocentric consciousness, or spiritual intelligence, helps us connect to the emerging forms of the future.[19] Without this kind of consciousness it is hard to find the future – with it, the future seems inescapable. The future is within us and around us. Its shape is already coalescing in our dreams, emerging from our play, emerging in the hasty decisions we make as we face overload at work. The future is forming here in our minds, already shaping the actions of our hands and moving our feet forwards. The world about us is also changing and we are connected with powerful forces that are already moving our world, and us, towards sustainability. The clues to a sustainable future are already there for us to find: in the next office, the factory up the street, the children's project at home, our own imagination. The future is a living presence now if we are prepared to respond to it.

Building or assembling the skills needed for diagnosis and action

Self-leadership is necessary, but it is not enough. As well as self-knowledge and an empathetic understanding of others, effective change leaders need skills.

First on the list are skills associated with effective diagnosis. If we are to attempt to change an organization we must first understand where the organization is on the path to sustainability and where it needs to go. Making the right diagnosis is as important in achieving organizational well-being as it is in achieving individual physical health. One of the major challenges for organizational change agents is that they usually have to make the analysis themselves and they have to do it on the run and *in situ*. It would be nice if our organizational change efforts began with a neatly packaged Harvard Business School case analysis, but unfortunately they don't.

If we work in the organization, then we are part of what we are analysing. Our viewpoint will be biased by the position we occupy – the view from below is always different, for example, from the view from above; the industrial engineer's view is different from that of the salesperson in the field. On the other hand, if we are external to the organization – for example, a consultant – we may have a more open mind; but we don't have the advantage of inside information. Whatever our role, as we start actively to find out more about the organization, looking at records, interviewing personnel and so on, we are already intervening in the ongoing system.

So forget objectivity in the traditional sense – we are inextricably part of the system we are trying to change. Forget also the models found in most management texts where managers, in particular, are assumed to be outside the system and all-powerful. This kind of model suggests that all we have to do to change organizations is to develop a plan and promulgate it throughout the organization. The rest of the organization is assumed to be rather like a piano, ready to respond with alacrity to the skilled interventions of those in authority who hold the exact script to be played out.

This is a fantasy – a pervasive fantasy, but one far from reality. The reality is that organizations are not machines but fields of political activity in which even the actions of CEOs can disappear with little trace. Whatever our role and our authority, we are not the only centre of power in the organization. And the organization is not waiting statically like a piano. Large organizations are more like ocean liners: they are moving with momentum on a trajectory powered by past decisions and by collective experiences embodied in a corporate culture. Change agents are intervening in an ongoing system that often has its own compelling internal logic built up over years and embodied in the programmed responses of people who have been there for years. It is also part of a larger world which at the same time is both holding it in place and pressuring it to change.

So we are studying a dynamic system of which we are part or become a part as we study it. We can't put it in a laboratory, take it apart and analyse it under a microscope. All we can do is immerse ourselves in it, understand that our own view will be biased and try to offset that by an empathetic identification with others who occupy very different positions. We can also gather data that can expand or contradict our biases. Moving around the organization helps, as does cultivating an open mind, observing and listening. The skills of action research are the most useful. In some cases we may wish to add more formal means of analysis such as surveys and financial analysis. These can help but are no substitute for being there with full awareness.

More specifically the action research and diagnostic skills we need are:

1 *a well developed systematic theoretical position*, a framework or multiple frameworks; that is, a model of how organizations operate which helps us select the kind of data that are useful for understanding and for future action. This model is always partial and limited and so we must be open to revising it on the basis of experience;
2 *a model of the ideal sustainable organization* combined with openness to others' ideal models. The future is mostly a collective creation, emerging from the active dialogue and interaction of interested parties. We need to be as clear as we can on what we want so that we can engage fully with others in that dialogue; but we need to be open to any emerging shared vision. Of course, there may be competing visions and resistance to visions in general: conflict is simply an element of the unfolding drama through which the future is defined: conflict is a signal that something important is at stake; it is a measure of progress on the path, not the end of the path;
3 *the ability to question and listen to others* for factual, value-based and emotive information; all three kinds of information are useful. Moving to sustainability necessarily involves values and emotions as well as facts;

4 *the ability to use varied data sources and methods of analysis*, to apply critical insight and make balanced judgements. If we want to make a map, it is useful to view the landscape from different viewpoints – triangulation increases accuracy;

5 *the ability to convey a concise diagnosis* to others in their terms. The emerging field of sustainability studies is already developing its own language – professional and technical jargon; some of this is useful as shorthand and for technical precision. But if we are to influence others, we need to be able to translate what is important into the everyday language of the workplace;

6 *the ability to monitor and evaluate the change process*: the process of diagnosis does not stop when the action begins. Diagnosis becomes even more crucial in checking whether we are achieving what we set out to achieve and whether we need to change the path we travel along as we reach a fuller understanding of where we need to go.

Diagnostic skills help define the path to sustainability. Moving down that path requires change agents to develop other skill sets too, particularly the skills of effective communication, of managing stakeholder relationships and project management:

1 *skills of effective communication*: the willingness to listen and ask skilful questions; the ability to adopt multiple viewpoints; the commitment to keep people informed and 'in the picture'; the ability to communicate clearly and simply with others in speech and writing; the ability to use images and emotions as well as facts in communicating with others;

2 *skills of managing stakeholder relationships*: direction setting (visioning) and defining the scope of responsibilities for parts of the vision; influencing and networking; delegating; developing, mentoring and coaching others; performance management and monitoring; team building;

3 *skills of project management*: making and taking opportunities; updating technical and organizational knowledge; problem solving; resourcing.

Figure 9.1 summarizes our analysis of the skills needed to become an effective change agent. These skills will be in great demand as more organizations embrace what Hirsh and Sheldrake refer to as 'inclusive leadership'.[20] Inclusive leadership, as they define it, derives from adopting the stakeholder perspective on organizations. It involves managers developing and maintaining an interactive exchange with all those who have a stake in the organization: investors, employees, suppliers, customers, the community, and representatives of the environment and future generations. Organizations need to perform instrumental tasks and to reach financial objectives. But this is most effectively achieved by creating a wider set of outcomes that meet the needs of key stakeholders.[21] The skills of relationship building will be particularly critical as organizations move forward on the path to sustainability.

Figure 9.1 *Skills of effective change agents*

Creating dialogue and shared scenarios

One of the central tasks of change agents is the creation of visioning capabilities in the organization. Gratton writes that 'the capacity to create and develop a vision of the future that is compelling and engaging [is] at the very centre of creating a human approach to organizations'.[22] But where does the vision come from?

Vision emerges from dialogue – both inner dialogue within ourselves and dialogue within the organization and with its external stakeholders. The task of the change agent is to work with others to create new meaning, for new meaning creates new realities. This is the process that Weick calls 'sensemaking'.[23] Dialogue is not chatter but rather engagement at the deepest level with ourselves and with others. Dialogue begins with cultivating awareness and with listening; it continues with responsiveness and an exchange that is a catalyst for creative change.[24]

Dialogue can change people's perceptions of themselves and of their organization. From these new perceptions a sense of collective identity and purpose emerges that can renew or transform the existing culture of the organization. If this happens, the leadership of change passes from the handful of change agents who began the change process to a much larger network within the organization. Leaders create leaders.

Leadership is about 'bringing everyone along' in a balanced way, not just in their minds so they understand it, but emotionally as well, in their hearts, so they are really energized and identify with it, and they themselves take part in the leadership.

Source: Frank Blount, former CEO, Telstra[25]

Our own experience in working with effective change leaders at all levels of organizations is that they have a profound belief in the capability of others. This belief manifests itself through challenging others to contribute even beyond what they thought was their best and supporting them in doing this. Typically, others say of such leaders: 'You know, he (she) believed in me more than I believed in myself. Through him (her) I learned that I could accomplish much greater things than I ever thought possible.' This is true empowerment and it is part of the process of creating organizations where everyone has the opportunity to lead in developing a sustainable workplace that offers exciting and meaningful work.

However, some conflicts of interests in organizations are intractable. When this is the case, leadership becomes the art of achieving what you believe is the best possible outcome in the circumstances, even if that does not match your ideal. Negotiations and compromise may be necessary to produce small wins that can be built on later. A general rule for change agents is that if you can't go around it, over it or under it, then negotiate with it.

Identifying and dealing with resistance to change

All change agents encounter resistance to the changes they attempt to introduce. There is an extensive literature on resistance to change and how to deal with it. Much of it is written for senior executives and embodies the assumption that positive change is mainly initiated by senior executives, who encounter resistance to change from middle management or the workforce. Our own experience is that senior executives are as resistant to change as anyone else and the initiative for change often comes from elsewhere in the organization. The reality is that most people resist change when others are attempting to change them; few do when they feel that they are in charge of change.

People are particularly likely to resist change when they see it as threatening their interests and when they believe that their knowledge and skills may be made irrelevant as changes take place. As we move towards sustainability, there will be those whose interests are threatened and whose current knowledge and skills become obsolete. Not all resistance to change is irrational. As change agents we need to understand that change is a political process in which people's power and status are implicated. There will always be those whose identification with the old order is so strong that they will actively oppose or passively resist change towards the new. There can also be legitimate disagreements – value conflicts – about the best way to proceed in progressing sustainability: disagreements about priorities, about facts such as the potential danger of certain substances, about strategies and tactics for moving forward. As change agents, we need to work to create an evolving consensus among interested parties. Active engagement of those who will be affected by the changes is often the most effective way forward. However, it does not always work. There can be delays, obfuscations, sidetracks, subversions. As in all fields of endeavour, persistence is a large part of success and persistence comes from a deep commitment to a meaningful view of the future.

Learning as we go

Quinn recalls a time when he and a student were writing a case study of a company and interviewed the CEO. The CEO recounted the story of the company's first five years as if it had been the unfolding of a clear strategic plan. This didn't match Quinn's understanding of how the changes took place and he challenged the CEO by giving his own version: Quinn saw it as a rather chaotic learning process. The CEO was somewhat taken aback by this, but then smiled and said: 'It's true, we built the bridge as we walked on it.'[26] Initiating and managing a change process, particularly in the area of sustainability where there are no standard models, will always mean building the bridge as we walk on it. Planning is important but it will be an evolving process and, despite our best efforts, the implementation will sometimes be disorganized and discontinuous. Learning as we go is the way we become skilled change agents.

Making it happen

The implementation of change requires relentless attention to detail. Rowledge *et al.* describe the implementation process of instituting life cycle management at Daimler Chrysler. Part of Daimler's programme to move to compliance plus involved deciding what restricted substances to track. They identified 1,700 substances of concern in their products and operations. Careful examination of regulations and scientific evidence on these substances led them to classify these substances into two groups – tier two and tier one, according to their estimate of the seriousness of the risks they posed. There were 103 tier one (high-risk) substances. For each of these substances, targets for recycling were identified and incorporated into the firm's product development strategy. Subsequently this has been used, in design and production, to select between alternative materials, parts and processes. This was simply one part of a change programme directed at achieving compliance.[27]

Disciplined application to detail underlies successful change implementation.

Contributing to living networks

An important part of making change happen is networking with like-minded people. Change agents spend real time in building networks to provide information about the systems they are working in, to act as channels of influence and for support in what is an emotionally demanding endeavour. But where do we find like-minded people?

Values researcher Ray has identified three major groups in the USA whom he refers to as modernists, heartlanders and cultural creatives. The modernists embrace mainstream materialist values, try to acquire property and money, value winners and are cynical about idealism and caring for others; the heartlanders hold conservative values, reject modernism, favour traditional gender roles and fundamentalist religion, are volunteers who care for others; the cultural creatives reject modernism and support the values of an integral culture that seeks to integrate life on the basis of diversity. They have a well-developed social consciousness, are optimistic and committed to family, community, internationalism, feminism and the environment. They are concerned about health, personal growth and spirituality. Cultural creatives share with modernists openness to change and, like heartlanders, care about community and personal relationships.[28] Ray's surveys estimate that 47 per cent of the US population are modernists, 29 per cent are heartlanders and 24 per cent are cultural creatives.

We expect that a disproportionate number of leaders in sustainable change programmes will be drawn from the ranks of the cultural creatives. Clearly, what Ray calls 'integral culture' is a value set that supports the views we have espoused in this book. Ray argues that there are about 50 million cultural creatives in the USA and that they are the leading edge of cultural change in the country. It seems that there are at least that number in Europe also.[29] We are not alone.

Other studies of changing values support these findings of a significant value shift occurring on a global scale. For example, Ronald Inglehart analysed data from the 1990–1 World Values Survey and showed a shift towards the values of an integral culture in a number of societies. He concluded that there was a global trend towards postmodern values that includes less interest in economic gain, less confidence in hierarchical institutions and a greater commitment to sustainability. The value shift also involves a search for more personal meaning and a deeper sense of purpose in life.[30]

Part of our networking can be a process of finding those who share these values so that we create the interpersonal links that are part of the flexible architecture of the sustainability movement. We can build the momentum for change most readily through networks of those who are committed to the cluster of values that support sustainability.

However, if this is the limit of our networking, we shall fail. It is just as vital to build networks with those who don't share our values for they too have to be part of the process of building sustainability. If we simply cut off from the modernists and heartlanders, we miss what we can learn from them and we vitiate the rich dialogue needed to build a shared future. We shall find as we dialogue that we share a common history and that they reflect back to us parts of ourselves we struggle with or deny. The tough-mindedness of modernists is a valuable characteristic at times and heartlanders often have a deep affinity with the land. If we are honest, we also are somewhat modernist and heartlandish. If we fail to acknowledge this, we shall be unable to work effectively in the richly diverse world of modern organizations.

Who are the leaders/change agents?

We have outlined the personal characteristics and skills of effective change agents. But what roles do change agents occupy and how do these roles affect the contributions they can make to the sustainability movement? Our list follows, and then we discuss how their distinctive contributions can make corporate sustainability a living reality.

Change agent roles

- *Internal*
    - line roles: the board of management, the CEO, the senior executive team, other managers and supervisors, general employees;
    - staff support roles: HR, OD, industrial engineering and environmental specialists, life scientists and IT specialists.
- *External*: politicians, bureaucrats and regulators; investors; professional business consultants; customers; community activists, concerned citizens and intellectuals; environmentalist activists; those who speak for future generations.

What are their distinctive roles?

We now take up the issue of how the various roles listed above can contribute to sustainability initiatives. As outlined, we divide them into roles internal to the organization and external to it. All these roles can make a distinctive contribution to moving organizations towards sustainability; in collaboration, they can have an irresistible impact. We begin our discussion with roles internal to the organization.

The internal roles consist of 'the line' and 'staff support'. The line consists of the board of management, CEO, senior executive team, other managers and supervisors and general employees.[31] The staff support roles consist of specialist professionals who provide support to those in the line. We will deal with the line roles first.

Boards of management

Boards of management can play a crucial role in setting the operating rules for an organization. Directors have heavy legal responsibilities and may be liable to major penalties if the organization is not compliant. They also have ultimate responsibility for appointing the CEO and signing off on the firm's business strategies. Boards are increasingly concerned with issues of sustainability as more companies face heavy penalties for failure to comply with environmental and health and safety legislation, as corporate reputations are damaged by the revelation of unethical practices and as ethical investment funds press for sustainable policies as the condition for providing investment capital. They are realizing that to press for shareholder returns at the expense of the interests of other stakeholders can be costly for themselves and the company and damage their own reputations as well as that of the corporation. Many are also realizing that sustainability represents a range of unexploited future business opportunities which can create future growth.

But boards of management often lack sufficient diversity to deal effectively with the shift from sole focus on shareholder value to meeting the expectations of a wider set of stakeholders. The changes we are advocating mean that the membership of boards needs to change so that they sample the diversity of stakeholders whose interests the board must now represent. Corporate sustainability has implications for corporate governance.

Line managers

Line managers include the CEO, senior executives, managers and supervisors or team leaders. Gratton views the line manager's role in the change process as being courageous enough to create broad involvement, to support the process of change, and to ensure that HR is centrally important to the business.[32] The CEO and senior executive team's central task is to ensure that sustainability strategies are an integral part of business strategy and that they contribute to profitability, to customer satisfaction as well as to the welfare of other stakeholders. Their role involves communicating that corporate objectives include sustainability and outlining what this means for the integrity of organizational structures, processes, products and services. Their actions must also match policy statements rather than contradict them: it is important that they model what they are espousing, allocate resources to support the change process and ensure that measures of business unit performance include progress on sustainability goals. As strategies are implemented successfully, line managers also have the responsibility for seeing that the resulting learning is communicated across the organization so that successful sustainability innovations are adopted and adapted.

The CEO   The role of the CEO is vital in terms of both symbolic and practical leadership. It is no easy role. Elkington describes the dilemma faced by Ford Motor Company Chairman William Clay Ford. Ford made a series of major sustainability initiatives, including a model citizenship report called *Connecting with Society* in which he gave his view that the popular sports utility vehicles were unsustainable given the petrol they consumed. He said that Ford aimed to be a model company for the twenty-first century, particularly in the area of sustainability. However, the report had only just been released when there was a recall of 6 million defective Firestone tyres that were shown to have triggered many accidents, including deaths. Ford vehicles, particularly sports utility vehicles, were the major users of the tyres. Firestone had attempted to cover up the growing history of accidents and is now mired in lawsuits as a result. Firestone was the supplier but Ford's reputation was also affected. The Ford Explorer was equipped with the Firestone tyres and had been a major profit generator, so profits slumped. Addressing the 2000 Greenpeace Business Conference, William Ford said: 'This terrible situation – which goes against everything I stand for – has made us more determined than ever to operate in an open, transparent and accountable manner at all times.'[33]

The CEO of a public company faces the dilemma that many market analysts and investment funds seek short-term returns and, as yet, place far too little emphasis on the importance of the issues we have discussed in this book. The CEO who is attempting to build a sustainable and sustaining corporate culture faces a daily performance evaluation by a share market which traditionally places little value on this. As we have discussed, ethical investment funds have demonstrated consistently superior returns and the size of these funds is growing. Nevertheless the CEO must deliver in the short term and find resources to invest in the future. This is no easy task, particularly in a recession; sometimes it feels to CEOs that they are running up an escalator that is moving in the opposite direction. Nevertheless many CEOs manage to generate short-term gains by 'picking low-hanging fruit' while quietly investing in building the capabilities of the corporation to generate medium to long-term performance, including performance due to sustainability initiatives.

Hart and Quinn saw CEOs as playing four kinds of leadership roles in the change process: motivator, vision setter, analyser and taskmaster. These roles are directed respectively to people, the future, the operating system and the market. They investigated the typical roles played by CEOs and linked these roles to three measures of firm performance: short-term financial performance, growth and future positioning of the organization, and organizational effectiveness (non-financial measures of performance such as employee satisfaction, product quality and social responsibility).

Hart and Quinn found that CEOs used the taskmaster role the most but the role did not influence any of the three performance measures. The analyser role, directed at creating improved efficiency, and the vision setter role were significant predictors of business performance and organizational effectiveness, but not of short-term business performance. The motivator role was, however, a particularly strong predictor of organizational performance on all three dimensions.[34] The research results also demonstrate that those CEOs who used all four roles achieved higher levels of performance than CEOs who did not.[35] Being an effective CEO demands a varied role repertoire and the flexibility to move in and out of different roles as the needs of the situation change. These qualities of the CEO are the qualities of any organizational leader, writ large: all leaders need to be able to understand the issues (analyser), inspire others (vision setter) and help them focus their energy (motivator).

Effective CEOs and executives are active in understanding the changing context in which the organization operates and place themselves where they will be sensitized to emerging changes in society. A problem in creating significant change in organizations is that many executives move in very conservative circles and live in elite enclaves cut off from mainstream social life. When organizations actively relate to the community this offers opportunities for senior executives, in particular, to break out of their circle of privilege from time to time and encounter others whose lives pose very different challenges.

Other managers, supervisors and team leaders contribute to the
strategic process and actively translate the strategies into practical action
plans. If they are to be effective, these plans will include achievable but
challenging sustainability goals and involve the introduction of processes
and systems that embody ecological and human sustainability principles.
Supervisors and team leaders, in particular, are the critical front line of
both incremental and transformational change. Their support and
feedback is vital to a successful change programme.

General employees

These often see themselves as having more limited power than executives
and managers. They certainly have more limited authority; but general
employees make or break organizational strategies. A strategy that is not
translated into the moment to moment, day to day operational work of the
organization is like a bird without wings – it never gets off the ground. To
use another analogy, senior managers are the architects of change but
general employees are the builders. The intelligence, commitment and
skills of general employees move an organization forward on the path to
sustainability. The moments of truth that test whether an organization is
serious about sustainability occur as members of the workforce face
customers across counters, on a telephone or on line, negotiate with
suppliers, respond to new legislative requirements, dispose of 'waste'. In
the process of change, there are also opportunities to innovate, to suggest
new or improved ways of doing things, to bring in knowledge acquired
elsewhere. Employees have another source of power: as a last resort, they
can vote with their feet and leave a company that is acting unethically or
not taking new sustainability initiatives.

Staff support roles

Staff support roles are usually occupied by specialists who do not have
the authority held by line managers. Their impact is achieved through
expertise and influence rather than authority. HR (human resource) and
OD (organization development) specialists, industrial engineers,
environmental specialists and IT (information technology) specialists are
particularly important in making change happen.

HR specialists are an integral part of the change planning process,
including working with and to the senior executive team. They must also

be active in creating and maintaining the guiding coalition that leads the change process and they need to provide technical expertise on HR issues. They are an alternative channel to the line for the expression of employee ideas and concerns as the change process evolves. Another important part of their responsibility is to ensure that the organization's reward system does not lag behind the innovations but supports behaviour consistent with the phase of sustainability being established. Building the skill base needed to support relevant sustainability practices is also their particular responsibility. Part of that skill base consists of the competencies needed to continually reshape the organization for future sustainable performance – the competencies for enhancing the organization's capacity for change. They build both technical and reshaping skills through recruitment, consultancies and education of employees.

Organizational development (OD) specialists are particularly important in the organizational reshaping process. Not all organizations have OD specialists or, if they have, refer to them in this way. By OD specialists we mean change agents with highly specialized skills around the process of corporate change. They are professionals with training and experience in techniques such as team building, conflict resolution, counselling and intergroup relations. They are accustomed to working with the hot human process of change as it occurs; they take emotional reactions as a normal part of any significant change process and are not fazed by them. They are accustomed to working in ambiguous situations where they have little authority and to collaborating with others to design the ongoing process of change. Working on the edge of chaos and keeping organizational change processes on track and productive is their specialty.

Industrial engineers In manufacturing and heavy industry, technical specialists with an engineering background play key roles in planning and operations. In most cases their training does not equip them with knowledge of how to make organizational change, particularly on the human side of the process. However, some bring good interpersonal skills learned in the workplace and considerable experience in making change. Where they have a grounding in BPR (business process re-engineering) this can prove invaluable in redesigning product flows to make them more efficient and sustainable. Their grasp of the technical knowledge needed in moving to sustainability can combine with the skills of HR and OD specialists to be a winning combination. All too often, however, specialists from these diverse backgrounds speak different languages, don't communicate with each other or appreciate the relevance of the other professionals' training and knowledge. This 'Tower of Babel' effect can be a significant obstacle in moving towards integration, particularly in the latter phases of sustainability where integration is vital.

IT specialists IT is an enabler of corporate success. No large, complex modern organization can afford to lag behind the leading edge of change in IT, particularly with the rapid development of e-commerce and virtual organizations. IT specialists are vital to the construction of the computer-based systems needed for co-ordination and control of a wide variety of processes, including complex supply chains. They need to understand the imperative for building sustainable systems and the requirement for them to be both efficient and user friendly. IT specialists can easily become lost in their world of rapidly changing technology and lose touch with the firm's business imperatives. In building new systems, it is relatively easy for IT specialists to carry across the inbuilt assumptions of existing 'old economy' systems and, in particular, fail to understand the revolution involved in the shift to strategic sustainability and the sustaining corporation. IT systems will only play a vital role in the development of more flexible, innovative strategies if IT specialists understand the nature of the revolutionary transformation involved.

In our work with organizations we have built networks consisting of experts in both human and environmental sustainability. We find that they have rarely interacted with each other before but are excited at the parallels they discover when they compare the development of sustainability principles in their respective fields. Few human sustainability experts have thought seriously about environmental issues and environmentalists are often quite untutored in the human sciences. There can be, however, a remarkable congruence between their values that makes the resulting dialogue between them very productive. In managing change programmes, therefore, there is a significant challenge in creating a collaborative relationship between the various experts in staff positions. Their expertise is vital in the practical process of developing systems and the most effective change programmes draw on their talent in a co-ordinated way.

As an organization progresses through the six phases of sustainability, there is an increasing requirement for a more holistic and integrated approach to both human resources and environmental management. This means that the HR and environmental management functions, in particular, must change and eventually merge or collaborate closely with a mutual understanding of how their efforts contribute seamlessly to the emerging philosophy and practice of sustainability.

External change agent roles

In the sustainability movement, external change agents have played major roles in bringing pressure to bear on organizations to adopt more sustainable strategies. This external pressure has been at times adversarial in both the human and ecological areas of activity. While there will be a place for adversarial activists in the foreseeable future, a shift in emphasis has taken place as more organizations move beyond compliance to launch sustainability initiatives on a voluntary basis. New collaborative alliances are taking place across the boundaries of organizations and external change agents have important roles to play in these alliances. Major and minor consulting companies have also moved to set up specialized practices to provide advice on a variety of sustainability issues.

Politicians, bureaucrats and regulators

The role of politicians, bureaucrats and regulators is to create 'third wave' economies that support 'third wave' organizations. This means having the courage to challenge the narrow assumptions of 'second wave' economists who dominate departments of finance in most western economies. It means being open to the new fields of ecological economics, industrial ecology and intellectual capital. The countries making most progress in this regard are the Netherlands, Germany, Finland and Denmark. They are already creating national policies that shift first and second-wave corporations forward into the growth industries of the third wave and are developing new export industries in, for example, alternative energy generation. In Denmark, for example, the wind power industry alone generates over US$6 billion a year and employs 15,000 people. Impressed by this, the British government has now allocated US$40 million over three years for research and development into alternative energy sources. From 1 April 2002 UK companies that do not use alternative energy also will pay up to twice the price for energy compared with those that do.[36] Developments like the diversification of energy sources represent significant strategic opportunities for both countries and companies.

Politicians however usually follow a new emerging consensus rather than lead it. Voter support for those political candidates who support sustainability regulation and incentives is therefore critical. Governments have an important role to play in setting the baseline for sustainability through regulation and raising the baseline where necessary as new environmental evidence emerges. On their part, bureaucrats and regulators can minimize or maximize the impact of legislation by inaction or action. Action often takes courage as particular politicians may not be enthusiastic to see powerful companies penalized, particularly those that contribute to party funds. Public pressure from activist groups can have a powerful effect in ensuring that legislation is not only enacted but also implemented.

Investors

Investors control the flow of capital to corporations directly and through brokers and funds. There is no more powerful pressure for change than the withdrawal of investment from public companies or the flow of capital to them. It is vital therefore that investors support companies that are working to implement sustainability policies and withdraw investment from those that are not. Companies with sustainable policies give better returns overall than those without such policies so, on financial grounds alone, this is a viable investment policy. Customers can exert similar pressures through shifting their buying to favour sustainable products and services. As these products and services are healthier, this is also a sensible pattern of consumer spending. Consumers are increasingly demanding transparency in terms of ingredients and components in products (for example, information on genetic modification of foods). Supporting increasing transparency makes an important contribution to advancing the sustainability movement because transparency makes informed consumer choice possible.

Community activists

Community activists, concerned citizens, intellectuals and scientists also have important roles in demanding transparency in company operations, assembling the best available knowledge about the impact of particular kinds of products and services (for example, chemicals), and bringing external pressure to bear on companies that avoid their responsibilities to their workforces, communities or the environment. In addition, as more companies move to an 'inclusive leadership' approach that welcomes the participation of a range of stakeholders in achieving corporate sustainability, there are emerging opportunities to collaborate on new initiatives. Community activists also have a vital role in speaking for the natural environment – they are often closest to it and best able to provide a voice to protect it.

Future generations

Finally, we have included future generations as change agents. The unborn generations are not, of course, yet present and so are unable to act for change that will serve their interests. They need spokespersons to stand for intergenerational equity. In our view, those best equipped to play this role are parents, educators, youth leaders and others who strongly identify with the children of the future and can speak for them.

Building alliances of change agents

Many change agents feel isolated and unsupported in working towards the creation of a sustainable future. Their activities often have little impact and are lost in the ongoing operations of large-scale, complex organizations. As the sustainability movement advances, there are increasing opportunities to lead by forming alliances between change agents working within an organization and others outside it. Such alliances can create a pincer movement of pressure for change in the first three phases of sustainability and so build momentum for compliance and for the movement towards compliance plus. In the latter three phases they can create increasing momentum by linking initiatives in different parts of the organization and in the community – initiatives that otherwise might be struggling on their own. It is vital to keep in mind that this is a social movement that extends beyond the corporation and, like all social movements, its success demands a disciplined co-operation despite inevitable differences of values and skill bases.

Constructing the sustainability agenda

So what is the agenda for collaborative action between change agents? The boxes contain summaries of the main points of the sustainability agenda we have discussed through the book. The first outlines the internal agenda, that is the changes in the workforce itself that are needed to build a relevant base of human capabilities. The next one outlines the external agenda, that is, the move towards stakeholder involvement and participation. The third box outlines the agenda for the ecological environment, that is, the changes that need to take place in the corporation so that it does not damage but restores and renews the natural world.

Human sustainability: the internal agenda

- Adopt a strategic perspective to workplace development.
- Build the corporate knowledge and skill base (intellectual and social capital) of employees – develop human potential.
- Foster productive diversity in the workplace (OH&S, gender equity, participative decision making, work–life balance).
- Develop the capability for continuing corporate reshaping and renewal, including visionary change leadership.
- Create communities of practice to diffuse knowledge and skills.
- Provide relevant expertise in the best way to organize work for high performance and satisfaction.
- Represent employees' concerns to management, while simultaneously giving employees an increased role in organizational decision making.

Human sustainability: the external agenda

- Reinterpret strategy around a wider range of stakeholders and develop co-operative strategies with them (responsiveness).
- Add, rather than subtract value for all relevant stakeholders.
- Build a culture of workplace learning and commitment to a 'generative society' through a declared and enacted value base.
- Initiate and sustain an ongoing dialogue with stakeholders to define key elements of social responsibility – set priorities (accountability).
- Define social goals, develop action plans to reach these goals, monitor and disclose performance against key performance indicators (transparency).
- Seek genuine feedback on performance from stakeholders – welcome and learn from criticism.
- Win, by responsible informed action, the support of all stakeholders for the organization's continued existence and growth.

Achieving ecological sustainability

- Design a production system that is an integral part of the ecology (like an earthworm).
- Conduct life-cycle assessment and a policy of resource stewardship.
- Eliminate waste and pollution particularly by product redesign and developing an industrial ecology.
- Form active partnerships with 'green', human rights and other community groups.
- Appoint independent experts to monitor the corporation's environmental 'footprint' (environmental auditing).
- Link action on human sustainability with action on ecological sustainability to create an integrated, seamless approach to corporate sustainability.

Owning your power and changing corporate culture

Corporate culture is strategy in action.[37] Culture arises out of the collective experience of the members of an organization; it provides a framework of meaning to interpret the stream of events people encounter in the workplace so that they can make sense of their work and their role in the organization and society. Culture is a guide to action – at best a living expression of the strategic intent of the organization. The role of change leaders is to actively engage in the process of meaning making so that they are an integral and powerful part of the process of cultural redefinition that must take place in order to create sustaining organizations in a sustainable society.

In this change process, actions are often more powerful than words, though words have an important place. Symbolic events are frequently the focus for significant shifts in cultural awareness. Part of the role of the change leader is to become an actor in the unfolding drama of change towards sustainability. Paul Bate refers to cultural leadership as 'multilateral brokerage in a jungle of meaning'.[38] This emphasizes the dynamic nature of the change process, the centrality of meaning making, and the change agent's function as a broker working the active dialogue of actions and words around the organization's future role. Bate rightly points out that change agents can't control cultural development – they can only 'initiate, influence and shape the direction of the emerging culture'.[39]

> The art of cultural coevolution is the art of managing dynamic complexity over time. Connecting things is relatively easy – the skill is in finding ways for them to connect in an organized, indirect, limited, yet coherently meaningful way.
>
> *Source*: R.D. Hames and G. Callanan, *Burying the 20th Century*[40]

As change agents and change leaders, we are only one source of influence in a complex changing reality. Nevertheless let us not underestimate the potential transformative power that we represent. As Korten has stated:

> The transformative power of the organism – both human and nonhuman – is the ultimate source of all that has value in the fulfillment of our own being. It includes not only the whole of the natural living capital, by which the planet's life support system is continuously regenerated, but also the human, social and institutional capital by which we utilize the wealth of the living planet to serve our needs and by which we may ideally come to lend our own distinctive capacities to further life's continuing journey.[41]

Change leadership involves owning our own power and using it responsively and responsibly.

Putting the jigsaw puzzle together

We began this book with an analogy. We wrote that constructing the sustainable organization of the future is like assembling pieces of a jigsaw puzzle. We have identified a range of organizations which represent parts of the puzzle because they have already begun inventing the future. No individual or group has yet grasped the whole picture; not all the parts of the puzzle are in existence; but when we make an inventory of what this organization is doing here and what another is doing there, the bigger picture emerges. We have used the sustainability phase model as an overlay to the puzzle – we think it clusters the pieces in a way that delineates an integral part of one section of the final picture. We all have a role to play in helping put the puzzle together, in unfolding the 'implicate order'. We can lead where we are now, by fulfilling the potential of the roles we hold in the organizations of which we are a part. If we act with integrity, standing with courage for the planet, for a healthy society and for future generations, our leadership will contribute to creating a new organizational reality – the sustaining corporation that contributes to creating a fully sustainable world.

Notes

1   P. Senge, 'Foreword', to D. Chatterjee, *Living Consciously: A Pilgrimage Towards Self-mastery*, Oxford: Viva Books and Butterworth-Heinemann, 1999, p. xiv.

2   J. Jaworski, *Synchronicity: The Inner Path of Leadership*, San Francisco: Berrett-Koehler, 1998, p. 6.

3   Ibid., p. 78.

4   Written by Dexter Dunphy.

5   Chatterjee, *Living Consciously*, p. 31.

6   C. Handy, *The Elephant and the Flea: Looking Backwards to the Future*, London: Hutchinson, 2001, pp. 74–5.

7   Quoted in Chatterjee, *Living Consciously*, p. 45.

8   R.E. Quinn, *Deep Change: Discovering the Leader Within*, San Francisco: Jossey-Bass, 1996, p. 9.

9   F. Luthans, K. Luthans, R.M. Hodgetts and B.C. Luthans, 'Positive approach to leadership (PAL): implications for today's organizations', *Journal of Leadership Studies*, 2002, 8(2), 3–20; F. Luthans, 'Positive organizational behaviour: developing and managing psychological strengths for performance improvement', *Academy of Management Executive*, 2002, 16(1), 57–72.

10   D. Dunphy, unpublished notes, The Skilled Practitioner Workshop, 2001.

11   Chatterjee, *Living Consciously*, pp. 51–4.

12   From A. Einstein, *The World as I See It*, reissue edition, New York: Citadel Press, 1993, quoted in V.D. Dimitrov, 'Complexity, spirituality and ethics', in *Integrating Purpose, Vision and Practicality*, Proceedings of the 4th Annual Conference, Spirituality, Leadership and Management Network, 6–9 December 2001, Canberra, p. 22.

13   See, for example, K. Wilbur, *Quantum Questions: Mystical Writings of the World's Greatest Physicists*, Boston, Mass.: Shambhala, 2001.

14   Jaworski, *Synchronicity*, pp. 56, 184.

15   Ibid., p. 38.

16   Quinn, *Deep Change*, p. 203.

17   Ibid., p. 204.

18   L.F. Buscaglia, *Living, Loving and Learning*, New York: Ballantine Books, 1982, p. 3.

19   For those who want to pursue further the idea of spiritual intelligence, a useful starting point is D. Zohar and I. Marshall, *Spiritual Intelligence: The Ultimate Intelligence*, London: Bloomsbury Publishing, 2000.

20   B. Hirsh and P. Sheldrake, *Inclusive Leadership: Rethinking the World of Business to Generate the Dynamics of Lasting Success*, Melbourne: Information Australia, 2001.

21   Ibid., pp. 211–12.

22   L. Gratton, *Living Strategy: Putting People at the Heart of Corporate*

Purpose, London: Financial Times/Prentice-Hall, 2000, p. 17.

23 K.E. Weick, *Sensemaking in Organizations*, Beverley Hills, Cal.: Sage Publications, 1995.

24 For a more extended discussion of the nature of dialogue, see E.H. Schein, *Process Consultation Revisited: Building the Helping Relationship*, Addison-Wesley, 1999, pp. 201–18.

25 F. Blount, 'Changing places: Blount and Joss', *Human Resources Monthly*, 1999, December, 10–14.

26 Quinn, *Deep Change*, p. 83.

27 L. Rowledge, R.S. Barton and K.S. Brady, *Mapping the Journey: Case Studies in Strategy and Action Towards Sustainable Development*, Sheffield: Greenleaf Publishing, 1999, pp. 178–83.

28 Quoted in D.C. Korten, *The Post-corporate World: Life After Capitalism*, San Francisco: Kumarian Press and Berrett-Koehler Publishers, 1999, p. 215.

29 'The invisible movement', *Trendspotter Newsletter* no. 2, Denmark: Novo Group Academy, October 2001, p. 4; website: www.novogroup.dk/academy; see also 'Storming the mindsets', *Future News*, 6(2), March 2001, Sydney: Futures Foundation.

30 Quoted in Korten, *The Post-corporate World*, pp. 218–19.

31 Of course, many organizations today do not have 'a line' in any simple sense – the term comes from traditional bureaucratic organizations. We use the line/staff distinction as a simple descriptive classification system.

32 Gratton, *Living Strategy* p. 125.

33 J. Elkington, *The Chrysalis Economy: How Citizens, CEOs and Corporations Can Fuse Values and Value Creation*, Oxford: Capstone, 2001, pp. 118–20.

34 S. Hart and R.E. Quinn, 'Roles executives play: CEOs, behavioral complexity, and firm performance', *Human Relations*, 1993, 46, 543–75; also reviewed in Quinn, *Deep Change*, pp. 148–51.

35 This result holds true regardless of firm size or the level of competitiveness of the firm's environment.

36 'Change is in the air as Britain rethinks energy policy', *Sydney Morning Herald*, weekend edition, 9–10 March 2002, World, 19.

37 P. Bate, *Strategies for Cultural Change*, Oxford: Butterworth/Heinemann, 1994.

38 Ibid., p. 243.

39 Ibid., p. 245.

40 R.D. Hames and G. Callanan, *Burying the 20th Century*, Sydney: Business and Professional Publishing, 1997, p. 35.

41 Korten, *The Post-corporate World*, p. 117.

Appendix
The corporate sustainability checklist

Characteristic	Activities[1]
	COMPLIANCE
Vision/goals	Develop an integrated, organization-wide plan for sustainability
	Implement systematic and on-going improvement in industrial relations, OH&S, EEO, EMS and community services
Change agents' key activities	Ensure top level commitment
	Select and develop change agents and nominate responsibilities
	Identify and regularly update the organization on risks of non-compliance with current legislation, possible future legislation and public opinion
	Organize workshops to define compliance roles
	Clarify roles of top management, compliance officers and other stakeholders
	Assign staff responsibilities to improve existing IR, EEO, OH&S, and environmental management systems
	Develop staff training systems
Corporate policies/ strategies	Foster an understanding of business ethics across the organization
	Work towards a comprehensive sustainability strategy
	Foster an individual sense of responsibility for the environment and the need to be alert to potential sources of pollution and resource waste
	Minimize adverse environmental effects of all activities and take steps to minimize waste and conserve energy

Characteristic	*Activities*[1]
	Take necessary measures to prevent avoidable accidental releases of pollutants
	Provide advice on the safe handling, use and disposal of the company's products
	Examine product liability requirements
	Take employee suggestions and feedback into account
	Minimize risk using a precautionary approach
	Build and sustain reputation
	Build a learning platform for the organization
Stakeholder relations	Establish positive relationships with community and government
	Avoid greenwash by reporting conscientiously
	Enlist NGOs as environmental and social monitors
	Establish volunteer relationships
	Assist public authorities in establishing well-founded environmental regulations
Human capabilities	Create OH&S, EEO, IR and community relations policies and involve employees in ongoing improvement
	Implement employee training programmes for OH&S
	Implement employee awareness programmes for human rights and EEO obligations
	Develop human sustainability auditing and reporting capabilities
	Identify human rights, OH&S and IR obligations of members of supply chain
	Establish relations with a third-party professional to conduct external audits
	Ensure ongoing compliance through implementing ISO 9000
Ecological capabilities	Implement environmental awareness programmes
	Develop ecological auditing and reporting capabilities
	Identify environmental obligations of members of supply chain
	Ensure ongoing capacity to address compliance through the implementation of voluntary standards or continuous improvement systems such as ISO 9001

Characteristic	*Activities*[1]
Tools/techniques	Develop a sustainability plan which covers the management and operation of facilities and the design, manufacture and delivery of products and services Involve employees in planning for the development of the sustainability plan Establish auditing and reporting systems Develop relationship with relevant regulators Communicate sustainability plan aims, objectives and benefits to employees and suppliers Press suppliers to be compliant through face-to-face meetings Ensure that contractors working on the organization's behalf apply acceptable human environmental sustainability standards Ensure that any transfer of technology is accompanied by information needed to protect the environment Assess in advance the environmental and human sustainability implications of new processes, products and other activities
Production/ service systems	Identify legislation and standards associated with all production and service systems Ensure assessment, monitoring and reporting systems are in place to address compliance requirements relevant to all products and services

EFFICIENCY

Vision/goals	Generate cost savings via the pursuit of efficiencies in ecological and human sustainability areas Generate efficiencies by reducing costs, adding value and innovation Develop an organization-wide approach that seeks to shift from cost to innovation in order to capture sustainable competitive advantages
Change agents	Allocate change agent roles to operational and line managers with relevant technical expertise Ensure top level commitment Develop change programmes that generate efficiencies in

Characteristic	*Activities*[1]
	specific areas – through the use of programmes – TQM, The Natural Step; EMS
	Pilot programmes and look for opportunities to widen the sphere of influence
Corporate policies/ strategies	Develop a systematic approach to the management and pursuit of efficiency; look for small wins and use these gains to spread the project, create a more programmatic approach
	Create corporate incentive schemes that reward employee performance and start to build social capital
	De-layer through the use of teams with the aim of increasing workplace commitment/outsource non-core activities
Structures/systems	Establish assessment systems to address OHS and community issues – that is, start to develop internal structures for external stakeholder information management
	Implement HRIS systems in order to track human resource performance
	Assess and report on social/environmental impacts beyond compliance requirements
	Establish environmental management systems and link into corporate-wide systems
	Assess product risk and other liability issues and look at building into value adding and innovation approaches (eco design)
Stakeholder relations	Identify key external stakeholders and engage in dialogue, symbolic activities
	Form alliances with suppliers and subcontractors in order to deliver on environmental criteria for product/service efficiency
	Focus on customer and look to add value to products by moving features to services
	Build new capabilities though shared learning experiences with other organizations
	Seek to build human capability through collaborative arrangements with other organizations

Characteristic	Activities[1]
Human capabilities	Develop increased returns from human resources; develop a systematic approach to human resource management Identify required competencies in middle managers and commence competency development Focus on appropriate employee skills development (communication, systems analysis, conflict management, problem solving) Reorganize in multi-skilled teams where appropriate Establish systems for employee empowerment Calculate cost–benefit ratios for human resources
Ecological capabilities	Develop skills required to identify and pick off low-hanging fruit Start to develop competencies in eco-design, supply chain management and procurement practices Develop and use systematic tools and measurement systems
Tools/techniques	Develop and use proven programmes – TQM; The Natural Step Implement TQEM and EMS Develop corporate-wide reporting systems for knowledge sharing
Production/service systems	Minimize environmental load and life cycle impacts Ensure packaging/design impacts along supply chain Commit to taking back products at the end of their lives Review all material and energy flows in physical and monetary units in order to identify efficiencies

STRATEGIC

Vision/goals	Scan the environment (present and future) to identify (a) potential threats to the sustainability of existing products and services; (b) potential opportunities for creating innovative sustainability products/services Ensure business activities generate competitive advantages through the pursuit of sustainability Develop a vision that defines core sustainability competencies and values

Characteristic	*Activities*[1]
Change agents	Benchmark against industry best practice Encourage feedback on new ideas in order to generate strategic insights Implement interpersonal skills training with a focus on developing the change competencies of the organization Develop systems of knowledge sharing among employees Work to develop close relationships with stakeholders – internal and external Work towards establishing enabling organizational structures – teams, virtual teams and networks Aim to develop long-term sustainability competencies
Corporate policies/ strategies	Integrate human and ecological sustainability systems to create dynamic core competencies Align the corporate vision on sustainability with practical polices and strategies for action Formalize commitment to sustainability at a board level Develop management plans and set targets for integration of environmental, financial, human competencies and knowledge management Create cross-functional sustainability integration teams Use TBL/balanced score card to demonstrate corporate performance Promote research and development into next-generation environmentally sound products and services Constantly undertake stakeholder analysis
Structures/systems	Develop systems for capturing and utilizing employee knowledge Develop systems for training, development and transfer of knowledge that focus on core competencies Develop structures – teams, project teams, virtual teams and communities of practice – that enable the pursuit of sustainability Align supply chains, stakeholders and logistics systems – examine e-commerce potential Develop performance management systems that monitor and reward sustainability performance of business units

Characteristic	Activities[1]
Stakeholder relations	Define and communicate strategic interests and potential benefits to stakeholders Develop codified rules for management and co-ordination of relationships Develop strategic relationships with NGOs, community organizations and other corporations Collaborate with non-profit and other commercial organizations and build reputational capital Leverage partnerships for sustainability such as communities of practice Develop key components of innovation competition Work with communities of practice to develop knowledge base – become an agent of change
Human capabilities	Support work/life balance for employees Provide diversity training Empower people by giving them the tools and motivation to innovate and express values through work Implement career and benefits planning Develop flexible workplace practices such as telecommuting or work sharing and videoconferencing; utilize new information technology to create project and virtual teams Ensure that good architecture provides a pleasant working and living environment
Ecological capabilities	Develop capabilities for monitoring and acting on a broad range of ecological and social information Develop key relations with stakeholders Incorporate core competencies on design/technology into strategies
Tools/techniques	Use triple bottom line reporting or balanced scorecard Conduct culture-building activities Initiate strategic competitor analysis
Production/service systems	Establish and incorporate systems of industrial ecology Develop industrial ecology synergies through supply chain management Increase focus on research and development

Characteristic	*Activities*[1]
	THE SUSTAINING CORPORATION
Vision/goals	Review basic corporate values; create codified set of company values Ensure top-level support for a strong sustainability position Re-examine organization values against changing external expectations by active workshopping with stakeholders Broaden stakeholder analysis to include society as a whole, future generations and the natural world
Change agents	Ensure that the senior executive team deeply internalizes and acts on sustainability principles Build strong collaborative networks between internal and external change agents to create momentum on progressing sustainability.
Corporate policies/ strategies	Build on sustainability achievements of previous stages Use external bodies to conduct social and environmental audits; cultivate transparency and accountability Communicate achievements to employees, community and other organizations and share learning with alliance partners – build reputational capital Develop new market opportunities; provide customized services Contribute to maintaining the biosphere
Structures/systems	Develop a networked, flexible corporate structure Form alliances and emphasize collaboration Create a strong corporate culture around core sustainability values
Stakeholder relations	Develop a shared vision with non-profit organizations Share employee work hours with non-profit partners Encourage active engagement in community activities Be proactive in pursuing sustainability agenda with governments and other community bodies
Human capabilities	Build personal and professional capability of the workforce; build intellectual capital within the organization and in collaboration with alliance members

Characteristic	*Activities*[1]
	Include ethical concerns in staff performance measures
	Ensure staff relations are based on potential for contributions, not status; support participative decision making
	Ensure staff recruitment policies are proactive towards minority groups; foster workforce diversity and equal opportunity
	Ensure highest standards in workplace health and safety
	Adopt family friendly policies
	Develop higher order employee capabilities (process skills, self-confidence, sharing)
Ecological capabilities	Contribute to ecological renewal
	Be proactive in negotiating with other corporations for the design and production of more sustainable products
	Assist smaller corporations to be more responsible by sharing knowledge and expertise
	Use life cycle assessment to reduce packaging, eliminate waste, increase dematerialization
Tools/techniques	Consolidate and integrate systems adapted in earlier phases
Production/service sytems	Redesign products to ensure environmental safety
	Redesign supply chains to become material processing loops to eliminate waste and pollution
	Dematerialize physical products where possible to emphasize service activities

Note

1 In constructing this list of activities, we have drawn, to some extent, on the following work: B. Nattrass and M. Altomare, *The Natural Step for Business*, Gabriola Island: New Society Publishers, 1999; Social Venture Network, *Standards of Corporate Social Responsibility* at http://www.svn.org/organization.html (accessed 18 April 2002).

Further reading

Beer, M. and Nohria, N., *Breaking the Code of Change*, Boston, Mass.: Harvard Business School Press, 2000.

Burnes, B., *Managing Change: A Strategic Approach to Organisational Dynamics*, 3rd edn, Edinburgh: Financial Times/Prentice-Hall, 2000.

Clarke, T. and Clegg, S., *Changing Paradigms: The Transformation of Management Knowledge for the 21st Century*, London: HarperCollins Business, 2000.

Conger, J.A., Spreitzer, G.M. and Lawler, E.E. (eds), *The Leader's Change Handbook: An Essential Guide to Setting Direction and Taking Action*, San Francisco: Jossey, 1999.

Dunphy, D., Benveniste, J., Griffiths, A. and Sutton, P. (eds), *Sustainability: The Corporate Challenge of the 21st Century*, Sydney: Allen and Unwin, 2000.

Elkington, J., *The Chrysalis Economy*, Oxford: Capstone, 2001.

Hamel, G., *Leading the Revolution*, Boston, Mass.: Harvard Business School Press, 2000.

Hart, S., 'Beyond greening: strategies for a sustainable world', *Harvard Business Review*, Jan.–Feb. 1997, 67–76.

Hart, S. and Milestein, M., 'Global sustainability and the creative destruction of industries', *Sloan Management Review*, 1999, 41(1), 23–33.

Hoffman, A., *Competitive Environmental Strategy*, Washington, D.C.: Island Press, 2000.

Kotter, J.P., *Leading Change*, Boston, Mass.: Harvard Business School Press, 1996.

Nadler, D.A. and Tushman, M.L., 'The organization of the future: strategic imperatives and core competencies for the 21st century', *Organizational Dynamics*, 28(1), 1999, 45–60.

Nattrass, B. and Altomare, M., *The Natural Step for Business*, Gabriola Island: New Society Publishers, 1999.

Roome, N., 'Developing environmental management strategies', *Business Strategy and the Environment*, 1992, 1(1), 11–23.

Rowledge, L.R., Barton, R.S. and Brady, K.S., *Mapping the Journey*, Sheffield: Greenleaf Publishing, 1999.

Stace, D. and Dunphy, D., *Beyond the Boundaries: Leading and Re-creating the Successful Enterprise*, 2nd edn, Sydney: McGraw-Hill, 2001.

Starkey, R. and Welford, R. (eds), *The Earthscan Reader in Business and Sustainable Development*, London: Earthscan Publications, 2001.

Sveiby, K.F., *The New Organisational Wealth: Managing and Measuring Knowledge-based Assets*, San Francisco: Berrett-Koehler, 1997.

Szulanski, G. and Winter, S., 'Getting it right the second time', *Harvard Business Review*, January 2002, 62–9.

Index